Saint Benedict, H. (Henri) Logeman

The Rule of S. Benet. Latin and Anglo-Saxon Interlinear Version

Saint Benedict, H. (Henri) Logeman

The Rule of S. Benet. Latin and Anglo-Saxon Interlinear Version

ISBN/EAN: 9783337160708

Printed in Europe, USA, Canada, Australia, Japan

Cover: Foto ©Thomas Meinert / pixelio.de

More available books at **www.hansebooks.com**

The Rule of S. Benet.

LATIN AND ANGLO-SAXON

INTERLINEAR VERSION.

EDITED, WITH AN INTRODUCTION AND NOTES

BY

Dr. H. LOGEMAN.

LONDON:

PUBLISHED FOR THE EARLY ENGLISH TEXT SOCIETY

BY N. TRÜBNER AND CO., 57 AND 59 LUDGATE HILL.

MDCCCLXXXVIII.

ON some pages of the Introduction to this volume, and also in the Notes at the end, I have had to mention gratefully the help I have received from various quarters.

But apart from the aid specified there, I must here give the names of two gentlemen, whose assistance to me has been very valuable. First and foremost my thanks are due to Dr. Furnivall, who with great kindness has facilitated the publishing of this book, both as my doctoral dissertation, to be presented to the Faculty of Letters at the Utrecht University, and as one of the issues for the Early English Text Society. I must also thank him heartily for the trouble he has taken in correcting my necessarily faulty English. Secondly to my brother, Mr. W. S. Logeman, who volunteered to extract by far the greater part of the text for lexico-graphical purposes. I need hardly say that this labour has been of material service to me, and I gladly take this opportunity of publicly acknowledging my obligations.

H. LOGEMAN.

CONTENTS.

---⧨---

INTRODUCTION.

TEXT.

[1] Those showing the order or sequence of the A.-Saxon words in construing the Latin.
[2] Part of a word put for the whole of it, as *pra* for *pravost*.

PAGE

[1] A Roman liquid measure.

INTRODUCTION.

I. Outlines of the History of Benedictinism in England until the Reformation.

THE Latin convent rule, known under the name of the Rule of S. Benet, was written by that Saint about the year 516 A.D.[1] Saint Benedict was not the first who found it necessary to lay down rules for monks to live by. He wrote only for those 'qui regulas *nigris monachis* ediderunt' (i. e. those that were **afterwards** called Black Friars, and Benedictines). Dugdale, on the page cited below, enumerates some six and more fathers who were the authors of Rules. Of these we may especially mention S. Basilius, and refer the reader to page 118[2] infra, where Benedictus of Nursia himself speaks of the Regula sanctis patris nostri Basilii, as 'bene viventium et oboedientium monachorum instituta virtutum.'

According to the commonly accepted idea, Pope Gregory the Great introduced Benedictinism, along with Christianity, into England in the year 596, when Augustine, prior of the Monastery of S. Andrew at Rome, came across with several

---

[1] See Dugdale's Monasticon, ed. 1817 and 1846, I, p. xxiii. S. Benedictus pater noster . . . . regulam monachorum edidit circa annum Christi 516.

[2] I here give the translation from the Durham MS., Bb. 1. 6 (see Wanley, p. 298), a collation of which was not given by Professor Schröer: 'Eac swylce þæra haligra fædera lif. 7 heora drohtnunga. 7 se regol ures halgan fæder basilii hwæt is hit elles butan ge timbrunga haligra manna. 7 ðæra munuca þ (read þe) wel 7 rihte libbað, 7 ge hersume synd.' See A. Schröer, Die Angelsächsischen Prosabearbeitungen der Benediktinerregel, Kassel, 1885–1888, p. 133. I may here thankfully mention the service rendered me by the Rev. Canon D. Greenwell, Librarian to the Dean and Chapter of Durham Cathedral, who, on my applying for the loan of the MS., volunteered to transcribe the whole of the Ben. Rule contained in it, and who, assisted by the Rev. J. T. Fowler, Librarian to the University of Durham, did so entirely as 'a labour of love.' Let me here publicly thank the reverend gentlemen for this extraordinary kindness.

other Benedictine monks [1]. Hook adds that 'Before Dunstan's time we may doubt the existence anywhere in England
of the Benedictine Rule in its completeness.' Lingard [2]
argues against this. According to this learned historian,
Benedictine writers have unsuccessfully tried to establish and
maintain that S. Gregory was a Benedictine himself. According
to him, it was not until Wilfrid's time (latter half of the seventh
century) that the monks of Britain got acquainted with the
Rule of S. Benedict. Be this as it may [3], all are agreed in
attributing a high character and a great authority to the
Rule in England when once introduced.

A few notes on the fate of the Benedictines in England
may be convenient to the reader. Dugdale, in his great
collection of materials for the study of Monasticism in England,
says [4] :—

'Tres autem apud nos celebres fuerunt monachismi veteris reformationes. . . .
Altera sub Dunstano fuit, in consilio Wintoniensi anno 965 regnante Edgaro,
magnificentissimo coenobiorum instauratore. Tunc primum monachis praescripta
fuit constitutio generalis tam ex Benedicti Regula quam ex veteribus consuetudinibus contexta quae dicta est Regularis Concordia Anglicae nationis [5].'

If this 'Regularis Concordia' is not Dunstan's, it owes its
origin at least to his mind, which pervades the time in which
he lived. His was the age of the revival of monasticism.
It is Dunstan's mind that speaks through Eadgar's mouth
when the latter prompts Aethelwold to a translation of the
Benedictine Rule [6]. What Dunstan aimed at, was to lead
back monastic life to its original purity and severe discipline
in accordance with the Rule of S. Benet, and to infuse the
spirit of monasticism into the whole of the English Church.
When, after sundry vicissitudes, Dunstan came to power
shortly after Eadgar's accession, the reforms sadly wanted

---

[1] See Smith and Cheetham, Dict. of Christ. Antiquities; and Hook, Church
Dictionary, in voce.

[2] Alterthümer der Angelsächsischen Kirche. Deutsch von Dr. F.
Rom. Breslau, 1847. When writing, I had not the English ed. at my disp........

[3] This is not the place for further investigations of the matter. I refer
to Lingard, pp. 64, 70, and 72.

[4] Monasticon Anglicanum, I, p. xiii.

[5] See infra, Ch. II of this Introduction, sub I.

[6] See Schröer, Die Prosabearbeitungen, pp. xiii-xviii; infra, p. xxxiv.

were carried into effect. And his faithful friend Aethelwold followed in his footsteps [1].

The institution of several affiliated congregations, as those of the Cistercian and Cluniac monks, shows on the one hand great interest in Benedict's Regulations; on the other hand, however, the fact that this revival was deemed necessary, clearly indicates that here and there the observance of the Rule had gradually become laxer. The same may be said with regard to the Councils held every now and then at London, and in other places. When we find one synod revive an enactment that no meat shall be eaten, it is a sure sign that for some time this precept had not been observed [2]. About the year 1421 we find that degeneration had again set in, and that a reform was contemplated. At a meeting in Westminster Abbey between King Henry V and the Abbots and prelates of the Order of Black Monks, more than 360 in number, a reform was decided upon [3].

Coming a hundred years down, we now approach Henry the Eighth's time, the age of the decline of monasticism, the time when monasteries were to be dissolved, along with the ties that had bound Henry VIII to Rome. That corruption had set in, is a fact recognised alike by both Roman Catholic and Protestant writers. 'It is not pretended that every single community of the very numerous houses in England,' says Weldon [4], 'where the Rule of S. Benet was followed, was at the time of its dispersion in the highest state of regular discipline,' and [5] :—

---

[1] I cannot but refer to B. ten Brink's words on this subject, which are very characteristic (Engl. Litt. Geschichte, 1877, I, p. 129); to Cockayne, Leechdoms, III, p. 412; and Bishop Stubbs, Memorials of S. Dunstan, Introduction, passim, but especially pp. cv and cviii.

[2] 'Sana de constitutione quam paulo ante concilium fecerant abbates ordinis Sancti Benedicti per Angliam constituti de carnibus non comedendis sacro approbante concilio his verbis diffinitum est.' Luard, Annales Monastici, II, 318, —nnales de Waverleia, MCCXXXVII. For other councils, see ib., IV, 547, 50.

[3] See Dom. Bennet Weldon, a Chronicle of the English Bened. Monks, etc., preface, p. vii, who quotes Thomas Walsingham, Historia Anglicana, ed. 1864, II, p. 337.

[4] Ib., p. xii.

[5] Liber Monasterii de Hyde, by E. Edwards. Preface, p. lxiii.

'The complaints'—against the inmates, as will be seen, of not a very serious
nature—'relate for the most part to certain anticipations by some of the more
youthful monks of the teachings of what has lately been called muscular
Christianity, as shown in their addiction to the practice of long-bow archery in
the Hyde meadows, and to that of keeping late hours, sitting for long discussions,
sometimes to the hour of eight in the evening and even beyond it (and, it is
much to be feared, occasionally over a potation to freshen their talk), instead
of betaking themselves to bed immediately after supper, according to the good
wont of their predecessors.'

And now a complaint on the part of the Roman Catholics,
which is at the same time a serious accusation :—

'In estimating the case with which so many venerable monasteries were
overthrown, it must be borne in mind that for some years previous to their
final suppression, many steps had been taken by those in power to render that
suppression more easy. One of these, and perhaps the chief, was the appoint-
ment by the Court of compliant and suborned men, already apostates at heart,
to highest positions in the religious houses. No one was more prominent in
this disgraceful intrigue than the highest ecclesiastical authority in the
kingdom, the primate Cranmer.'

As a proof of this, D. Weldon[1] instances the case of a
man who was recommended for a vacancy, and who was—
in an introductory letter quoted—said to be 'very tractable,
and as ready to set forward his prince's causes as no man more
of his coat' (1538). And the late Professor Brewer, a Protestant
historian of Henry VIII[2], has an admission bearing on this
subject, when he says: (Nothing) . . . . 'warrant(s) us in
believing that the era preceding the Reformation was more
corrupt than that which succeeded it.'

We now understand the preamble of the Act 27 Henry VIII,
intitled ' An act concerning the suppression or Dissolution of
certain Religious houses and geven to the Kings Highness
and to his Heirs for ever.

'For as much as manifest sinne, vycyous carnal and abominable living
ys daily used and cōmitted in such littell and small abbayes and priories
and other religious houses of monkes chanons and nonnes where the con-
gregation is under the number of XII'[3], etc.

How the new hope to which Mary's accession gave birth

---

[1] Weldon, pref., p. xiii.
[2] The Reign of Henry VIII, from his accession to the death of Wolsey, by
the late J. S. Brewer, M.A., ed. by James Gairdner, of the Public Record
Office, I, 1884 ; see p. 600.
[3] Monasticon Anglicanum, Appendix to Vol. VIII, p. 1654.

was cut short with the end of her brief reign, and the
succession of the Protestant Elizabeth, who undid all, and how
the Benedictines fared unto this very day, all this and more
the curious may pursue in the works I have cited in the
foot-notes. I may fitly close this section of the introduction
by two more passages from Professor Brewer's book, which
are worth quoting :—

'The greater monasteries were necessarily modified by the circumstances
of the times, and their religious characters impaired. They admitted a
number of lay inmates, or, at least, kept open house for persons not connected
with their foundations' (I, p. 50) and (ib., p. 51):

'That in so large a body of men, so widely dispersed, seated for so many
centuries in the richest and fairest estates of England, for which they were
mainly indebted to their own skill, perseverance, and industry, discreditable
members were to be found (and what literary chiffonier, raking in the
scandalous annals of any profession, cannot find filth and corruption) is
likely enough, but that the corruption was either so black or so general as
party spirit would make us believe, is contrary to all analogy, and is un-
supported by impartial and contemporary evidence[1].'

II. BIBLIOGRAPHY OF THE VARIOUS TREATISES, FOUND IN THE COTTONIAN MS., TIB. A. 3.

THE manuscript from which the present copy of the
Benedictine Rule is taken, is the Cotton MS., Tiberius A. 3.
It is described by Wanley on pp. 193[2]–199 of his catalogue.
The MS. is slightly injured, but has been rebound and
beautifully pasted up. At p. 198, section LXI, Wanley records
the very gaps that I have noted below (on p. 1, ll. 1, 2, etc.),
so that these injuries must be anterior to him, and therefore
also to the fire of 1731.

The MS. is a miscellaneous one, containing a varied col-

---

[1] Just now a notice reaches me of a book only recently published, 'Henry VIII
and the English Monasteries ; an attempt to illustrate the History of their
Suppression.' By Francis Aidan Gasquet. Vol. I. The book, which lays
blame on Protestants as well as on Roman Catholics, is characterised as being
'most conscientiously fair.' For a full statement of the case against the
monasteries, I refer the reader to Ch. V of R. W. Dixon's History of the
Church of England. Vol. I, 1878 (London : Smith, Elder, and Co.).

[2] Wanley, by a misprint, 793.

lection of interlinear versions, prayers, confessions, and other treatises. The authorities of the great public libraries are not, so far as I know, keeping registers of the MSS. published or transcribed. The work in arrear is of course enormous; but an inverted Wanley to begin with,—to which the present is a humble contribution—would be an invaluable boon to students of the Oldest English, and would be a foundation for librarians to work upon. I therefore proceed to give notes of where the various pieces in the MS. Tiberius A. 3 are printed, if they have been edited at all; and I hope that all who have ever turned over the leaves of MSS. to hunt for unpublished matter, will be glad of my attempt; especially those who have diligently copied out page after page, only to find that this had been already done by some one else. Since Wanley's time the pagination of the MS. has been slightly altered, and my statements refer to this new pagination.

That some one will take this work up for all MSS. is a consummation devoutly to be wished.

The greater part of the MS. was copied out by Junius (see below, p. xxxii, on the value of these transcriptions), and his copies are kept in the Bodleian Library, at Oxford. It is to the various MSS. of this collection that the words ' MS. Junius' (infra) refer.

Contents of the MS. Tiberius A. 3.

No. I (fo. 3).   Regularis Concordia Anglicae Nationis Monachorum Sanctimonialiumque.

MSS. Jun. 52. 109 (now = No. 46).   Wanley, pp. 92 and 99.   VII.

Of this, the Latin text has been printed in full at least twice: (a) in R. P. Clem. Reyneri Apostolatus Benedictinorum, and (b) in the later editions of the Monasticon Anglicanum, see edd. 1817, 1846, I, p. xxvii. The Anglo-Saxon text has never been printed in full. Besides the smaller quotations given from it by Wanley himself, other extracts have been put in type several times. Selden printed the prologue and the greater part of the epilogue in his notes to Eadmer. See his Works, ed. 1726, II (tomus 2), pp. 1612-1621 (see MS. Junius, 18 ; Wanley, p. 103). Selden, in accordance with the usage of his time, ' edits'[1] the MS., and though he does not mention the MS. from which his text is taken, it is highly probable that our MS. is the one. Th. Wright, in his Biographia Litt.

---

[1] See Skeat, Preface to the Gospel of S. Matthew, p. viii.

Brit., Anglo-Saxon period (I), p. 459, prints the 11th chapter by way of specimen. Quite recently the prologue and part of the first chapter have been published—critically edited, as the title page says—by Dr. Edward Breck, 'Fragment of Aelfric's translation of Aethelwold's De consuetudine Monachorum,' etc., Leipsic. W. Drugulin's printing office, 1887.

An edition of the whole text is preparing by Mr. W. S. Logeman. I may here add that the work is generally supposed to be one of Dunstan's, but it has been attributed also to Aelfric, whilst of late, independently of each other, Professor A. Ebert (Allgemeine Gesch. der Litt. des Mittelalters III, p. 506), and the above-named Dr. Breck, have fathered it upon Aethelwold, Abbot of Abingdon, and afterwards Bishop of Winchester.

II–XVII, inclusive, are all of a nature that makes us turn to Cockayne's Leechdoms (London, 1864–1866) to see if any are printed in it. As a matter of fact, I find the following state of affairs :—

No. II (fo. 27 b).   Leechdoms, III, 198.
MS. Jun. 43. Wanley, p. 88.

No. III (fo. 32 b).   Leechdoms, III, 184 (without the Latin text).
MS. Jun. 44. Wanley, p. 89 (imperfect? Wanley).

No. IV (fo. 35 b).   Unprinted[1] (but copied by me for publication).
MS. Jun. 43. Wanley, p. 88.

No. V (fo. 36).   Unprinted.

No. VI (fo. 36 b).   Unprinted.

No. VII (fo. 36 b).   Leechdoms, III, 150.
MS. Jun. 44. Wanley, p. 89.

No. VIII (fo. 37).   Unprinted, but copied for publication.
MS. Jun. 44. Wanley, p. 89, sub VIII.

No. IX (fo. 37 b).   Leechdoms, III, 154 and 168.
MS. Jun. 43. Wanley, p. 88, sub II and V. There is, however, a discrepancy in the two concluding passages of the texts. Having at the moment of writing no access to either MS., I am unable to solve the difficulty, which was perhaps also felt by Wanley. At least, he says, very prudently; 'Idem Codex, inquit, ch. Junius,' etc.

No. X (fo. 39 b).   Leechdoms, III, 176.
MS. Jun. 44. Wanley, p. 89, sub V.

---

[1] I consulted Professor Napier on this subject. He was so kind as to put his bibliographical knowledge at my disposal whenever I wished to draw upon it.

No. XI (fo. 40).   Leechdoms, III, 180.
MS. Jun. 44.   Wanley, p. 89, sub IX.

No. XII (fo. 40 b).   Leechdoms, III, 180.
MS. Jun. 44.   Wanley, p. 89, sub VII.

No. XIII (fo. 40 b).   Leechdoms, III, 146.
MS. Jun. 41, sub II.   Wanley, p. 87.

No. XIV (fo. 41).   Leechdoms, III, 156.

No. XV (fo. 41 b).   Unprinted (copied).
MS. Jun. 44.   Wanley, pp. 89 and 90, sub XI.

No. XVI (fo. 42).   Unprinted (copied).

No. XVII (fo. 42 b).   Leechdoms, III, 144.
MS. Jun. 41.   Wanley, p. 87.

Nos. XVIII–XX, and Nos. XXIII, XXIV inclusive, (ff. 43–44), are small tracts, very short notes, in fact ('Notulae' Wanley), on Adam, Noah, Fasting, the Virgin's Age, and on Crime. They are shortly to appear in the Anglia XI.

No. XVIII.
MS. Jun. 44.   Wanley, p. 90, sub XIV.

No. XXI is Latin (fo. 43 b).

No. XXII (fo. 44).   Leechdoms, III, 228 (partly, only, and from the MS. Caligula A. XV).

No. XXIII.
MS. Jun. 44.   Wanley, p. 90, sub XIV.

No. XXV (ff. 44–57). A collection of confessions and prayers as yet unprinted. They will shortly appear in the Anglia. Only the latter part (Wanley, p. 196), beginning : 'Dæt sceal geþencan,' also appearing in an Oxford MS. (Wanley, p. 51), was used by Thorpe in Ancient Laws, II, 260.
MS. Jun. 63.   Wanley, p. 93.

No. XXVI (ff. 57–60 b).   'Missa, cum rubricis Saxonice.' I am not aware that it has been printed.

No. XXVII (fo. 60 b) has been published several times; see Wülker's Grundrisz, p. 476 (III, § 568).
MS. Jun. 66. Wanley, p. 95. Zupitza (Zeitschr. f. D. Alt. 31. 28 ff.) has recently treated of the relation of the two MSS. known to exist. I must here mention a note in the preface to Wanley's Catalogue. Amongst some books that used to be in the library of Christ Church, Canterbury, he names (p. 8) a 'Locutio Latina glosata Anglice, ad instruendos pueros (forte Aelfric Bata).' I have no means of de-

terminining whether this is the identical copy that is now in the
Cottonian Library. It would seem not, from the fact that it is mentioned
as a separate book, whereas both the Oxford and the London copies are
part of a collection of treatises. The query rises, were they always
so? The Oxford MS. is to be published by Zupitza.

Nos. XXVIII–XXXI (fo. 65). Latin.

No. XXXII (fo. 65 b). Leechdoms, III, 238 (here, as in
some of the cases quoted before, only as ' variae lectiones ').

MS. Jun. 41. Wanley p. 87. See Wülker's Grundrisz, III, § 571;
Anglia X, p. 457 ff.

The notae that Wanley mentions on p. 196 b of his catalogue (Nota de
Archa noe, de S. Petri Ecclesia, et de Templo Salomonis, Saxonice,
fo. 73 a, b) have not yet been printed, but I presume they are
shortly to appear in the Anglia (xi). MS. Jun. 44. Wanley, p. 90,
sub XIV.

No. XXXIII (fo. 73 b). Cockayne's Narratiunculae, p. 39;
cf. Wülker's Grundrisz, § 602.

No. XXXIV (fo. 77 b). Aelfric's Homilies (ed. Thorpe),
II, 240.

No. XXXV (fo. 83). Is in Napier's ed. of Wulfstan's
Homilies.

MS. Jun. 69. Wanley, p. 95.

No. XXXVI (fo. 87). Kemble's Salomon and Saturn, p. 84.

MS. Jun. 69. Wanley, p. 96. It will be included in Professor Napier's
first volume of Homilies, to be edited for the Early English Text
Society.

Nos. XXXVII–XLVIII (fo. 88 b), inclusive, will all be
found in Professor Napier's Wulfstan.

No. XLIX (fo. 93 b). Latin.

No. L (fo. 94 b). I. Edited in Thorpe's Anc. Laws, II, 260.
Nos. 2–6 inclusive are also to be found there, but printed
from other MSS. See above, under No. 25.

MS. Jun. 59. Wanley, p. 93.

No. LI (fo. 97). Printed by Kluge, Internationale Zeitschrift für Vergl. Sprachforschung, ed. Techmer, II, 118.

MS. Jun. 52. Wanley, p. 92.

Nos. LII and LIII (fo. 101 b). So far as I know, unprinted. One would expect these to be included in Cockayne's
Leechdoms.

No. LIV (fo. 102). See Kluge, E. Stud., VIII, 472. It
contains a reminiscence of the A.-S. poem, the Seafarer.

No. LV (fo. 103). 'Que sunt instrumenta Bonorum, Latine et eadem Saxonice. Sectio excerpta ex Regula S. Benedicti,' says Wanley. It is a copy of chapter four, of the work which, as I have said above (p. xv) and below (p. xxxi), has been edited, with some variae lectiones, by Professor A. Schröer; but he has not given a collation of this Tiberius MS.

Nos. LVI, LVII (fo. 105). These will probably be included in Professor Napier's collection of Homilies.

> MS. Jun. 48 (by a misprint in Wanley: 47). Wanley, p. 90 (for No. LVII).

No. LVIII (fo. 106). Leechdoms, III. p. 286. See Wanley, p. 110 (C. C. C. C. L. 12).

No. LIX (fo. 106). See Wülker's Grundrisz, §§ 564–566, p. 475.

No. LX (fo. 107 b). 'Votiva Laus.' Latin.

No. LXI (fo. 118). This is our Benedictine Rule. See below, sections III and IV.

> MS. Jun. 92. Wanley, p. 103. Junius copied only part of the gloss into a printed text : ' Regula S. Benedicti Latine Duaci impressa, A. D. 1611, Saxonice per Junium glossata ex Cottoniano codice qui inscribitur, Tiberius A. 3.' When preparing my text for the press, I was not in a position to compare Junius's copy.

No. LXII (fo. 163 b) Regulae S. Fulgentii Latine, cum interlineata versione Saxonice.'

> MS. Jun. 52. Wanley, pp. 91, 92. Wanley, in bestowing this name on this collection of monastic precepts, evidently followed Junius, who, at the beginning of his copy, says: Benedicti regulam interlineatam, quam habet Cottonianus codex qui inscribitur, Tiberius A. 3, mox excipiunt S. Fulgentii regulae, similiter interlineatae.

> The Precepts, as in the present MS., begin thus :—
>
>   'DICEBAT VERO SANCTUS FULGENTIUS.
>
> ' Juxta[1] regulam patrum vivere semper stude ; maxime autem secundum sancti confessoris tui benedicti ; Non declines ab ea in quoquam : nec illi addas quippiam, nec minuas ; Totum enim quod sufficit habet, et nusquam minus habet ; cujus verba atque imperia sectatores suos perducunt ad celi palatia ;' and then follows immediately—
>
>   ' A KALENDIS AUTEM OCTOBRIS USQUE IN PASCHA
>
> ' hora nona hoc faciunt,' etc.
>
> These words : ' A kalendis autem Octobris,' etc., to the end of our

---

[1] I leave out the interlinear gloss, and here tacitly correct the Latin. These rules will be printed separately elsewhere.

so-called Regulae S. Fulgentii, at fo. 168 b, form part of a treatise printed in Migne's Patrol. Cursus completus, Vol. 66, p. 938, where it is headed: Ordo Monasticus S. P. Benedicto attributus. It is this fact that makes it all but necessary for me to say a word on the subject.

The reason why these Precepts have been ascribed to S. Benet seems to be this. A monk at S. Germain du Pré[1] stated that they were found in a 'vetus quoddam MS. Cassinense,' which enjoys a high reputation for genuineness.

This circumstance seems to have been sufficient reason for Arnoldus Wion to print the Precepts with the edition of the Benedictine Rule in 1593 at Venice, and thus silently[2] sanction S. Benet's authorship. The argument is, however, a very shallow one, and so long as no other proofs are adduced, 'hoc opusculum non pro vero fetu magni S. Benedicti vendere praesumimus' (Migne, Vol. 66, p. 938).

The words at the beginning: *Juxta regulam* to *celi palatia*, headed by *Dicebat vero sanctus Fulgentius*, and especially the latter, must have given rise to Junius's error.

Nos. LXIII and LXIV (fo. 168 b) are Latin monastic precepts which, *variis lectionibus*, also occur in MS. Titus A. 4, ff. 107 and 117.

No. LXV (fo. 174). 'Aethelwoldus de consuetudine monachorum Saxonice.' It has been printed by A. Schröer, Englische Studien, IX, 291. See E. Breck, as quoted *supra*, passim.

MS. Jun. 52. Wanley, p. 91.

No. LXVI (fo. 177) is a Latin fragment, and, I think, unprinted.

No. LXVII (fo. 178). This did not originally belong to the MS. It most probably belonged to MS. Tib. A. 6. See Wanley's note, and Prof. Earle's ed. of the two parallel Chronicles, p. xxv (Oxford, 1865). See Wanley, p. 84 (MS. Laud, G. 36, II).

MS. Jun. 66. Wanley, p. 95. It appears from Wanley's note that in his time it belonged to MS. Tib. A. 3.

No. LXVIII (fo. 179). See Leechdoms, III, 218.

No. LXIX (fo. 179 b). Latin, and, so far as I know, not printed.

---

[1] R. P. Jacobus du Brevil monachus S. Germani a Pratis; see Migne, Vol. 66, note at the end of the treatise there, p. 942.

[2] I have not seen this edition, but presume that Wion does not expressly attribute the Precepts to S. Benet.

III. The Latin Text. Nineteenth-century Editions.
Manner of Editing.

WE have already seen (p. xv) that S. Benedict of Nursia
wrote his Rule about the year 516. No earlier writers have
yet been pointed out as his sources. It is quite probable that he
had none [1]. The Rule no doub t originated in the saint's desire
to provide his own followers with a code of laws to live by.
However much he venerated his *foregengan*, as the conditions
under which his monks lived differed from those of his
predecessors, he must have been mainly, if not quite, original in
the choice of his precepts. No doubt, his reading the works of
a S. Basil and others may have made him feel the desira-
bility of writing regulations of his own. But I should be
surprised to hear that after-search had established a definite
and direct relationship of matter between our Rule and any
one of the works whose key-note it has more or less struck [2].

The number of commentaries that our Rule has called forth
would seem to be legion. This Introduction is hardly the
place for their enumeration. Neither can we allow ourselves
to copy out the encomia of which S. Benedict and his followers
can boast. Suffice it to refer for these to Migne, (see below)
volume 66, which contains the greater part of these encomia,
and references to more works on the subject.

Our Latin text has been edited several times. Apart from
the older editions, such as the one of 1593 (printed at Venice
by Fr. Arnoldus Wion), I here enumerate those nineteenth
century edd. that have come to my knowledge :—

(*a*) MIGNE. Patrologiae Cursus Completus, vol. 66, p. 215
ff., Regula S. Benedicti cum commentariis.

These commentaries make the edition a very useful one.
However, the work is very difficult to be got at, its enormous
bulk—over 200 volumes—makes few persons care to buy it.

---

[1] See Guéranger, as quoted infra, 'sanctus spiritus per beatum Benedictum
. . . Regulam Monachorum edidit' (p. vi).
[2] See however: Concordia Regularum, auctore S. Benedicto, . . . auctore
Fr. Hugone Menardo . . . Parisiis, 1638.

(*b*) *Guéranger.* Enchiridion Benedictinum, complectens Regulam vitam et Laudes sanctissimi occidentalium monachorum Patriarchae, accedunt Exercitia S. Gertrudis Magnae et Blosii speculum. Andegavi. Typis Cosnier et Lachese. MDCCCLXII, contains page 1, ff. Regula S. Patris Benedicti Juxta exemplar Cassinense.

(*c*) Pax. Monastic Gleanings. No. 1.

The Rule of Our most holy Father S. Benedict, patriarch of monks; in Latin and English. Translated by A Monk of S. Augustine's Monastery, Ramsgate. London, Burns & Oates, 1872.

(*d*) Regula Sancti Patris Benedicti juxta antiquissimos codices recognita, a P(atre) Edmundo Schmidt. Cum Permissu Superiorum. MDCCCLXXX. Ratisbonae, Neo Eboraci et Cincinnatii. Sumptibus, Chartis et Typis Friderici Pristet, S. Sedis Apostolicae Typographi.

This contains twenty-two pages of Prolegomena, in which the author treats of the relations of the MSS., and in which he wishes to establish that S. Benet prepared *two* drafts of his Rule. The work appears to be printed privately. At my request, however, the author kindly placed a copy at my disposal, for which I here beg to thank him most heartily.

(*e*) The Rule of our Most Holy Father Saint Benedict. Edited, with an English translation and Explanatory Notes by A Monk of S. Benedict's Abbey, Fort-Augustus. Jussu Superiorum. London, Burns & Oates, 1886.

(*f*) 'Die Winteney Version der Regula S. Benedicti, lateinisch und englisch zum erstenmale herausgegeben' has just appeared at Halle (M. Niemeyer), with a most interesting Preface. Before the work was published, the editor, Herr Dr. A. Schröer, professor at the University of Freiburg, presented me with a copy of the advance sheets of the text. For this courteous act I here express my sincere gratitude, as well as for other kindnesses received at that gentleman's hands.

The English work is a thirteenth century text, taken from the MS. Cott. Claud. D. III, whence the Latin text is also transcribed.

Herr Schmidt used fifteen Latin texts for his edition ; Professor Schröer only those four of which he published the Anglo-Saxon version [1]. As Herr Schmidt used a collation of our codex (Schmidt = F) as well as one of the MS. Tib. A. IV (= Schröer's T, Schmidt's G), the total number of Latin codices to which I shall subsequently have occasion to refer to is nineteen. I designate them as follows :—

A. Cod. Tegernseensis. Royal Libr., Munich (clm. 19408).
B. „ Mondseensis. R. and Imp. Libr., Vienna (2332).
C. „ Fuldensis. Bibl. Fuld. (D. 3).
D. „ Parisiensis. Nat. Libr. (4208).
E. „ Frisingensis. Royal Libr., Munich (clm. 6255).
F. „ Londinensis I. Cott. Libr., Tib. (A. 3).
G. „ Londinensis II. Cott. Libr., Tit. (A. 4).
H. „ Veronensis I. City Library.
I. „ Bruxellensis. Library of the Dukes of Burgundy (8305).
K. „ Romanus. Vatican Cod. Lat. 5949.
L. „ Einsidlensis, No. 236.
O. „ Oxoniensis. Bodl. Libr., Hatton MS.
P. „ Faucensis. Library of the Cathedral Chapter at Augsburg.
Q. „ Veronensis II. Library of the Cath. Ch. at Verona.
R. „ Sangallensis. Chapter Library, 916.
S. is Schröer's C Winteney Version. MS. Cott. Claud. D. III. Cf. p. xxvii.
T.   „   A. (MS. C. C. C. C. 178). Schröer, Prosa Bearb., p. xix
                 (Anglia, vi. 430).
U.   „   O. (MS. C. C. C. O. 197). Schröer, ib., p. xxi.
W.   „   Wells fragment, belonging to the Dean and Chapter of Wells
                 Cathedral. Schröer, ib., p. xxv.

For further particulars about MSS. A–R, the few privileged persons who possess the book may be referred to Schmidt's Preface, pp. xii–xv, from which part of the above has been abstracted. For G, see also Schröer, Die Prosabearbeitungen, p. xxiii. For F, see supra, Ch. II. The collation of our text, undertaken for Herr Schmidt by a friend, appears to be rather incorrect.

It must not be supposed that there are no more Latin texts than those enumerated. I have casually come across others in the Library of Durham Cathedral, in the Lambeth Palace Library, in the Phillips Library at Cheltenham, and

---

[1] See A. Schröer, Die Prosabearbeitungen der B. R., p. xxvi, and now the above-mentioned preface, p. xi.

(of the fourth chapter only) in MS. Tib. A. 3, fo. 103 (see above, p. xxiv).

In the MS. Tib. A. 3 (fo. 118, above, p. xxiv), our Latin text occurs in an exceedingly corrupt state. 'Scatetque mendis,' justly observes Schmidt (p. xiii). Guéranger, Schmidt, Migne, etc., have, in their editions, largely deviated from the MS. readings. Lower down in this Introduction, in §§ 7 and 8 of No. V, some remarks will be found bearing on the edition of the Latin text, to which I beg to refer the reader. It will be seen from those, what my position is with regard to hitherto prevalent modes of editing Latin texts. The principles there stated have led me to deviate as little as possible from the MS. readings, nay, I have tried to keep to them always, except in cases where their spelling would make the text absolutely unintelligible to the ordinary reader. No one will for a moment feel doubts as to the meaning of *debead, prospiciad, habbatis*, etc., but I deem it possible that the spelling *medicetur*, as lemma to *he smæge* (96. 2), might throw those off the track who did not at the moment think of the phenomenon which will be found discussed, infra, No. V, § 63. Hence, such spellings have been banished from the text, but I have been careful to mark these divergencies in the foot-notes, whereas the spelling differences whose meaning was obvious, I have put in the text itself.

I have adhered to the paragraphs of the MS., as well as to its peculiar [1] punctuation. The contractions have all been expanded [2], and to denote them, the letters not actually found in the MS. are printed in Roman type, whereas the rest of the Latin text is in italics.

In the first few pages of this Rule, some gaps occur ; see the Text, p. 1 ff., passim. The Latin letters, so far as they may be supposed to have disappeared, are added in brackets. The headings of the chapters are almost always majuscules in

---

[1] So peculiar that I afterwards, but too late, wished I had adopted a less embarrassing plan.

[2] I am unable to agree with E. Kölbing, E. Stud., III, 469 note, in so far as he says that it is unnecessary to denote these contractions.

black ink, but mostly tinged with red. The first line, or part
of it, of the Latin text in each chapter is usually also in
capital black letters, no red ink being applied here. In this
edition they have been denoted by small capitals. The illumi-
nated capitals found in the MS. at the beginning of the
chapters are mostly of a red, green, or blue colour; once or
twice they have been forgotten. The glossator or glossators
has or have sometimes added Latin words in the line of the
gloss above the Latin[1]. These additions are sometimes words
that also occur in other Latin texts, so that we may suppose
the then glossator to have copied these from another Latin
text. In this case the added word has been inserted in the
text, and in the *Latin* foot-notes attention has been drawn
to this by the words: *added* or *supplied* by glossator. Of a
different nature are the words that are scribbled over the
Latin text, without being at all found in the other texts.
They may be termed Latin glosses, and though comparatively
rare, are found, e.g. where the word *debere* or *debemus* (see text,
Cap. IV, passim) is added to explain the infinitive used as
an imperative. Of this nature is the gloss ɫ *plane* to *sane*
(78. 17). These words, although Latin, are always put in
the line above, as partaking of the nature of glosses. They,
too, may be due to more than one scribe, but they are
now found in the MS. in the characteristic handwriting of
the Anglo-Saxon scribe. Attention has mostly been drawn to
these additions in the Anglo-Saxon foot-notes.

IV. The Anglo-Saxon Text. Manner of Editing.
The 'Paving Letters.'

The prose paraphrases of the Rule of S. Benet in Anglo-
Saxon that have been edited by A. Schröer[2] have no connection

---

[1] Our MS. is a copy; so that if more than one glossator has been at work—
which I have every reason to believe—the external traces of their work
are effaced. The reader will see that the existence of more than one glossator
must be assumed, by referring to the work, and especially the notes (e.g. note
to 10. 7, p. 121; and 47. 3, etc.)

[2] (a) Bibliothek der Angelsächsischen Prosa, von C. W. M. Grein, fortgesetzt
von R. P. Wülker, Zweiter Band: Die Angelsächsischen Prosabearbeitungen

whatever with the present interlinear text. Of course, some words are the same, both in the interlinear and paraphrastical translations, but the greater number of them are different. This constitutes the principal claim of our text to a separate edition. It would be an interesting task to compare the vocabulary of the two versions together. There is no doubt that where the meaning of an Anglo-Saxon word can be demonstrated from glosses, there is a chance of its being the correct one. But still the glossator may have misunderstood his Latin[1], a fact of very frequent occurrence; and in some cases, through lack of other instances, we may be unable to control his rendering, which, of course, is not checked by any context. But in the case of a running text, the translation, even if corresponding word for word, is free, and we cannot always depend on the translated word being an exact equivalent of the original. Where we have an interlinear translation—a sort of crib—as well as a paraphrase, we may be certain that those words which occur in both translations are accurate renderings.

So far as I am aware, the thirty-ninth chapter, which Thomas Wright published in his 'Biographia Britannica Literaria' (I, p. 442, Latin and gloss), is the only part of the present Benedictine Rule that has been edited, excepting, of course, the few specimen lines that may be found in Wanley's and in other catalogues. But the MS. appears to have been extracted from for lexicographical purposes, and consequently words and phraseological quotations from it are to be found in the various A.-S. dictionaries. Part of the glossing was copied into a Latin printed text by the indefatigable Junius. His texts, however useful they may be to the student of literature, should not be used for linguistic purposes. Junius

---

der Benedictiner Regel. Herausgegeben von A. Schröer. Kassel, 1885–1888. (b) Die Winteney-Version der Regula S. Benedicti, Lateinisch und English. Mit Einleitung Anmerkungen, Glossar und einem Facsimile zum ersten Male herausgegeben von Dr. M. M. Arnold Schröer. Halle a.-S. Max Niemeyer, 1888. See supra, p. xxvii.

[1] It seems like biting sarcasm when in the historical tract in MS. Faustina, A. 10 we read of the 'scearpþanclan witan þe . . . þisse engliscan geþeodnesse ne behofien' (Cockayne, Leechdoms, III, 440; i. e. the keen-witted sages that . . . do not need this English translation.)

appears to enjoy the reputation of being a faithful copyist, but when collating his copy of the so-called 'Regulae S. Fulgentii' (above, p. xxiv) with the MS., I observed that this reputation was entirely unfounded [1]. He adds words not in his MSS. He leaves out words found in his original, or transposes them. He does not distinguish between ð and þ, which he consequently uses indiscriminately [2]. He entirely disregards the punctuation of the MS., and he adds numbers of chapters after his own pleasure or notions of how they ought to have been. Lastly, he corrects his text without giving the reading of the MS.

The convent to which this MS. belonged is not known. Nor is there any author on whom we have reason to father our version. The likelihood indeed is that this interlinear version *gradually* developed, so that it cannot be assigned to any one person.

The object of this edition is to furnish the student with a text as it is found in the manuscript, with all its gaps, imperfections, and absurdities. I am of opinion that however stupidly a scribe may have mangled his original, the reading of the MS. is still the only thing of which we are sure. I have tampered so little with the MS. that I have left even the most palpable errors unchanged; here, however, I have followed the example set by former editors, and starred the forms which without doubt are merely clerical errors. It need hardly be said that I should not have followed this plan, were this text destined for the use of those desirous of learning the rudiments of Anglo-Saxon. Moreover, if the present were the only version extant, I might have taken into consideration the wants of those students who wished to read this text for the 'realia,' and I should thus

[1] See H. Sweet, Introduction to Gregory's Pastoral Care, p. xix, whose sole blame is that Junius 'sometimes swerved from the path of literal accuracy in a few unimportant particulars.' See, on the contrary, Zupitza, Zeitschrift für Deutsches Altertum, 31. 2; Breck, Fragment, etc. (supra, p. xxi), p. 5. MacLean, Anglia, 6. 448.

[2] It is generally assumed that the scribes themselves did not distinguish between the ð and þ, and used them promiscuously. But if even any distinction is to be found, editors should take care not to obscure this find by not adhering strictly to the writing of the MSS.

have been compelled to make a more or less readable text of
it. But for this there is, of course, no occasion. Those who
wish to read S. Benet's precepts for the sake of their contents
will find their wishes gratified in the present volume by
looking up the Latin text; and if any one desires to read it in
Anglo-Saxon, the very handy editions of Professor Schröer are ·
now available. There can be no doubt, to my thinking, that
it must be the aim of an editor to give the text as the
manuscript records it. Of course he may then set to work
and, by dint of exterior and interior criticism, try to eliminate
some mistakes, but—in the case of an edition like the present
—I am of opinion that this should be done in foot-notes.
Nothing can be gained by imprudently introducing one's own
—if I may so express it—one's own Anglo-Saxon amidst the
language—though a corrupted specimen of it—of our fore-
fathers. Indeed a great deal may be lost—unity.

Now, doubtless, it may be objected that when, e. g. the
word *gebetrode* is found in the MS. as *gebcorode*, there can be no
doubt that this was not a mistake, but simply a *blunder*, and
that therefore no purpose is served by retaining it in the text.
True, partly! But even here there is this consideration, that
to watch the mistakes of scribes is not without interest, for
the study of culture in a given period.

In accordance with the principles laid down, I have given
the text of this Rule exactly as it is found in the MS. Only
the following must be observed. The *i*, which is in the
MS. written undotted, has been printed with a dot over
it. Absolutely wrong forms are starred. Elucidations to
forms in any way remarkable, will be found in the foot-notes,
or in those at the end of the volume [1], or, when the matter is
one of phonological or grammatical interest, in the fifth division
of this Introduction. Italics denote the expansions of the
scribal contractions, when no foot-note is appended. Other-

---

[1] In most cases attention has been drawn to these by the words *see note*.
The editor is sorry to own that, owing to a want of foresight, no very definite, at
least no very scholarly, principle can be laid down as to what notes may be
found at the foot of the page, and what at the end of the volume. As a rule,
palæographical notes are at the bottom of the page, and elucidations of
different nature on p. 119, etc. But various causes prevented this rule being
always adhered to.

wise, those letters are italicised to which attention has been called in the foot-note. Thus *þæt* means that the MS. has the contraction þ, as no foot-note is there. But the letters *nce* in *gesw*ince (1.6) are italicised merely to call the attention to the note. Whenever I have thought it necessary to propose an emendation, it has been only when some reason for the corruption could be adduced, either from a graphical error, or a psychical process. But where these reasons were more or less obscure, I have stated them in words.

Our Anglo-Saxon text is a copy, i.e. the glosses have not been put over the Latin text only in our MS. Both have been copied from another text or from other texts, most likely at the same time, and possibly by the same scribe. The chances are—indeed, there is every reason to believe—that our MS. was copied often. That the last copyist had an interlinear translation before him, is evident from the frequent occurrence of wrong forms that can only be explained by influence of the lemma on the gloss, or vice versa (see foot-notes, passim). When an original Latin text was first glossed, we may a priori assume two possibilities. Either the glosses were *copied* into our original Latin from a ready-made Anglo-Saxon translation, or the glossators worked without a model of any kind.

Let us consider the first assumption. If this were true, the Anglo-Saxon text must have been supplied either from the text commonly attributed to Aethelwold[1], or from some other hitherto unknown text. We need, of course, not speak of the latter possibility, as the establishment of this point, as well as its rejection, are utterly beyond determination. As to the text edited by Schröer, it is not likely to have been the original, for, as we have already seen, the vocabulary of the two is somewhat different.

We are therefore led to the theory of the gloss-origin. And, indeed, even if we could have for a moment thought of the other theory, the evidence in favour of the former is so overwhelming that there can be no doubt about it; and I

---

[1] Thus Schröer, ib., p. xvii. I am not sure that he has established his point.

have but to refer to the appearance of the text, passim, without entering into particulars in any way.

We find then that our version developed,—just like the glossaries that Henry Sweet has so ably treated of in his Oldest English Texts, p. 7—out of a few interlinear glosses, that have multiplied gradually until, in our MS., the Latin is very nearly fully-glossed, every copyist having contributed some more glosses to those which he found in his original. The scribe of our MS. has also acted as a glossator. His work can be traced, e.g. in the words *gesawen* and *visum* (as its lemma, 13. 3), that he himself put instead of the *ealra*, *omnium*, which is a misreading that does not belong to the text.

That we can still be positive about the fact that more than one scribe has been at work is rather curious, considering that through the last copy all external traces of former glossators are lost. Yet a place like (13. 1)

leorn forebeon i. cnihtum
præesse   discipulis

can hardly be otherwise explained than as the work of two glossators.

THE 'PAVING' LETTERS.

Those who happen to have looked into the text of our Rule before reading this part of the Introduction will have been struck at seeing numerous letters enclosed—in our print[1]— in square brackets spread all over the volume. In the notes they will be found referred to as 'paving letters' or 'gloss-letters.' The word, as well as the matter, I now proceed to explain.

As to the letters themselves, they are found in our MS. Tib. A. 3, over most of the Latin words, both in our Benedictine Rule, and in those tracts that Wanley styled the Regulae S. Fulgentii (supra, p. xxiv), but, so far as I have been able to find out, they do not occur anywhere else. No one I could consult—I may thankfully and especially mention Dr. E. Maunde Thompson, now Chief Librarian of the British

---

[1] Not so in the MS. See next paragraph.

Museum—knew of their existence in any other manuscript. The only man who mentions them is that accurate worthy, Wanley, who, at p. 199 of his Catalogue, speaking of these letters, says: 'N.B. Super voces Latinas, exaratas esse Literas Saxonicas, quae, quo ordine construendae sunt, ostendunt.' Had Wanley written in English, his would have been the task, which now devolves upon a foreigner, of bestowing an English name on these 'Literae.'

He would, no doubt, have followed the ordinary school-crib *ordo*, which gives the English construing order of a Latin author, and would have called these unfortunate waifs ' *order*- or *sequence*-letters.' But when I talked to Dr. Thompson on the subject, he said that the Rugby boys' slang term for this process was *paving*—paving smooth (I suppose) the rough road of learning Latin. The term struck me as a happy one, suiting Wanley's *construendae*, and so I adopted it, though perhaps without due consideration of how it would puzzle readers to whom 'paving' suggests only laying stones on a carriage-road or a footpath.

That Wanley is right in saying that these 'paving' or sequence letters show the order of construing Latin into Anglo-Saxon, is not so apparent at first sight as on closer investigation. The idea must have been, of course, to put the letters over these words that wanted construing, in such a way that they had but to be arranged in the alphabetical order thus indicated, in order to yield an intelligible meaning [1]. Now it is, e. g. not clear why the scribe at one time begins with *a* and goes on to the end of the alphabet, whereas at another time he proceeds only as far as *g* or *l*, or almost any letter, and begins again at *a*. The Latin wanted ' paving,' not the gloss-text. A friend suggested to me that it must have been the Anglo-Saxon text whose syntactical word-order was thus pointed out. 'In order to get an Anglo-Saxon translation, not glosses'—thus my friend writes—'some one put in those " paving " letters to indicate the word-order of the vernacular text. A later copyist, not being able to read the text well, copied the paving letters,

[1] See below, V, § 6.

but omitted the glosses.' I am inclined to think that this
view is not correct. It must be admitted that the several
blunders—see the starred forms—for which we must blame
one or more of the scribes, point to an imperfectly legible
text [1] at one time or another. But is it likely that the gloss
should have been unintelligible so wholesale, and the paving
letters quite clear? Must we not *a priori* accept the fact
that the Latin text stood in need of comment? What could
have been the object of him who thus tried to transmute
the interlinear translation into a more or less paraphrastical
one? I do not wish to lay undue stress on the fact that
the gloss-letters are in Latin characters, like the Latin
text, whereas the A.-S. text is naturally written in A.-S.
characters. I only say that, although it perhaps remains an
open question, the likeliest thing seems to be, that we must
look upon the gloss-letters as ' paving ' the Latin text.

At one time we find two gloss-letters over one Latin
word, not only where this is glossed by *two* Anglo-Saxon
ones, but also where only one A.-S. rendering is given. At
another, a few non-paved words may be seen intervening
between two sets of paved ones. Sometimes these non-paved
words must be taken into account when construing the
sentence, whereas a little further on we may find an instance
where they need not be taken into consideration. From this
it is clear that, whatever explanation we fall back upon to
solve the difficulty—and none other but the one propounded
by Wanley seems plausible, or even possible—we must not
strain it; we must rather be content to apply the key somewhat loosely; for there can be no doubt that our ' paving '
letters have suffered by the frequent transcribing which our
text has undergone. In consequence of this we may expect:—

    a. Letters to have been put over the wrong words ;

    β. Letters not to have been transcribed ;

    γ. Letters to have been misunderstood as part of gloss-
        words, which in reality are nothing but gloss-letters ;

---

[1] To this cause the same gentleman also attributes the phenomena I have
discussed below, V, § 4.

δ. Parts of a word—initial letters, mostly—to have been taken as 'paving' letters, and written separately accordingly.

For the case of *a*, I refer the student to the text passim. For *β*, I would remind him of the fact that unless this assumption be right, the frequent occurrence of a single gloss-letter over a Latin word, amidst a number of non-paved Latin words, cannot be explained. Of the cases under *γ* and *δ* some instances should be adduced:—*asutol, esefor, drenc, aða, bæt*, which must be read respectively as [a.] sutol, [e.] se for (ma) [d.] renc (cf. note to 69. 12), [a.] ða, etc., whereas in *h algena* (sanctorum) the case would seem to lie the other way about.

All this tends to make it tolerably certain that Wanley's supposition is correct, however many difficulties we may find in our way. In the MS. the gloss-letters are always found over the Latin words, sometimes by the side of the A.-S. gloss (either before or after it), sometimes under it, or even over it. To print them in exactly the same place was not feasible, as that would have taken up too much space. I have therefore had to make shift, and to print them in the same line with the A.-S. glosses: this was at once practical, and in accordance with the principle followed throughout in this edition, that whatever must be held to belong originally to the Latin text, whether written by the Latin scribe or by the last glossator, is put in the line of the lemmata, whereas all that partakes of the nature of the gloss—whether A.-S., Latin, or 'paving' letters—has been put in the line assigned to the glossarial renderings.

V. The Language of the Text. Crude Forms. 'Mero-graphy.' Evidence of the Latin Text. English Sounds. English Inflections.

§ 1. The language of the present text will be considered in this chapter in its most striking peculiarities. In all essentials, I think, we shall find it a document of the later periods of Anglo-Saxon. External criticism cannot be called in to bear

out this statement, for, as we have seen, there is no person on
whom to father it, nor is there any external reason to attribute it to an inmate or to inmates of any particular convent.
Considering that the only evidence we have—the palæography
of the MS.—gives us the limit of about 1020–1030, and
further remembering that we have some reason to believe
that the MS. was copied more than once, we may perhaps
roughly assign it to the first years of the eleventh century.

§ 2. The text will not be treated exhaustively. Such
treatment had better be reserved for the works of a standard
author of the period. Now that we have a statistical grammar
of two representative works of King Alfred's, in Prof. Cosijn's
Altwestsächsische Grammatik, it is highly desirable that some
one should take up this labour and commence a similar work
for, say, Aelfric. A work which is fit for such treatment
should yield material not only for phonetic studies, but also
for the study of inflections, and also of syntax. Our text
lacks the former to a certain extent, and the latter altogether.

§ 3. For the want of inflections, to a certain extent, I
refer to what in a letter to the *Academy* (for July 21, 1888),
and borrowing a term from Sanskrit philology, I have
called 'crude forms.' A glossator wishes to write down the
sense of the Latin word merely as an aid to his memory ; and
without regard to either number or case, he just jots down the
word—no more. It is not so much the nominative which he
selects, as 'the word' in the abstract, which of course in Teutonic
philology always coincides in form with the nominative.
I shall here enumerate some cases of crude forms :—

siðfæt (itinera, 3. 12), *twyfeald* (dupplici, 12. 17), *hyrde*
(pastoris, 12. 8 ; 17. 5), *leas* (gewitnesse ; falsum testimonium,
19. 13), *lænctenfæsten* (quadragesime, 45. 13, etc.), *vers*
(versuum, 50. 2), *mid gewunelic þeaw* (68. 5, 6 ; probably mid
was added afterwards to indicate the case ; more solido),
gewordenum forecnyll (facto primo signo, 82. 11), *wrað* (iratum,
116. 13).

Here the crude form is always singular, as also where we
find *hæc*, neuter plural, glossed by the neuter singular *þis* (5. 3).
But once I found ' utentibus' glossed by *brucendas* (92. 6),

which looks very much like a plural crude form. This may be also the case with *bebodn* (preceptis, 21. 17 ; 55. 13 ; and also 54. 2).

Conversely we find a singular glossed by a plural in *gymeleastum* (42. 7), and a nominative by a genitive in *calra heardnessa* (96. 7), but these must surely be due to a mistake. A similar occurrence is when verbal forms are glossed by infinitives. We cannot be astonished at this, if we think of what a school-boy in the present time, who had to prepare a piece of Latin for translation, would do. Suppose he found the form *taxavimus* in his text; the ending would naturally be clear to him, and he might ask, What is *taxare*, and having remembered it, or having been told, he would *perhaps* write down *we write*, if he took the ending into consideration, but it is quite possible that he would jot down *to write* only. In the same way we must bear in mind that it was quite as often the aim of the glossators to aid their own memory, as to further the use of the text by *others*. This is lost sight of, I think, by those scholars, who look upon any gloss as a *mistake* which does not in all particulars of tense, person, or number, case, etc., correspond with the lemma. For instances, see *leon* (fueris, 75. 4), *underfon* (subjaceat, 91. 8), and *infaran* (96. 13 ; ingredere, which, however, may not be in point, as the glossator was liable to the mistake of looking upon *ingredere* as an infinitive). See note to (97. 2).

§ 4. A phenomenon akin in character to the above, is one which, for want of a better name, I was forced to call ' merography,' because only part of the gloss was in these instances written. It would seem as if the glossator, when writing down only a few letters, thought: 'If I see but this part, I shall remember the whole easily enough ;' or, in cases where the ending is given only : ' I know the word well, it is only the case which I am in doubt of.' Hence, we find forms like the following [1]:—

*becu*man (5. 17), æm *tigað* (5. 17), lea *des* (10. 8), *for* ma (23. 5), eal *dre* (26. 11), *h*læd *dre* [2] (28. 1), hlæd *dran* (28. 9), *monðæs*,

---

[1] The parts which I supply are printed in Roman characters.

[2] The *h* is here, possibly, a corruption of a ' paving ' letter *b*.

monð *es* (39. 10), *on ænde* byrdnesse (41. 15), *ead* modnesse
(53. 8), *under* fo (56. 13), *ge* mæn *sumunge* (? 70. 5 ; cf. 69. 6,
or must we read *gesomnunge?*), *becumen* dum (? 75. 2),
sin gendra (77. 5), ræd *an* (83. 17), anfeald *lice* (101. 16),
genan (probably a mistake for *genam* ian ; 105. 17),
wege dihtað (110. 16, 17), *pra* vost (111. 9), *to wurpon* nesse
(113. 15).

Perhaps also in *rihtwisnesse* (injustitias 33. 11, but it may
more likely have been understood by the glossator as: *in
justitias*), and in *geunrotsaded* (62. 18) which must be supposed
to stand for *geunrotsad* or *geunrotsed*.

See, for another view of the origin of these glosses, IV,
p. xxxvii, note.

§ 5. As regards the lack of syntax, it is but natural that
syntax could not be expected in a collection of glossarial
renderings, constituting a text, like the present. Slight traces
of it may however be found, as when a gloss follows the
government of a preceding English word, instead of the
lemma, e. g. *heardlices*, as gloss to *asperum* (6. 4), being
a genitive dependent on the words *ænig þinc*, going before.
Cf. also the following :—*on ðam*, referring to *hiwe* (masculine, 14. 13), but gloss to in qua ; *hareowlicum hi fylian
regole* (magistram sequantur regulam, 18. 9); which may be
also owing to the tendency in Latin, of mixing up dative and
accusative forms.

In *þam geræddum* (qua perlecta, 41. 13), the gloss is wrongly
put in the masculine ; the glossator evidently thinking of the
godspelle which goes before ; whereas in reality the *qua* refers to
lectio.

§ 6. I must remind the reader, at this point, of how
narrowly we have missed possessing a valuable contribution
to the study of English syntax in our document. If we had
but the original, instead of a much defiled third or fourth-hand
copy, how the ' paving' letters would repay the trouble of an
investigation ! For there can be little doubt that if we could
re-arrange the Latin words in the alphabetical order of
the original position of these paving-letters, we should
find that the words were then put in the Anglo-Saxon word-

order, or nearly so. Why this is not now the case, may be
seen above, p. xxxvii.

§ 7. In making my choice as to what I should take up
and what reject, I have been guided by the principle of
noting only that which may be thought in any way to supple-
ment Sievers's Standard Grammar. It is to his second edition
that my quotations of his sections refer, which, however, I
do not always cite. I also give what is characteristic of the
period to which the present text belongs.

In what follows, the evidence will be found to be based,
with one or two exceptions, on material drawn from our Old
English text. But, when lately investigating this matter,
I came to the conclusion that a careful analysis of a Latin
text may sometimes yield valuable matter for phonetic investigation too. In a letter to the *Academy* [1] for Sept. 22, 1888,
I tried to lay down the general principles by which we
should be guided when working at a Latin text for this
purpose. What will be found there, may be summarised as
follows :—Where we know a Latin text to be written in the
country whose language we are investigating—in our case,
English,—and where we know that the spelling-differences
presented by the text under consideration are deviations from
the ordinary Latin taught in the Middle Ages; that is, where
we have reason to suppose that the peculiar spellings in this
text are due to an *English* scribe, we may take those Latin
spellings into account to corroborate the evidence of the
spelling in our English text.

Now although our MS. dates from the eleventh century,
i. e. about four centuries after the reported introduction of
Benedictinism into England, yet the ultimate source is a
Latin original. The fact, however, that the other MSS.
appear *not* to present the peculiarities of this manuscript,
enables us to rely more on the following evidence, especially
in conjunction with that of the Anglo-Saxon. I have here
brought together the little evidence that our text yields.
But my knowledge of Middle Latin is so slight that I am by

---

[1] See also the subsequent numbers of that periodical.

no means confident of having been at all consistent in distin-
guishing between what is general, and what is peculiar to the
English scribe. (See above, p. xxix.)

§ 8. That *ae* becomes *e* (passim) is, of course, quite general,
but perhaps the reverse process may be thought to illustrate
what will be found stated below in § 15. Cf. *desiderænt* (24. 13),
item (31. 13), *occupæntur* (82. 4.) The general levelling of
unstressed vowels may be perhaps exemplified by *corda* (19.
10), *murmurantis* (25. 10, 11), *opore* (35. 16), *leganter* (38. 15),
memoriter (39. 16), etc. As to what has been said of the
possible existence of nasal vowels, if any importance is to be
attached to the examples in §§ 41, 70, we may here instance
atiphona (43. 7), *emendaverit* (= -*int*, 59. 4), *injugat* (80. 16,
etc.). Do, perhaps, spellings such as *completori*, *subsellis*,
versum (40. 11, 46. 6, 50. 2, for *completoriis*, etc.) prove that
our scribe was accustomed to indicate vowel-length by
doubling the letter ?

As to § 42, cp. *sompno* (2. 9, 28. 2), *comtempnentes* (28. 16,
where *p* is added below the line), *amplicet=applicet* (21. 1), etc.

For the pronunciation of *b=v*, cf. in our text *habitavit*
(3. 16, etc.), which, however, is of very frequent occurrence
(as in the O.S. *Heliand*, e.g. *bar=far*). See Sweet, O.E.T.,
p. 185. If, as I have reason to suppose, this change obtains
only in this ending, -*abit*, -*avit*, I doubt whether it is anything but a graphical, or a continually occurring, blunder.

As to § 50, see *debead* (63. 12), *prospiciad* (68. 14), capud
(73. 15), *hospidum* (75. 8), *deliquid* (79. 15), and compare *jube
addare*, which is, of course, *jubeat dare* (91. 5). Hence in
(64. 14) I put *agad* in the text, not *agat*, on account of the
deo following.

Medicetur (96. 2, þæt he smæge, MS.)=*meditetur*, is equally
interesting, as the word *secende=setende* (below, § 63). Ad
§ 66, cf. *siens*=sciens (97. 5).

As to § 72 compare *habbatis* (79. 8), *coherceat* (15. 12), *in has
signato* (75. 3 = in (h)*assignato*), as well as *omnibus* (MS., evidently a corruption of ominibus=hominibus, 30. 6), *ospitum*
(61. 15), *ospite* (88. 12), *abitant* (91. 11), *ortu*(s) (112. 15), etc. ;
nichilum (4. 8) is, I believe, quite common elsewhere.

We shall now have to examine the Anglo-Saxon text.

§ 9. SOUNDS.—A. Stressed short *a* before nasals has passed through the second *o*-stage (Sievers, § 65), and has again become *a*. passim, e.g. *underfangen* (97. 4), *langsumum* (97. 7). Stressed short *a* otherwise placed is stable; the only cases where it is found as *o* are *ut to foranne* (65. 16; cf. § 20), and *upahofennesse* (22. 7).

Half-stressed and unstressed *a* passes into *e* and *o*. Cf. *andsweras* (3. 1), andswore (112. 6, 112. 9), and for the latter case *cadmodren* (14. 9), *forhiegenden* (15. 4), *witen* (72. 13), and befrinonne (26. 12).

§ 10. O. Stressed short *o* is sometimes found as *eo* before *r*, *f*, and *h*: *feorwyrðe* (interitum, 57. 5), *godes leof* (ambrosianus, 38. 7, but *lof* and *lofsang*, passim), to geleohgenne (92. 8). I also find *ŏ* represented by *u*, *stuwe* (36. 10) and *lucað* (110. 12), which latter is possibly a mistake for *lociað*.

§·11. Stressed long *o* is represented by, possibly its umlaut, *e* in *werigende* (vagari, 112. 17), but *u* in *du*=do (103. 7).

§ 12. Unstressed *o* becomes *a* in *abbade* (116. 2; Latin influence?). It is rendered by *u*, e. g. in *furður* (26. 13), and often by *e* in the case of the ending *-æst* of the superlatives (e. g. *leofestan*, 3. 9, etc.). Cf. also *nygeða* (37. 4), *nigeða* (37. 11).

§ 13. U. There is little to be said of the *u*'s in stressed syllables : on a possible nasal *ŭ*, see below, § 41.

u, in unstressed syllables, is represented by *o* in *hohfolnesse* (54. 1 and 57. 18), and by *a* in *oðram* (14. 9).

§ 14. Ĕ, Ǽ. Genetically speaking, *e* is either palatal or guttural. Traces of this may be seen in the fact that *g* is retained longer before guttural *e*'s than before palatal ones, where it soon runs into the palatal spirant (j). Thus we find the prefix ge- (=ga) unswervingly represented in this way. It is not until the end of the eleventh century that we find it represented by *i* (Vices and Vertues, ab 1200, passim, icleped, idon, etc.).

§ 15. Short *ĕ*, stressed, half-stressed, and unstressed, very frequently becomes *æ* ; conversely *æ*, in all three positions is often written *e*. The natural inference is, that the two sounds

have run together, and are assimilated.   In fact, three
originally different vowel values may be said to have dwindled
down into one.   *e* = West Teutonic *i* ; *e* = *a* + *i*, and *e* = *æ* =
W. S. *a* before non-nasals + palatal vowels (Sievers, § 49 ;
Sweet, History of Engl. Sounds, second ed., § 413).

Cp. *ændebyrdnesse* (14. 3), *ælfræmedne* (20. 5), *ælles* (28. 4),
bigænge (86. 3), *þænce* (104. 16).

wæfuls (32. 14), *monðæs* (39. 10), *Infiænde* (68. 1), *hei aspendæ*
(98. 9), etc.   In *ælmæssan* (99. 16), and in *hæftemæst* (76. 5), the
non-italicised symbol may owe its sound to a confusion with
mæsse, -mæst, due to and explained by popular etymology.

§ 16. Æ.—Both short and long *æ* are often found in our
text represented by *a*. *þarrihte* (23. 16), *stape* (28. 13),
hwar (36. 1), *radan* (72. 10), *mage* (72. 15).   They are also
written *e*: *seið* (2. 18), *stepe* (31. 9), *gemenlica* (communis,
34. 12), *geedleht* (51. 17), *efterfilige* (54. 10), *afered* (prostratus,
78. 11), and lastly, both short and long *æ* is expressed by the
symbol *ee*: *geedleehte* (51. 3), *gepeef* (101. 16).

§ 17. *æ* is *ea* possibly in *eallþeodscipa* (89. 5), if it is not
a mistake, influenced by *eall*; *gehealdenne* (61. 2), which must
then be supposed to be wrong for *getealde* (but cf. note, infra,
on p. 123), and perhaps in *teallic*, = *tællic* (54. 7).

§ 18. *æ* is *y* in *gystes* (94. 5).

An *i* has developed after a long *e* in the case of *hei aspendæ*
(98. 9).   It may be due to the analogy of the *e* in some cases,
e.g. aweig (1. 7), etc., where a *g* followed.

§ 19. Ē has developed into *ea* in *fealaspreocala* (35. 5 ; cf.
infra § 30); into *eo* in the same word *fealaspreocala*, as well as
in *beotwux* (51. 8), and in *neodbehcofe* (69. 14, but regularly
behefe, 81. 14, etc.).

§ 20. *e* becomes *o*, *swoðunga* (fomenta, 59. 11), and possibly
in *ut to foranne* (65. 16), where, however, the *o* may equally
well be the representative of *a* ; cf. § 9).

§ 21. ĕ has become *y* in *bið beiyten* (adquiritur, 65. 9), and
i in *æthwigan* (92. 16).

§ 22. ĕ in unstressed syllables is very frequently represented
by *a*; thus in *forasþræc* (1. 2), *foraglæwlice* (18. 7), *forabeon*
(11. 9, 24. 13), *forahradian* (55. 4, 5), *forascawunga* (73. 11);

in the following two verbal forms: *he gemuna* (meminerit,
16. 14), *of acerfa* (amputet, 108. 11); then in the gen. sing.
m. g. *lareowas* (10. 8, etc.), *bebodas* (22. 2).

Conversely, the ending -*as* of the plural being written -*es*
occasioned the corruption *asyndrodest* (56. 9).

§ 23. This *a* for *e* is most probably phonetically correct in
the above-mentioned cases. In *to smeagenda* (26. 11), *hlæddra*
(28. 7), it may be from the influence of the respective lemmata.
The lemma has probably also influenced the gloss in the case of
gewrita (32. 5, scriptura).

§ 24. Syncope of *ĕ* follows the rule as laid down by Sievers
(§§ 144, 293). Hence we find forms like *regolicere* (63. 10),
regollicere (103. 15), by the side of *regolicre* (113. 16, 115.
16), etc.

§ 25. I, ẏ. Although of different origin, these two vowels
may, in the stage to which the language of the present Text
belongs, be safely considered together, as they are both levelled
under one sound, probably the *i*. That this should be under
the former sound, is first of all made likely by such spellings
as *forþig* (17. 16), *ingehide* = *ingehygde* (94. 12), in both of
which cases the *ig, i* represents the long *ī*, and is secondly
borne out by the subsequent history of the letters, both of which
are diphthongised into the present *ī*. Hence we find such
spellings as *kin* (genus, 10. 6), *cinehelm* (31. 14), *mycel* having
again (cf. Sievers, § 31 note) become *micel* (72. 15, etc.).

§ 26. I, *y* are rendered by *u*, in *wursan* (11. 4), and in *cwude*
(24. 14), *oferfull* (71. 9), *gefullan* (81. 4).

§ 27. *e* for *i* resp. *ẏ* is found in the following instances:—
gef (3. 1), *smeðe* (officium, 23. 1), *þen(g)* (71. 7), *tender* (75. 17),
gement (decreverit, 78. 17), *begeme* (intendat, 96. 5), etc.

§ 28. For an apparently long *i* in *lilic*, see § 42.

§ 29. EA, EO. That these were stressed on the second ele-
ment, in the period to which this text belongs, and that, consequently, the first *e* had become a half-vowel is, to my thinking, beyond doubt. I adduce in support of it the following
forms:—*iornfullestan* (1. 12), *iarcie* (16. 17), which may easily
be multiplied from the present and other texts. *eode* is spelt
(58. 17) *gode*, and in conjunction with forms like *gercordgenne*

(74. 2), *hadgenne* (107. 4), but especially *gebisgode* (82. 4, which cannot be anything but *gebisiode*, cf. also below, § 68 *f*). I have no hesitation in looking upon this *gode* as a case in point. See Sievers, § 212, anm. 2, and § 214, sub 7.

§ 30. *ea* and *eo* interchange. See *neorwan* (24. 8), and for *feola, feala*, supra, § 19, Paul Beiträge 4. 345, 6. 55. The former is found monophthongised in a great many cases in full syllables, as well as in half, and unstressed ones. The monophthong *e* thus born, is sometimes found interchanged with *æ*.

nextan (4. 6), *ege* (13. 13 bis), *geþehte* (19. 7), *hlehtregamene* (21. 11).

þeh (21. 17), *seel* (58. 8, 102. 8, etc.).

þrege (15. 9) and *þræiungan*, (59. 7) *foreglæwlice* (18. 7), *glæwnesse* (58. 9, 59. 14).

gimleslice (63. 9) and *gimlæslic* (MS. *gunlæslic*, 62. 2), as against *gemeleasan* (15. 3) and passim.

§ 31. The spelling *scamen* (76. 11) and *gescad* (109. 2), etc., is no monophthonging at all, because the vowels never were diphthongs, see § 66. *Salmos* (51. 9) is Latin influence.

§ 32. In *andwyrde* (presentem, 30. 11) and *beþyrfendra* (93. 15), *ea*, probably through *e*, is represented by *y*.

§ 33. *eo* is *e* in *ceriende* (20. 15), and possibly in *ateriað* (89. 10), but see note. Hence in *cyrigende* (55. 12), *eo* becomes *y*.

In *forrane* (29. 13) and *forsig* (64. 13) *eo* has become *o*.

§ 34. U, in consonantal value, presents the usual contractions: *noldon* (2. 7), *sutol* (9. 7), *gesutulað* (29. 10 ; cf. *geswutulað*, 29. 11), for which see Sievers, § 172 note, who does not mention *ucan* (52. 7), *ucrþena* (66. 12), and see note to *uwucan* (52. 4).

It is superfluous in *hwucrædenne* (107. 11), whilst *ðryruyssum* (32. 12), *anfealde* (91. 4, etc.), *þeahfæstnysse* (100. 13), are mistakes due to the misreading of *r*(p), *f*(ᚠ) and *h* respectively for *w* (p).

Is *awyrtlian* = *awyrtwalian* (108. 7) a mistake, or the outcome of a phonetic process?

§ 35. I, in consonantal value, need not be treated separately,

as it has become identical in sound, as well as mostly in
symbol, with the spirant palatal *g*, for which see below, § 68.
Thus we find *gcoralice* (23. 2), as well as *geond* (11. 4);
iornfullestan (1. 12), as well as *iond* (50. 1).

§ 36. R is omitted, whether phonetically or graphically it is
difficult to say, in *foahrædigeude* (106. 11), *tobedde* (109. 15,
inflati), *hicce* (32. 9), *bæd* (54. 7). R is inserted in *mæssepreostrum* (100. 10, see note, but preosta 101. 6), *ætbredendrum*
(32. 13), *hefigran* (65. 7, cf. 66. 9), and of course by mistake
in *frynd* (20. 11, inimicos).

§ 37. We may further note a case of svarabhakti in *merigenlicum* (66. 13), and *merrigenlice* (37. 14), as also two
instances of metathesis, *hærdlicor* (24. 6), and *wryhta* (33. 16,
etc.). In the case of *merrigenlice* it is also possible that the
ig, resp. *rig*, represents only the vocalisation of the *g*. Cp. the
spelling *meriendlice* (44. 7, 45. 16, 46. 4).

§ 38. L has disappeared in *æfwyrðe* (16. 6), and has been
doubled in *welleorniaþ* (100. 4).

§ 39. M. Apart from the ending of the dative plural, where
an older *-um* is usually supposed to have dwindled down into
-an, *m* is often found represented by *n*. Graphically speaking,
the difference is so slight that e. g. in a word like *wylne* (fervore, 9. 19) we must perhaps assume a scribal error; on the
other hand, forms such as *þan* (40. 4, 69. 2) and *medenlicum*
may be phonetic.

A case of assimilation may occur in *belippendan* = *belimpendan* (73. 11, but see note). For *lilic* = *lim(p)lic* (21. 11),
see § 42.

§ 40. N. Not written in *fudung* (9. 19), *windrucen* (20. 13),
drihtelican (50. 1), *gedihtere* (51. 4; cf. *gedihtenre* 50. 17), *ære*
(semel, 54. 7), *þearflices* (82. 3), *si geþeoda* (injungatur, 84. 3),
wacmodes (84. 5), etc.

Added in *geþeondan* (57. 14), and assimilated to *d* in *edde-
byrdnesse* (78. 17), doubled in *inn code*, which was misunderstood or mistranscribed and written *in ncode* (103. 18).

§ 41. Misreading a word so as to put an *n* where it was
not, or *vice versa*, is admittedly of very frequent occurrence,
owing to the fact that *n* is often denoted by a stroke over

the preceding letter. All our instances may be due to this.
But if Sievers is right in assuming the existence in early
Teutonic of nasalised vowels (ib. 45. 5), and if Zupitza's
account of Kent. Glosses 795 *strenð = strengð*, etc., is correct[1]—
that is, if we may lay down the principle that certain sound
values are thus symbolised in a preceding letter, it is just
possible that some of the cases above indicated owe their
origin to this principle, and that this aided the spreading of
the then only apparent loss of *n*. Cf. § 70.

§ 42. P. Omitted in *cam dom* (abbreviated in the MS. as
cā dō, 14. 6); *iýl* (jactantiam, 22. 7), *gelimlic* (96. 3) This
last word occurs also (21. 11) under the form *lĩlic*, where
the sign of length ⁻ must be taken as indicating *m*.

§ 43. An epenthetical *p* obtains in *luftempre* (dulcius, 3. 8).
No doubt under the influence of the lemma a *p* is retained
in *psealmas* (38. 7). The word *reps* = Latin *responsorium* is
perhaps another instance of metathesis, as to which see
Sievers, § 204. 3; otherwise the form may be explained as
representing *re*(s)*p*(on)*s*(orium) and not *resp*(onsorium).

§ 44. B. The close relationship that exists between *m* and
its corresponding stop *b* explains at once forms like *emfaran*
(83. 6), and perhaps also *gemysgunge* (occupationem, 89. 16),
and *si forhæmed* (abstineatur, 71. 12), although in the latter
word a mixing up with *hæmed* is the more probable origin
of the extant form.

§ 45. *b* is misread as *h* in *heode* (56. 8), and *hetelicum*
(=betchtum, 31. 1).

§ 46. F, V. In the instances to be mentioned lower down,
both F and V express the voiced labial spirant, and hence
they are here mentioned together—*rers, verse* (41. 7, 47. 13,
50. 2, etc.), in each case as gloss to a Latin *versus* (or oblique
cases), the writing of *v* may be due to Latin influence. Not
so in *pravoste* (54. 10), *pravostum* (104. 4), *pravostscire* (111. 15);
see also *se sylva* (12. 16), and *weouedes* (62. 1), and compare
Sievers's remark that this representation by *v* is characteristic
of the oldest English (§ 192. 2).

[1] 'Das *n* behielt natürlich in allen diesen fällen seine gutturale natur,
Z. f. D. A. 21. 11.

§ 47. An original voiced *f* (= Gothic *b*, or Latin *f*) before *n* admittedly often becomes *m*, 'especially in the later period' (Siev., § 193. 2, and see note). Bearing this in mind, we must be struck to find *stefne* and *efnum* constantly, which forms are indicative of an older period; and on the contrary, the following English adaptations of the Latin word *antiphona* : *antiphonas* (81. 1), *antiphonam* (41. 1) ; *antemn* (79. 1), *antemne* (38. 5) ; *antemp* (56. 10, 79. 12), and *antempne* (42. 12 ; 43. 4).

§ 48. Are any traces found of an interchange between *f* and *w* ; and is this phonetic, or, as is certainly very possible, merely graphical? The constancy of the occurrence of the gloss *anfealde* to *potestate* in our text (which I have starred ; 91. 4, and passim) would almost make me inclined to think that the change was phonetic. If so, we may look upon *liw* (61. 13) as an analogue. Here, however, the *w* has been changed into *f* (contemporarily).

f is dropped in *frore* (solacio, 10. 1), and has been added, no doubt erroneously, in *yfefle* (31. 5).

§ 49. T.   The resemblance in shape of this symbol to *c* may often account for forms like the following : *orseclena* (9. 18), *uncruman* (109. 6). Whether *wice* (poena, 25. 12), *secende* (ponens, 28. 14) must not be viewed in a different light, is a matter which will be found treated of below, § 63).

§ 50. Traces of the voicing of final *t* to *d* are numerous :— *gemed* (modus 45. 8, 72. 14), *gild* (33. 10), *tramod* (118. 2). Of this last word, Schröer's texts have on p. 133 of his edition, *tramet*, which is also in the Durham MS. in the corresponding passage on fo. 123 b. Schröer asks (glossary, in voce) if the word is masc. or neuter. The following references may give an answer to this question. Gospel of S. Matthew, ed. Skeat, p. 2, l. 10 : *tramelas* ł *wegas* ł *stige* : tramites ; and Prudentius glosses, Germania 23, p. 398 b. *tramelas* : paginas.

t, the outcome of the combination -te**þ**, becomes voiced in the following cases : *si gebed* (emendaverit, 25. 13), *anded* (confitebitur, 29. 14), *agild* (deliquerit, 80. 4), *hæd* (91. 3) and as the result of -de**þ** being contracted in : *asend* (mittit, 36. 13), *led* (ducit, 117. 3).

Observe the spelling *geledt* (impediatur, 87. 4).

§ 51. *t* is dropped very frequently. Finally in *gejcah*
(17. 14), *higeleas* (75. 17). Cp. also *sceornesse* (39. 13),
cræfican (= cræftican, 94. 10), *swa of* swa (94. 5), etc.

Inwardly in *drihne* (1. 8), *tihende* (suadentem, 4. 7), *tearum*
(61. 1, probably a mistake for *teartum*) influenced by the
thought of *tearum* = lacrimis ; *wæsmas* (82. 3).

Initially it is, with a following *e*, misread for *æ* in **ælendne*
(= *telendne*, detractorem, 20. 15), and **arlicor* (= teartlicor,
115. 5).

§ 52. *t* is found added after *s* in *gewist* (38. 6), in *cost*
[certainly in (88. 3), and probably also (20. 7), if *pacem* may
be taken to mean *pacis osculum*], and through a mixing up
of forms in *asyndrodest* (= asyndrodas, privati, 56. 9). Owing
to influence of the lemma, it is added in *peniant* (serviant,
65. 15). See a very interesting article, Mod. Language
Notes I, 3, and ib. I, 97.

§ 53. *t* becomes *ð* in *si gescyrð* (53. 13), *wurð menð* (87. 15),
and also in *swa hwæð swa* (1. 11). This latter instance,
unlike the former which is *isolative* (Sweet, H. E. S., § 47),
is *combinative*, influenced by the following *s*. Other combinative changes of *t*, but through a preceding *s*, are found
in these words: *apreht* (78. 10, 98. 7), and *prengestan* (1. 9).
Instead of becoming *þ*, the *t* of *st* is dropped in *æt nyxan*
(2. 7).

§ 54. D. This sound is very frequently unvoiced. *Myrrent*
(stirpator, 62. 3), *mænifealt* (113. 15). It is retained etymologically in *gemildsa* (39. 7). The frequently occurring forms
abbot in the nominative as well as in the oblique cases (e. g.
79. 8, 80. 15, etc.) are not likely to be all due to the form
of the lemma ; they may on the contrary present examples in
point here.

Illutclipol (35. 11) and *stuntmælum* (38. 10) may be
instanced as exemplifying the unvoicing of a *d* at the end
of a syllable, and the following words as a specimen of the
same process inwardly, so far as they may be thought to
indicate phonetic and not merely graphical changes.

fotum (alimentis, 68. 15), *wið meten* (mercedi, 85. 13,

probably a blunder), *atreogenlic* (agenda, 37. 12), *to motgenne* (superbiendi, 110. 4, cp. § 69), *stete* (111. 15). For the apparent change of *d* into *g*, see below, note to 5. 9 (p. 119).

§ 55. *d* is represented by *ð* in the following cases : *æfwyrðe* (16. 7), *beon gesæið* (22. 3), *belaðod* (65. 6, 65. 13). See for *wiðscripel* (10. 16, 17), where *d* is influenced by the following *s*, § 53 above. Owing to the want of length-designation in our MS. it is difficult to decide whether *wið* here represents *wið* or *wíð*. In the former case the change would be combinative and internal; in the latter isolative and external (Sweet, H. E. S., § 46. *f*).

§ 56. The close relationship existing between the *d* and *n*, *n* being formed exactly in the place of the *d* but with free breath-passage, throws more or less light on the following instances, most of which, if not all, may represent truly phonetic changes. See also below, § 92.

ablicendum earum (2. 10), *tundgan* (3. 3), *angitfullum* (13. 3), *gewitendlicum* (16. 11), *meriendlice* (44. 7, etc.), *ion* (per, 49. 2), etc. etc. See Sievers, § 198.

d is represented by *n* in *gegearcon* (exibetur, 25. 3), is doubled in *gepreadd* (104. 6), and assimilated to *n* in *cumenne*, etc. (95. 11).

§ 57. Þ, Ð. The sound symbolised by these letters is in our text often found represented by *d*. Cp. *nytwyrdnyssum* (19. 6, 65. 14), *sodes* (89. 7), *læigd* (98. 2), *sede* (115. 15). This *d* by unvoicing becomes *t* in *underfeht* (16. 1), *det* (108. 6, where the possibility of Latin influence is not excluded). It is assimilated to *t* in *ættan* (77. 16).

þ, *ð*, as sign of the 3 p. s. are often omitted; cp. *sæig* (24. 9), etc.

Inwardly, *þ* has disappeared in *swyrian* (59. 14), and possibly in *lareow*. So says Sweet, as regards this last word, in the Anglia, III, p. 152. But is this derivation correct? Speaking *a priori*, a *þ* is more likely to be added by analogy than to disappear phonetically between *r* and a *vowel*; *lateow* from *ladþeow* is no fit analogue. Or must we presuppose, for a transitional stage, **lapreow*? Even then our *swyðrian* is but a meagre analogue, occurring as it does only once or so, as against the constancy with which *lareow* obtains. On the whole, Reimann (Die Sprache, etc., cp. § 64, p. 36),—who assumes *larþeow* to be a twelfth century neologism,—seems to me most likely to have hit the mark.

Original *dh* is represented by *dd* in *auddettan* (21. 15), *þ* is written *f* in *stæfuysse* (55. 5), a very probable phonetic interchange.

§ 58. s. *S* is assimilated to *t* in *blettian* (33. 3), and is prothetic—if phonetic in this place, which is at least doubtful —in *stalu* (= *talu*, detractionis, 110. 7).

§ 59. c, κ. Both these symbols express either a guttural or a palatal voiceless stop. In our text the following words occur with *k* by the side of forms with initial *c*. *ofkyrfes* (abscisionis, 60. 2), *gekynd* (5. 14), *kyð* (69. 10), *beon gekydde* (29. 9), *kyre* (18. 4), *kyn* (9. 17), *kin* (10. 16), *kapitol* (47. 9), etc.

c is sometimes voiced: *begimð* (76. 4), *drencg* (potus, 78. 1), *godgundre* (81. 10), *geswing* (84. 4), *swingan* (109. 3).

c is represented by *t* in *fæte* (37. 13) and *geferlætenn* (102. 13). For the reverse process, see § 49 above, and for the explanation, § 63 below.

§ 60. As regards the pronunciation of this *c*, I have already stated that it is either palatal or guttural. The guttural pronunciation occurs of course before guttural vowels, and possibly also in a few cases before purely palatal vowels, but only when the *c* is there owing to a secondary development. Thus, when we find *re* glossed by *þince* (33. 9), it is difficult to believe that the *c*, which has grown out of *g*, and is thus a purely guttural stop, can be palatal in the oblique cases. Before guttural vowels a palatal pronunciation is not likely to have obtained.

§ 61. What is the nature of this palatalisation? Sievers expressly and distinctly states, in various sections of his grammar, that the palatal *c* = *tsch* (§ 196. 3), i.e. a 'pronunciation resembling the present English *ch*[1]' (§ 206, anm. 3).

---

[1] Sievers does not restrict his statement to any later period. The following may therefore be of interest. That this assibilation of the *c* cannot be established for the older periods—I here refer to the Corpus Glossary—may be seen from Dieter, § 43, who gives *mertze* (Wr. W., 32. 25) as representing

However strange it may be that the author of the 'Grundzüge der Phonetik' must have here made the slip of con-
founding palatalisation with its consequence, assibilation,
the fact is proved by referring to p. 62 of the third edition
of the Grundzüge, where a correct statement is given. But
the words quoted above still stand in the A.-S. grammar, and
the wrong notion there expressed, pervades the whole treatment of the *c*.

§ 62. Let us examine the facts on which Sievers's theory
is based. They are :—

(1) The transition of *ort-geard* into *orceard*, afterwards
orcerd, ordceard.

(2) The transition of *fetian* into *fecc(e)an*.

Now the interchange of guttural *c* and *t*, i.e. of the voiceless guttural and dental stops, is no matter of wonder; and
as such, the matter might be explained without more ado [1];
but there is more which tends to explain the change. A
palatal *c*, as in A.-S. *rice*, before having attained the present
stage of pronunciation—assibilation to *tsch* in *rich*—must
have passed through the *tj* stage—i.e. exactly through the
place where the *tg* (i.e. *tj*) of *ortgeard* must have been formed.
No wonder then, that *t* + palatal vowels, or rather *t* + palatal
semi-vowels, should be confused *in writing* with *c* + palatal
vowels, i.e. semi-vowels. Hence the transition of *ortgeard*
into *orceard*. Hence possibly also the form *feccean* by the
side of *fetian*, although the possibility of two distinct verbs
being apparently merged into one is not excluded [2]. Thus
then I believe with Sievers, that *orceard* proves a pronunciation *ortjard*, but no more. I shall now examine the re-
maining grounds against this supposition. The *c* originally
sufficed because, as is very likely (Siev., § 206), palatalisation is an Anglo-Saxon phenomenon. But when the palatals
began to develope, *k* was sometimes used to denote the
guttural sound. This at least is very probably the meaning

the middle Latin *mercem*. If *c* had then been *tsch*, the scribe would not have
had recourse to the unusual *tz* to express this sound, then so akin to that
of *c*.

[1] See Mod. Language Notes II. 222, III, 126, 192.
[2] Whence does Bosworth-Toller get his preterite, *fehte* ?

of *k* (Sievers, § 207); but that the distinction was not always
kept up, that is, that the distinction was evidently too
delicate to be palpable to the untrained ear, is clear from the
list of words above, § 59, where the *k* occurs before vowels
originally palatal as well as those originally guttural. But
however rough and obtuse an ear may be, the distinction between *k* and *tsj* must be sure to be heard and to find expression
consistently. How then was it afterwards expressed? By
the adding of *h* to the palatal *c*; but this did not happen
until the beginning of the Middle English period (Koch,
§ 172 ff.). I do not believe that the *ch* of the Northumbrian
documents represents *tsj*, but I wish to reserve my judgment
until the grammar of these texts, which may be expected from
the hands of Professor Cook, has placed before us the necessary
material on this subject.

§ 63. We may now safely conclude that the evidence in
Anglo-Saxon does not do more than prove that palatal $c = tj$
at the utmost, not yet *tsj*. See also on this subject the
remarks of Professor March, Englische Studien, I. 315.

Hence it is that I have left the above-mentioned forms
fæte, geferlætenne, etc., unstarred, since they are just as likely
to represent the palatal *c*, as would be done by this symbol
itself, and it is probably owing to this confusion of *c* and *t*
that we find such forms as *wice, secende*, cp. supra, § 49.

§ 64. A word must be said about the *c*-epenthesis, although,
of this phenomenon proper, I have not found an instance in
our text. Traces of it may, however, be perhaps discovered.
For instances of it, see Sievers, § 210; Cosijn, Altwests.
gramm. I, § 131, i.e. Sweet, Pastoral Care, p. 482 f.;
Zeuner, Die Sprache des Kentischen Psalters, § 39; Dieter,
Sprache und Mundart der ältesten Englischen Denkmäler,
§ 45, p. 63; Reimann, Die Sprache der Mittelkentischen
Evangelien, § 28, sub 3; Schröer, Die Winteney-Version der
R. S. B., p. xxvii, etc.

§ 65. What is the nature of this epenthesis, i.e. what is
here the sound of *sc*? I think that *c* must be supposed to
indicate the change of *s* (not only of *sc* as Zeuner has it,
note 2 on p. 80) into the *palatal* sibilant, and I am happy

to find that the only writer who does speak of the nature of the sound—Reimann, l. l.—is of the same opinion. It is curious that so far as my instances go, the older periods present this insertion only between *s* and *l*, *m* or *n*, not before *p* and *t*[1], as in modern South German. Here *stein* and *spalte* become[2] *ŝtein* and *ŝpalte*; there it is only such words as *sniden* which would become *scniden*. Now in German this *ŝ* from *s* has run into the sound *sc*, (etymologically) *sch* = *sk*. In modern English an original *sk* has often also become '*sc*' (i.e the palatal sibilant), as in *shadow* from *scadu*. In § 31, I have stated that the spelling *scamen*, etc., does not present a case of monophthonging. This must be now further explained.

§ 66. If the above view of the *c*-epenthesis be accepted, we need not be surprised to find this *c* written so comparatively rarely. Even in Anglo-Saxon times we may safely assume pronunciation to have been in advance of spelling, so that when the former began to change, the latter followed only tentatively, and not always consistently. Suppose therefore, that the sound-change, under certain conditions, of *s* to *sc* = *ŝ* were pretty general, it is quite possible that in the majority of cases it should yet be written *s*, especially since the difference between the two is not so very great. Now the *sk* before palatal vowels would easily become *stj* (cf. §§ 60–63); and owing to the presence of the *s*, it would further dwindle down to *sj* (= *ŝ*).

If it be objected that I here give a pronunciation to the *c*, which was denied it in the §§ cited, I must emphatically state that this is owing to the influence of the *s*[3]. That a stop should be slurred over sooner *between two continuants* than that at the beginning of a syllable (ri-ce) a *tj* should develop a sibilant, no one will care to deny, I think. Another possibility must here be disposed of. Could *sk* have developed into *ŝ* through the intermediate stage of *sχ*? (= *s* + the un-

---

[1] I now find *cæsctra* (castellum) in the Northumbrian Gospel of S. Matthew, 21. 2.

[2] By *k* in the rest of this section I denote the guttural voiceless stop, and by *ŝ* the palatal sibilant.

[3] See Mod. Language Notes, as quoted in § 52.

voiced palatal spirant). It is possible, but not likely. Spellings
like *schyldo* (Mt. prologue 17. 12) and *bischead* (corr. from
bigschad. Praef. Eusebii, 9. 13), as well as *sgiire -monn* (dis-
pensator, Luke 12. 42) in the Northumbrian Gospels, would
indeed seem to favour this view, but for a reason pointed
out above, I do not wish to lay too much stress on these
forms. For my own self, I am inclined to look on the above
forms as all indicating the pronunciation *śyldo* (= sgyldo),
biśead, *śiiremonn*, etc. But there is more. Do spellings like
schamian occur? i. e. *sch* before guttural vowels?

As to *sk* before the guttural vowels, whatever may have
originally been the impetus that set *sk* changing into what
is now spelt *sce* (Sievers, § 76), it did change in this direction,
and as soon as forms like *sceamu*, *sceadu*, had developed themselves, the way was open to change in the same manner as the
sk before palatal vowels. Sievers, in reply to Kluge (Anglia,
V, anz. 83) has treated of these *ea's*, etc. in the Beiträge,
(Paul and Braune) 9. 205 f. His reasonings have not con-
vinced me, and I continue to hold with Kluge that the *ea*
in *sceamu* is no real diphthong. Thus we find that *ce* in
sceop is the symbol for one sound (just as *sh* in *shall* is
the expression for only *one* sound), and the *o* has not become
diphthongized by the palatal *c*, i. e. the stress is on the *o*.
Now when the palatal *ś*, as developed out of *s* in the case
of *scniden*, had come to be expressed by *sc*, and when the
sound thus symbolised was also expressed by *sce*[1], we need
not be surprised to find that the *j*-sound originally expressed
by the *e* now got sufficiently known to be inherent in the
symbol *sc* (= *ś*) and that consequently a return to the spelling
scame may gradually be observed. This is what I meant
above when saying that slight traces of the *c*-epenthesis
might perhaps be found in our text.

§ 67. I have said that we must expect to find *sc* written
for *s* only rarely, whereas it may have been pronounced
so much oftener. We may now go further, and say that

---

[1] This nearly always in conjunction with *a* and *o*, so that they can be
looked upon as the diphthongs *ea* and *eo*, which by this time had also the
stress on the *á* and *ó*.

a spelling *mænnisnesse* (68. 11) need not be a mistake for *mænniscnesse*, as *s* probably had here the value of *ś*. See also *flæslican*[1], Cura Past. 234. 14. (Cosijn, I, § 131.)

Cosijn (I, p. 123) instances *menniscu*, *-escu* from the Pastoral Care (71. 12), without *sc* making the preceding vowel long through position. Was *sc* already palatal *ś*?

§ 68. G. The following selection of forms, which might easily be multiplied, bears out the various statements of Sievers in his Grammar on the pronunciation of this letter :—*beiym* (47. 7), *aiyldenne* (19. 4), **asmaidan* (29. 11, read asmaiand= *asmeagend*), *adli* (morbida, 60. 4), *scyldine* (36. 3), *sæde* (36. 6), *gesæið* (22. 3). *secce* (38. 12), *cræftican* (94. 10), *forhicgende* (12. 14), *underfænc* (16. 12), *þince* (33. 7), etc. etc. The combination *hg* occurs twice: *geleohgenne* (92. 8), *gelohgenlican* (63. 5). See also above, § 29. As regards the transition of *g* to *w*, it is exemplified in our MS. e.g. in *suwian* (11. 5, cf. Siev., §§ 214. 8, 416. 8), but the form *forgæwað* (107. 14) by the side of *forgæian* (75. 8) is rather curious. (Cf. note to 86. 17.)

§ 69. To one statement of Sievers's (§ 216, 3) I must take exception. He says: '*dg* has caused *cg* in *micgern*, fat (for **midgern*, O. H. G. *mittigarni*), which is extant in comparatively late texts only. This transition presupposes for its time (tenth century) a pronunciation of *cg* as *dz*.' I must claim for this *cg* the pronunciation *tj*, and refer my readers to § 63. O.H.G. *mittigarni* presupposes A.-S. **midgern*. This would readily become **mitgern*[2], i. e. *mitjern*; see above, § 62, where I have shown how this combination could be written *micgern*.

The pronunciation of *cg* as *dz* is therefore not proven.

---

[1] This word has lately been treated of by *Osthoff* (Beiträge, 13. 401 ff.; see especially p. 407). I suppose that the Kentish word *flæc*, which Kluge cites in his new ed. of his Etymol. Wörterbuch, is part of *flæchaman* in the Kentish Psalm 143. Zupitza, Z.f.D.A. 21. 12, thinks that this is a mistake. The suggestion may be hazarded that *c* (=*ś*) should stand for *sc*, but I cannot support this spelling at present, except by the selfsame words *þercce ðerccedum*, which Zupitza instances from the Kentish Glosses, and by the Northumbrian *oncæccen bið* (denegabitur, Luke 12. 9). Cp. perhaps the spelling *ftðerfete flæsð*, =*fiðerfete flæsa* (71. 11), for the *d* presupposes an *a*, rather than *ea*.

[2] Cf. *motgenne* ∾ *modgeane* (110. 4), and *gemodigenne* (114. 10).

§ 70. N, i.e. guttural *n*. This is usually, and in our MS.
also continually, expressed by the letters *ng*, *nc*. While referring the student to § 41, I may here comment on the
possibility that there may be something more than mere
accident in the occurrence of the following forms:—

forspennigum (11. 3), *geondsprecend* (= geondsprengend, 12.
1), **gespinð* (i.e. geswinð, 82. 5; cp. 80. 2), *ginran* (106. 11),
etc. etc. In the first two instances *g* and *c*, in the last two
n, may denote what I have written *ñ*.—See *Zeuner*, Die
Sprache des Kent. Psalters, § 32.

§ 71. If *midlum* (59. 1) is not an adverbial dative, then *ñ*
is here denoted by *m*.

Note also *aflingede* (84. 5)=*afligede*, *alinge* (78. 10), *alenge*
(79. 4), and *cantincas* (41. 5) by the side of the more usual
canticas.

§ 72. H. We find an *h* added in some words, e.g. in *hæftemæst* (76. 5), *upahræred* (94. 14).

On the other hand we find: *efenlyttan* (consortes, 6. 14),
nexode (molliti, 10. 9), *ofreow* (19. 8), *wilce* (26. 11), *wanon*
(30. 13), *wælreow* (58. 12), *rægelhuse* (98. 15), *reod* (108. 8),
rædlice (109. 13), *lyst* (auditus, 113. 12), etc. This dropping of
the *h* most likely denotes a voicing of the *hw*; this is also
expressed by the following spellings, *æiwheþera* (81. 11) and
whænne (103. 2).

h is misread as *b* in **bræd* (promptus, 35. 6) and **bada* (14. 7).

§ 73. Doubling of consonants, and conversely haplography [1],
is exceedingly frequent in our text. I am not sure that in
each case a phonetic corresponding process is thereby inti-
mated. I select the following instances:—

goddra (53. 17), *fett* (pedes, 66. 2), *estmettas* (20. 1), *be-
healdenne* (29. 6), *aworpones* (34. 8), *hederne* (80. 2).

§ 74. INFLECTIONS. I begin my notes on the inflections
by giving a couple of instances of the absolute cases. They
are of course imitations from the Latin, and although not
restricted to interlinear translations, they are very frequent
there, owing to influence of the lemmata.

---

[1] The writing of one symbol instead of two.

aw(ec)cenduthe gewrite (2. 8), *rihtwisnesse dihtendre* (14. 2), *gedihteure endebyrdnysse* (50. 17), etc. etc.

§ 75. SUBSTANTIVES. Nominative. *intingu* (occasio, 91. 6, misreading?). Twice I have noticed the use of an accusative instead of a nominative case, *neode* (57. 19) and *forgimeleaste* (68. 8). See, however, (69. 16), where *neod* under the same circumstances is used in the nominative case.

Genitive. *cræftis* (22. 11), *biscopis* (107. 8). This ending -*is* may be owing either to influence of the respective lemmata, or it may be the natural reflex of -*ys*, which is very common in some texts. See Sievers, § 44, anm. 2. Is *breðer* (13. 12) perhaps wrongly influenced by the preposition *on*?

Dative and Instrumental. *gebeda* (orationi, 21. 13), *gebeda* (oratione, 21. 14), *eallra sawla* (anima, 19. 11), *dara* (noxa, 56. 17), are instances of a dative form, which (only in the two last words) may be due to Latin influence.

Accusative.—*repse* (Si quis dum pronunciat responsorium, 79. 11). Whence this dative form? Is this (as well as the accusatives instead of nominatives recorded above) to be looked upon as a trace of the mixing up of forms, to which Sievers, § 1, anm. 2, has drawn attention?

§ 76. Nom. Acc. Plural.—*broðra* (fratres, 57. 19), *gebroðra* (73. 13), *gebroðran* (3. 9, 105. 3), *beboda* (13. 4, 13. 6, etc.), *andsweras* (3. 1), *kynna* (9. 15), and other instances probably exemplify this same principle.

§ 77. If we did not find the words *geongra cildra* (pueri parvi, 106. 11), I should be inclined to look on *cildra* (pueris, 105. 14) as a misreading for *cildrū = cildrum*.

§ 78. The dative plural ends in -*ou*, -*an*, -*um*, passim. There is no need to give instances. *Heofonum* (28. 8, 36. 9) may be a dual (Kluge, Beitr. 8).

§ 79. Of dative forms of the ADJECTIVES we notice the following, which are worth mentioning:—*orsorgi* (securi, 10. 3), which *i* may be due to the Latin ending[1], and forms like *ungehyrsumnde* (12. 8), *gecwemlice* (78. 5) as exemplifying the form-mixing spoken of above.

§ 80. Of plural forms compare the following:—*godu* (13. 2),

[1] Another possibility is, that, with the *ge* following, the word may be *orsorgige*.

feawa (35. 10), *þurhtogenes* (74. 11), *sinderlices* (85. 1), in most
of which cases the presence of the lemmata makes us doubt
whether the changes are not merely graphical blunders.

§ 81. The dat. plur. ends in *-on, -an, -um.*

§ 82. As regards the NUMERALS, a form *sex*, which, if it is
not caused by Latin influence, resembles the Northumbrian, is
found (reference missing).

§ 83. Of the Ordinals, I note the following forms which
are not found in Sievers, or of which he doubts the cor-
rectness :—

9. *nygeþan, nigeþan* (37. 4, 11).

30. *þritteoga* (43. 9).

40. *feowerteogaða* (43. 10).

50. *fifteogaða* (42. 13, 43. 10), *fyfteoða* (45. 19),*fiftugeðan*
(43. 6).

60. *syxteogaða* (42. 11, etc.).

70. *seofonteoða* (42. 14).

80. *hundeahteoða* (43. 13), *hundeahtoða* (43. 13).

90. *hundnigenteoða* (43. 14, 51. 3), *hundnigenteoðan* (76.
2, 3).

100. *hundteontiga* 7 *eahtateoðan* (48. 16), *hundteonteoðan*
(49. 16, 17).

§ 84. PRONOUNS. In *c, us, y*, as possible pronominal gloss
to *nobis*, see below, notes to (27. 2). *Inc* may be a pronoun
(19. 5), but there is no corresponding lemma. A peculiar
case of a declined 'genitive' (see Sweet, A.-S. Reader[2], p. lix)
is found (54. 3), *abbodes heores* (abbatis sui).

þis (a neutral singular) is gloss (5. 3) to the neuter *þis.*

Seo, as a masculine pronoun, occurs (43. 11) and (70. 4), and
possibly also (36. 13). It thus bears out the statement of
Sievers, § 337, anm. 2. Conversely *se* would seem to be a
feminine pronoun in *se romanisca laðung* (aecclesia, romana,
44. 3).

§ 85. VERBS. Only a few verbal forms are interesting
enough to be noted. Of these we find the following third
persons : *beheald* (respicit, 30. 16), *stynt* (97. 1), and some
others where there is no suffix (see Cosijn, Altwestsächsische
Grammatik, I, § 148, p. 200). *sweg* (118. 5), *sæig* (30. 6), etc.

§ 86. Of plural forms, the corrupt *sed gat (22. 2) points to *secgat*, which antiquated form (Sievers, § 360) may itself have been the cause of the corruption ; cf. *secgat* (17. 17).

§ 87. Of infinitival forms, we may notice *hatian* (jubere, 11. 17), which, however, is probably a mistake for *hatan* ; *gecian* (vocari, 17. 17), which, according to Sievers, § 408. 3, is mostly found as *cigan*. The rarer forms in *-on* occur pretty frequently. See, for instance, *ahȳrdon* (2. 12), and *unwrigon* (33. 7), as infinitival gloss to the imperative *revela* (supra, § 9). Of infinitives in *-a*, I found *lysta oððe gehȳra* (audire, 21. 12).

§ 88. Of the verb *sculan*, the text has the following notable forms :—*scel* (debet, 26. 3, 102. 8), *scell* (69. 2), *scȳll* (112. 7), *scealan* (debent, 81. 9), and *scealan* as infinitive (32. 10).

§ 89. The 'participium necessitatis,' which Sievers mentions in § 350 as found in later texts, and as formed after the Latin, occurs pretty frequently in our text. For the form given by him we may instance *to campiende* (5. 14), *to specende* (26. 7), *to smeagenda* (*a* is owing to the lemma, requirenda, 26. 11), *to andedende* (46. 10).

By the side of this we find even more frequently, however, forms in *-enne*, e. g. *to campienne* (1. 9), etc.

§ 90. That this future participle should also be found declined might be expected. Accordingly we have *eardigendes* (5. 11), and *be gegearnendum to ræde gebroðra* (de adhibendis ad consilium fratribus, 17. 10). In this case *to* is, as a matter of course, suppressed (31. 5, I find *aræriende*, for *ariende* or *æriende*,—as gloss to *parcendo* : here *to* would also seem to be omitted).

§ 91. The same notion is sometimes expressed by adjectives in *-lic*, e. g. *þa sendlican* (dirigendi, 113. 4), *on doulicum þingum* (in faciendo, 23. 12), which same ending I have once found glossing a present participle, *becumendlicum* (87. 12). Here *supervenientes* was possibly mistaken for *superveniendi*.

§ 92. 'Formed on the pattern of the Latin :' these words of Sievers's convey the impression that Latin only is answerable for the development of this *d*. I think that, viewed in the light of § 56, *d* will probably prove to be of a purely phonetic origin. When once the *d* began to develop phonetically, its growth and spreading may have been aided by a more or less conscious association with the Latin participle; but I hold that analogy and phonetics both share the paternity of the new form.

§ 93. I may here mention *beon gelogodre* (reponantur, 98. 15). How the passive voice of a verb can be glossed by what is apparently the dative feminine of a past participle, I am unable to understand. With partial dittography the same ending is probably found in *lehyd(dad)edre* (100. 1, 2). See however note on p. 124. Compare (26. 16) where the infinitive *aperire*, which may be construed in a passive sense, is glossed by an apparently masculine dative (*geopenodum*). Equally strange datives occur (66. 15) *þa utgangendum*, (74. 12) *þa gehyrendum*, and (87. 12) *ofer becumendlicum*. But they may perhaps exemplify the mixing up of datives and accusatives, which is characteristic of the later Anglo-Saxon.

§ 94. To any one who has looked into the text, or into the foregoing §§, many Kenticisms must be apparent at a glance. Thus we have the *e = æ* (*supra*, § 15, etc.; Sievers, § 151, 1); the *e = y* (§ 27, Siev. § 154); absence of diphthongisation of *e* into *ea* (§ 30, Siev. § 157. 2), to mention only the most striking peculiarities. But it will also have been seen that these do not appear throughout, and that West-Saxon influence is traceable. Now has a Kentish text been copied by a West-Saxon scribe or *vice versa*? I think a case like *betehtum* (31. 1), which was misread as *hetelicum*, is singularly instructive. *Telendne*, (= tælendne) which was misread as *ælendne* (20. 15), tells the same tale. An interchange—graphical—of *h* and *b*, *te* and *æ*, and of *h*, and *li* is quite common. Was it not the *strange* forms *betehtum, telendne*, instead of *betæhtum, tælendne*, which led to the confusion? If so, the Kentish text must have been the original, and the West-Saxon the copy.

THE RULE OF S. BENET.

Iɴ ɴoᴍɪɴᴇ ᴅoᴍɪɴɪ ɴoꜱᴛʀɪ ɪᴇꜱᴜ ᴄʜʀɪꜱᴛɪ Iɴᴄɪᴘɪᴛ ʀᴇ(ɢᴜʟᴇ) |
foraspræc fæderes þæs haligan þæs eadigostan benedictes
ᴘʀoʟoɢᴜꜱ ᴘᴀᴛʀɪꜱ ᴇxɪᴍɪɪ ʙᴇᴀᴛɪꜱꜱɪᴍɪ ʙᴇɴᴇᴅɪᴄᴛɪ)

hlÿst eala bearn beboda lareowes 7 aḥÿld eare
Aᴜꜱᴄᴜʟᴛᴀ ꜰɪʟɪ ᴘʀᴇᴄᴇᴘᴛᴀ ᴍᴀɢɪꜱᴛʀɪ ᴇᴛ ɪɴᴄʟɪɴᴀ) *aurem*

heortan þinre 7 mÿnegunege arfæstes fæderes lustlice
cordis tui et ammoniti(onem) pii patris libenter

underfoh 7 fremfi gefÿll þæt þu to him þurh gehÿrsum-
excipe et effica(citer) comple ut ad eum per oboedi- 5

nesse geswince gehwÿrfe forþam þurh ungehÿrsumnesse asolcenesse
entie laborem redeas a quo per inoboedientie desidiam

þe þu aweiggewite cornostlice nu min spræc is asend
recesseras ; Ad t(e) ergo nunc meus sermo dirigitur

swa wið cweþende *aþenum lustum drihne criste
quisquis abren(un)tians propriis voluptatibus domino christo

þamsoðan cinge to campienne gehÿrsumnesse þa þrengestan
vero regi militaturus oboedientie fortissima

7 þa þurh beorhtan wæpna swa underfehst ealra ærest þæt ,
atque precla(ra) arma assumis. In primis ut 10

þu swa hwæð swa to donne þu on god fram him beon
quicquid agendum in(choas) bonum ; ab eo per-

gefremmed þam iornfullestan gebede bid se þe us iallinga
fici instantissima oratione dep(oscas). ut qui nos iam

bearna gemedemode on getele getellan *ut þæt he na sceole*
in filiorum dignatus est nume(ro) computare ; non debeat

---

5. *fremfi,* see note. 6. *geswince, nce* not clear. First *s* of *asolcenesse* not
at all clear. 8. *aþenum,* read *awenum.* 9. *þam-,* *a* may be *æ.* *ð* of
soðan may be *d.* 10. *beorhtan, tan* is by no means clear. 11. After
on part of the MS. is torn away. 12. After *bid,* part of the MS. torn away.
13. *ut,* Latin in glossator's hand. It is in none of the other texts.

1. ʀᴇ not very clear. 3. Aᴜ-ꜱᴄᴜʟᴛᴀ in two lines by way of illumination
by the side of *In nomine—foraspræc—prologus—fili.* 5, 6. *oboedientie,*
MS. *oedientie; inoboedientie,* MS. *inoedientie.* 7. *t* of *t(e)* not clear.

æhwænne be urum ýfelum da   beon geunrotsode swa soðlice
aliquando de malis act(ibus) nostris   contristari;   Ita   enim

him on ælcere tide be   his   on   us   is to earcienne ł
ei   omni tempore de bon(is) suis in nobis   parendum

hýrsumienne þæt he ne na þæt an swa swa ýrre fæder his
est;   ut   non   solum   ut irat(us) p iter suos non

oðer hwile bearn beerfwerdige ah swa   swa egeful hlaford
aliquando filios   exheredet, sed nec(ut) metuendus dominus

swa geýrsod fram ýfelum urum þæt he swa swa þa wyr
5   *irritatus   a malis nostris   ut   nequissimos*

þeowan to þam ecan na betæce to wite   we þe him fýlian
servos perpetuam   tradat ad poenam qui   eum   sequi

noldan to wuldre   uton arisan   æt nýxan æt sumon cýrre
noluerint ad gloriam; Ex:urgamus ergo tandem   aliquando

aw . . cendum us gewrite 7 secgendum   hit is us
excitante   nos scriptura Ac dicente ho(ra) est jam nos

of slæpe uparisan geopenedum eagum uri . . | god-
de sompno surgere. Et   apertis oculis nostr(is) | (ad d)eifi- (118

cundan leohte mid ablicendum earum 7 utan gehýran þagod
10 *cum lumen;   attonitis auribus audiamus   divina (co)-*

amlice clipiende hwæt us mýngie stefn   to dæg
tidie clamans quid nos ammoneat vox dicens. hodi(e si v)ocem

gegehyrað nelle ge ahýrdon cowre heortan   eft
ejus audieritis nolite obdurare corda vestra. (et) iterum;

se ðe hæfð earan to gehýranne gehýre hwæt
Qui habet aures audiendi; audiat quid sp:ritus (dic)at

gelaðungum 7 la hwæt sæigð cumað la gebearn gehyrað
aecclesiis; Et quid dicit; Venite   filii   audite me

. . . htnes ege 7 ic lære eow ýrnað lifes leoht þa hwile ðe
15 *(timorem domini   docebo vos; Currite   dum lumen vite*

ge habbað   þýstru deaðes eow þæt ne gegripan 7 secende
habetis (ne) tenebre mortis vos   comprehendant; Et querens

meniu   folce þam he þas ðinc clýpað his wrýhtan
dominus (in) multitudine populi cui haec clamat operarium

t seigð la hwýle is man se ðe wýle lif 7
suum (ite)rum dicit. Quis est homo qui vult vitam et

---

1. After *dudum* part of the MS. torn away.   4. One letter erased between oðer and *hwile*.   5. After *wyr* part of the MS. torn away.   6. to?, very indistinct.   8. In *aw . . . cendum* two letters indistinct, probably *aecccewlum*. 9. *u* of *geopenedum* reads like an *i*.   Read *urum*.   11. Read *dæghwamlice*. 15. Read *drihtnes*.   18. *t*, last letter of *eft*.

7. *s* of *exsurgamus* add. afterwards.   8. *dicente*, see note.

gewilnað . . . on dagan gode þæt gef þa gchýrende andsweras
cupit (vi)dere dies bónos ; quod si tu audiens respondeas.

. . . gð þe gode gif þu wilt habban þæt soðe lif 7 þæt
Ego (di)cit tibi deus ; Si   vis habere veram   et per-

ece lif   . . . cond tundgan þine fram ýfele 7 þine
petuam vitam (proh)ibe linguam tuam   a   malo et labia

weleras 7 þæt hi na sprecan . . . n gecýr fram yfele 7 do
*tua   ne loquant*ur   *(dol)*um *; Deverte a malo et fac*

god smea oððe sec sibbe   . . . ýlig hýre 7 þonne þas
bonum.   inquire pacem   (et) sequere eam ; Et cum haec 5

þineg gedoð eagan mine ofor   7 mine earan to cowrum
feceritis.   oculi mei super (vo)s et aures mee ad preces

benum 7 ær þonne   geclýpian me ic secge eow æfre ic her com
vestras. Et antequam me in(vo)cetis dicam vobis.   Ecce adsum ;

est luftempre   . . . ere stefne   gelaðgendre la ge
Quid dulcius nobis (ab h)ac voce domini invitantis nos

þa leofestan gebroðran efne mid his arfæstnesse   geswutulað
fratres karissimi ; Ecce   pietate   (sꝺa demonstrat

us   lifes weg begýrdum mid geleafan oððe mid
nobis dominus viam vite; Succinctis (e)rgo fide   vel obser- 10

gehealdsumnesse goddra dæda lendenum . . . . u gebroht
vantia   bonorum actuum lumbis (n)ostris perducatum

bodung utan gan his siðfæt þæt we gearnian hine se ðe
evangelii pergamus itinera ejus ut (ꝺ)ereamur eum qui nos

geclipode on his rice   geseon . . n ðæs rices healle on inne gýf
vocavit. In regno suo ridere; (In) cujus regni tabernaculo si

we wýllað   buton | midgodumdædum ýrnende nateshwon
volumus habitare. nisi | illuc bonis actibus currendo minime

ne bið becumen* abutan axan mid þam witigan drihten
pervenitur; Sed interrogemus cum   propheta   dominum. 15

secgende him   la hwa wunað on ðinan inne   oððe
dicentes ei Domine quis habitavit in tabernaculo tuo aut

la hwa gereð on ðinre haligan dune æfter þýssere ax-
quis requiescet in monte sancto suo? Post hanc interro-

---

1. Read *geseon*.   2. Read *swigð* or *swgð*.   3. *eond*, see note.   4. Read
facn.   5. *ylig*, read *fylig*.   8. *est*, c in MS. ; Latin in glossator's hand.
In no other text. . . . *erc*, read *pissere*. 9. *n* of *gebroðran* erased. 11. . . *u*,
read *urum*. *gebroht*, see note. 13. . . *u*, read *on*. 15. *abutan*, read
ah utan.

---

1. *audieris* would seem to have been corrected into *audiens*. b. *et* (after
pacem) pasted over. 11. a of *observantia* corr. from *e*. 12. Erasure of one
letter after *pergamus*. 17. *e* add. above line (*requiescet*).

unge   uton   gehýran   andswariende 7 gesutuliende
gationem fratres audiamus dom:num respondentem et ostendentem

his   healle oððe innes   7 seccende se ðe   ingæþ
nobis viam ipsius   tabernaculi   ac dicentem ; Qui ingreditur

butan smittan   swýlce wýrcð rihtwisnesse 7 se ðe sprýcð soð-
sine   macula et   operatur justitiam :   Qui loquitur veri-

fæstnesse   heortan on his 7 se ðe na deþ facn on his tungan
tatem   in corde suo   qui non egit dolum in lingua sua

se ðe na dýde nextan his   yfel   se ðe hosp   na underféncg
5 *Qui non fecit proximo suo malum. qui obprobrium non   accepit*

agen   his nextan   se ðe þone awýridan deofol sum ðinc
adversus proximum suum. Qui   malignum   diabolum aliqua

tihende him sýlfan mid his sýlfan tihtinge fram gesihðum
suadentem sibi   cum ipsa   suasione   a conspectibus cordis

forsconde se gewrohte   his lýtlan hwædan geþohtas
sui respuens   deduxit   ad nichilum. et parvulos cogitatus ejus

7 heald   betæhte   non
tenuit et allisit ad christum ; Qui timentes dominum de bona

hi sýlfe þanc deð upahafene þa sýlfan on
10 *observantia sua non se   reddunt   elatos   sed ipsa   in*

him sýlfan goda na fram him sýlfan magon   beon
se   bona non a   se   posse   sed a domino fieri

ahwenende   7 hi mærsiað
existimantes. et operantem in se dominum magnificant. illud cum

na us
propheta dicentes. non nobis domine non nobis. sed nomini tuo

ah forðan paulus se apostol be   his bodunge
da gloriam. Sed   nec   paulus apostolus de predicatione sua

him sýlfan ah forðam ne tealde
15 *sibi aliquid   imputavit dicens ; Gratia dei sum. id quod*

se ðe wuldrað   wuldrie he
sum ; Et iterum ipse dicit. Qui gloriatur in domino glorietur ;

þanon sweigð   sæde
Unde et dominus in evangelio ait ; Qui audit verba mea

þas þinc | ic *onlocie hine wisum were
hæc   et facit ea | similabo cum viro sapienti. qui edificavit (119 b.)

---

9. *betæhte*, first *t* not clear.   18. Above *ea* the gloss is partly cut away; an *h* is recognisable, and part of a letter which looks like *g*, so *hig* ? Read *onlicie*.

---

8. *parvulos*, MS. *pa:rulus*.   13. *sed*, MS. *se*.   18. *a* of *ea* partly cut away.

comon   floðas   bleowan
domum   suam   supra   petram.   Venerunt flumina.   flaverunt venti

7 hi ætspurnon on   ðam huse   7   hit   ne feoll forþam þe
et   impegerunt   in   domum   illam   et   non   cecidit; quia fun-

hit wæs gestaðelod   ofor þam stane þis gefyllende
data   erat   super   petram;   Hæc complens dominus;

anbidiað   mid dædum
expectat   nos cotidie.   his suis sanctis monitis   factis   nos

we sculan forþi   for   bote
respondere   debere.   Ideo nobis propter emendationem ma'orum 5

þises lifes dagas to fyrstum sind to alætenne
hujus vite   dies   ad   inducias relaxantur;   dicente apostolo;

nyte ge la þæt ge godes geþyld   eow
An nescis   quia   patientia   dei   vos   ad   penitentiam   te

læt   þa synfullan
adducit;   Nam pius dominus dicit;   Nolo mortem   peccatoris.

þæt he gecyrre   þonne   we axiað
sed   ut   convertatur   et vivat: Cum   ergo   interrogassemus

be wunungum
dominum   fratres   de   habitatore   tabernaculi ejus.   audivimus 10

eardigendes   bebod   ah gyf we gefyllað wunigendes þenunge
habitandi   preceptum.   Sed   si   compleamus habitatoris officium.

we beoð   sin to gereccanne
erimus   heredes regni celorum;   Ergo   preparanda   sunt

7 lichaman   haligre   beboda   gehirsumnesse
corda   et   corpora   nostra   sancte   precep'orum   obedientie

to campiende 7 þæt hwonlic þæt þe on   us   gekynd acumenlic
militanda   et quod minus   habet   in nobis natura possibile.

ac uton biddan   his   gife þæt he iarcie   fultum
rogemus   dominum ut gratie sue   jubeat   nobis adjutorium 15

þenian   7 gif fleonde helle   wite   life we wyllað
ministrare; Et si fugientes gehenne poenas ad vitam   volumus

becum   to ðam ecan   tigað 7 þa hwile æt þisum
pervenire   perpetuam.   dum adhuc vacat. et in hoc   corpo-

lichaman þe we sin   ealle þas þinc þurh þisne leohtes weg
re sumus: et haec omnia   per   hanc   lucis   viam

---

7. Second *e* of *nytegela*, being written too close upon the *l*, is not quite clear.
8. *þa*, read *þæs*.   17. Read *becuman*. *tigað*, end of *æmtigað*.

7. *vos*, not in other texts; *te* is crossed out.   10. *habitatore*, MS. *habita-*
torum; see note.   15. *jubeat*, MS. *habeat*, a wrong transcription for *jubeat*,
which all other texts have? The gloss *þæt he iarcie* would lend support to
this view.

gefÿllan ÿs to ÿrnanne 7 is to donne   nu
v⟨acat⟩ *implere currendum* et *agendum est modo.* | (120 a.)

þæt hit on ecnesse   framme is to settanne   fram
quod in perpetuum nobis expediat; Constituenda est ergo a

us drihtenlices scole þeowdomes on ðære we hihtað ænig þinc
nobis dominici scola servitii. in qua institutione, nihil

heardlices ænig   us to gesettanne we hopiað   gif
asperum nihilque grave nos constituturos speramus; Sed etsi

hwæt litles forðstepð stiðlicor dihtende rihtwisnesse gescad for
5 *quid paululum restrictius dictane aequitatis ratione propter*

bote   oððe drohtnunge soðre lufe forðstypð
emendationem vitiorum. vel conversationem caritatis processerit

þærrihte   ac þu na forfleo   hæle se ðe
non ilico pavore perterritus refugias viam salutis que

nis buton mid stige to onginnenne mid forðsteppinge
non est nisi angusto initio incipienda ; Processu vero

drohtnunga   heortan onunasecgendlicere lufe
conversationis et fidei dilatato corde inenarrabili dilectionis

werednesse urnen   beboda godes fram his
10 *dulcedine curritur via mandatorum dei. ut ab ipsius*

æfre lareowdome   oð
nunquam magisterio discedentes. in ejus doctrina usque ad

deaþ on minstre se þurhwunigende þrowungum
mortem in monasterio perseverantes. passionibus christi

þurh geþyld þæt we beon dælnimende rices his
per patientiam participemur. ut et regni ejus mereamur

efenlyttan
esse consortes. AMEN. EXPLICIT PROLOGUS REGULE BEATI BENE-
15 DICTI ABBATIS. PATRIS MONACHORUM.

   I. *De generibus monachorum vel vita.*

   II. *Qualis debeat esse abba.*

   III. *De adhibendis ad consilium fratribus.*

   IIII. *Que sint instrumenta bonorum operum.*

20   V. *De oboedientia discipulorum qualis sit.*

---

5. *forðstepð*, probably copied here by mistake by scribe, who must have seen
it a line lower down. Cf. infra, note to l. 3 (*hihtað*). 7. *þærrihte*, *æ* or *a*
not clear; first *r*, but for context, might have been put down as *f*, the *l* of *ilico*
being blended with it.

---

6. *conversationem*, MS. *conservationem*. 7. *pavore*, MS. *pavorem*. 9 *o*
of *dilatato* corr. from *a*. 19. *Q* of *Que* wrongly rubricated in the MS. as *D*.

19. *XXV.* This is a mistake for *XXIV*, and the mistake is continued throughout in this list, so that ch. *XLIIII* as given lower down (*De his qui* etc.), ought to be ch. *XLIII. esse* not in the MS.   21. *XXVII.* A word erased after *abbatis*, probably *junguntur*, which is therefore added in brackets. 22. *XXVIII. communicatos, o* of *os* corr. in MS. from *i* by writing *o* over *i*. 24. Second *e* of *debeant* above line.

---

8. *occurrunt* supplied here as the reading of all the MSS. used by Schröer.
Cf. A. Schröer, Die Winteney-Version der Regula S. Benedicti, p. 10. The
text of the Winteney Version (S = Schröer's C) has *occurrerint*, and our text
(fo. 146 b) has *veniunt*. From *XLIII* down to the closing of the bracket the
omission in the MS. has been supplied from our text (corrected). 12.
XLVII. The heading for this chapter not being in our MS., it is supplied
from the readings of the other MS.; cf. Schröer, W. V., p. 96.

EXPLICIUNT CAPITULA. INCIPIT LIBER BEATI BENEDICTI |

ABBATIS. PATRIS EXIMI MONACHORUM MILITUM CHRISTI.

DE GENERIBUS. EORUM VEL VITA.

feower   kynna [b.] [c.] beon   [a.]sutol   is
Monachorum quattuor   *genera*   *esse*   *manifestum*   *est.* 15

þæt forme mynstermanna þæt is mynsterlic campiende [h.]
Primum coenobitarum *hoc est monasteriale militans*

under regule. oððe abbude.   [b.] syððan þæt oðer kyn is
sub regula vel abbate ; *Deinde secundum genus est*

dan.* orseclena þæt is westþensetlena. [g.] þissera [h.] þaðe na
anachoritarum id est heremitarum horum qui non

drohtnunge *wylne mid niwum [p.] ac mid mynstres [o.]fadunge
conversationis fervore novitio ; sed monasterii probatione

[u.] *landsumere [h.]lcornodon ongean þone deoful mænigra
diuturna didicerunt contra diabolum multorum 20

---

18. Before *dan.* erasure (see note).   *g. þissera* added in margin, possibly by the original glossator.   19. Read *wylne.   ac mid?* *c* may have been there, but it has been made into first stroke of *m*, which now, by mistake, of course, looks like *m* with four strokes.   20. Read *lancsumere.*

---

7. *LXVIIII* and following numbers are not in the MS.; *ut in monasterio* etc., the title of ch. *LXVIIII* follows in our MS. directly after the *ad mensam tarde* of the title of ch. *XLIIII*, without a capital letter or rubric being used for *ut,* so that it looks like one chapter. A page must have been skipped here. 12. EXPLICIUNT, MS. EXPLICIT.   18. *horum* added in marg., possibly by glossator.   19. *conversationis,* MS. *conversionis.*

[1.] mid frore, callunga gelærede [i.] winnan [q.] bene getȳde
    solacio jam docti pugnare;   et *bene instructi*

of broðorliccre fæɪɪ ædene to anfealdan gewinne westenes
    fraterna ex acie ad singularem pugnam heremi

georsorgi. ge buton frofre oðres mid aɪɪɪe [t.] hand
    securi jam sine consolatione alterius sola manu

[u.] oððe [u.] earme agean leahtras flæsces [i.] oððe geþohta
    vel brachio contra vitia carnis vel cogitationum,

gode gefultumiandum [v.] winnan [q.] 7 hi nihtsumiað
5 *deo auxiliante pugnare sufficiunt;*

þæt þridde [c.]   [d.] þæt atelicost [b.] kin [a.] sȳlfde-
    Tertium vero monachorum teterrimum genus est. sarabai-

mera [a.] þa on ænigum regole na afandode uel oððe afundennessa
    tarum. qui nulla regula approbati experientia

lareowas [h.] [n.] [m.] ofencs.[n.] ahge .. des on gekynde
    magistri sicut aurum fornacis; sed in plumbi natura

nexode [i.] þa git. [r.] mid weorcum. healdende [o.] weorulde.
    molliti adhuc operibus servantes seculo

[p.] truwan. leogan. [b.] gode þurh scere [a.] sȳnd acnawene
10 *fidem. mentiri deo per tonsuram noscuntur;*

þa twȳfealde þreofealde oððe soðes anlepic gangende ambulantes
    Qui bini aut terni. aut certe singuli sine

butan hȳrde hig on drihtenlicum heordum. ac heora agenum
    pastore, non dominicis sed suis

beclȳsde fore æ heom is gewilnunga. lust
    inclusi ovilibus pro lege eis est desideriorum voluptas.

þoɪɪne hi hwæt wenað tellað oððe geceosan þæt secgaþ halig
    cum quicquid putaverint vel elegerint. hoc dicunt sanctum

7 þæt þæt hi nellað þæt 7 hi wenað | na beon alȳfede. þæt
1ɜ et *quod noluerint. hoc putant | non licere. Quar-* (122 a.)

feorðe soðlice kin is [a.]   þæt is genemned wið
    tum vero genus est monachorum quod nominatur gȳro-

scriþel þa on eallon heora life geond mislice sciru þrim
    vagum. qui tota vita sua per diversas provincias. ternis

---

1. *frore*, i. e. *frofre*, and see note on this word. *bene*, Latin copied into gloss. 7. *u* in *ænigum* of irregular shape. *vel*, Latin; see note. 11. *gangende* in the MS. is gloss to *ambulantes*, which has been put in by glossator spontaneously. It is not found in the other texts. 17. Uncertain whether *scira* or *sciru*.

---

2. Erasure after *heremi*? 13. *eis* above the line. 16. *est* above the line and erasure.

---

oðer feoweru dagum geond mistlicora þinga hus cumliðiað
aut quaternis diebus per diversorum cellas hospitantur

æfre worigende 7 næfre staðolfæste agenum lustum
semper vagi et numquam stabiles. et *propriis volup-*

7 gyfernesse 7 forspennigum þeowgende geond ealle þinc
tatibus et *gule illecebris servientes* et *per omnia*

wursan þam sylfdemerum þara enlra drohtnunge be ðære
deteriores sarabaitis ; De quorum omnium miserrima conver-

earmræstan beteie hit is suwian þonne sprecan. þisum forlætenum
satione melius est silere quam loqui; His ergo omnissis ; 5

[c.] to [e.] mynstermanna [d.] þæt strengoste [d.] kyn
ad cenobitarum fortissimum genus

[c.] gedihteu [b.] fultumiendum [h.] [a.] uton cuman.
disponendum. adjurante domino veniamus ; QVALIS

DEBEAT ESSE ABBAS. (CAP. II.)

se abbud seðe forabeon [d.] wyrðc is [c.] [f.] on mynstre [h.]
ABBA QVI PREESSE DIGNVS EɬT *monasterio. semper*

gemunon [a.] sceal þæt he is gesæd 7 naman oððe [m.]
meminisse debet quod dicitur et nomen majoris 10

middædum [m.] 7 gefyllan [k.] [c.] [b.] [h.] don
factis implere ; Christi enim agere

[c.] spelunga [f.] [a.] he is *gelyst ðænne his [i.]
vices in monasterio creditur. quando ipsius

he is geciged to forenaman secgendum [a.] [k.] [e.] ge under-
vocatur pronomine. dicente apostolo; Acce-

fengon gast gewyscednysse on ðam we cleopiað
pistis spiritum adoptionis filiorum ; in quo clamamus

arwurða fæder [a.] [a.] 7 forð [c.] naht [h.] butan [g.] bebode [g.]
abba pater; Ideoque abbas nihil extra preceptum 15

[g.] þæt feorsi [h.] na sceall [h.] oððe læran. [d.] [a.] oððe
domini quod absit debet aut docere. aut

gesettan [e.] oððe [f.] hatian [f.] ahsi hæs [b.] his [b.] oððe [c.]
constituere vel jubere. sed jussio ejus. vel

lar [c.] *bysn [o.] godcundre [e.] rihtwisnesse [c.] leornincg
doctrina. fermentum divine justitiae in disci-

---

1. oðer, read oððe ; feoweru, read feowerum. 12. Read gelyft. 18. byɛn,
read byrma (=beorma) ?

---

5. Er. of one letter (e ?) after ergo. 7. dum crossed out before -te of
adjurante. 13. pro added afterwards.

cnihtas [g.] [dm.] [p.] geþancum geondsprecend mýndig sig [a.]
pulorum   *mentibus conspergatur; Memor sit*

æfre   [b.] þæt [n.] [e.] his lare [g.] [g.] oððe [h.] leorninc cnihta
semper. abbas   quia   doctrine   sue   vel   discipulorum

gehýrsumnesse [h.] æghwæðera [k.]   [k.] on ðam egesfullan [l.]
oboedientiae.   utrarumque   rerum   in   tremendo

domc [l.] godc to donne he [c.] is he [c.] is [e.] oððe [f.] 7 wite [a.]
judicio   dei. facienda   erit | erit   discusio.   Sciatque (122 b.)

se abbod [b.] gýltes [d.] hýrdes onsigan [c.] [f.] swa hwæt on
5   abba   culpe   pastoris incumbere   quicquid   in

sceapum [g.] se hiredes ealdor [g.] nýtwýrðnesse hwonlicor swa
ovibus   paterfamilias   utilitatis minus potuerit

mæg gemetan swa micel [d.] eft [d.] *srig [c.] he bið gif unstilre
invenire;   Tantum   iterum   liber   erit, si inquieto

oððe ungehýrsumude [g.] hýrde [e.] ælc. [f.] geornfulnýssa
vel inoboedienti   gregi pastoris fuerit   omnis   diligentia

bið forgifen 7 gif adligum [c.] heora [c.] dædum [c.] call [b.]
attributa.   et   morbidis   earum   actibus   universa

býð [a.] [b.] gýman gegearcod hýrde [e.] heora [e.] on dome [g.]
10 *fuerit   cura   exhibita.   pastor   eorum   in   judicio*

drihtnes tolýsed [f.] ut *þæt *ece mid þam witigan
domini absolutus   dicat   cum   propheta   domino;

[b.] þine rihtwisnýsse [b.] ic ne be hýdde on minre heortan
Justitiam tuam   non abscondidi   in   corde   meo.

þine [e.] soðfæstnesse [e.] 7 halwendan [f.] [f.] þinre ic sæde
veritatem tuam   et   salutare   tuum   dixi.

hig [g.] forhicgende [h.] forsawon [g.]   7 [a.] þonne [b.]
ipsi autem contempnentes   spreverunt   me. Et   tunc

æt nýxtan [e.] ungehýrsuman gýmene [f.] his [f.] sceapum to wite
15 *demum   inoboedientibus   cure   suae   ovibus: pena*

[a.] bið hcom swýðrenda sesylva [c.] [c.] deað [b.] þonne
sit   eis   prevalens   ipsa   mors; Ergo   cum

ænig [g.] underfehð [f.] naman [i.] [h.] þæs abbodes. on twýfeald
aliquis   suscipit   nomen   abbatis.   dupplici

---

1. *dm* stands above *g*, *p* under *g*, both to the right. See note on *geondsprecend.*   7. *srig*, read *frig.*   11. *ut* in line of gloss by hand of glossator.
þæt ece, i. e. *þ̄ ece*, read *secce*?

---

10. MS. *earum*, an *o* above the *a*, which does not seem to me to be
one of the 'paving' letters, but a correction by glossator of *earum* into
eorum.

---

he sceal [a.] lare [e.] his [d.] leorn [c.] [c.] forebeon i.　cnihtum
debet 　　*doctrina* 　*suis* 　　　　　　*preesse* 　　　　*discipulis.*

þæt is calle [b.] godu. [b.] 7 halige middædum [e.] swyðor
id est omnia 　　*bona* 　et *sancta* 　　*factis* 　　　*amplius*

þænne [f.] [f.] mid wordum he atiwige angitfullum leorniccnihtum
quam 　　　　verbis ostendat; ut capacibus* 　　*discipulis*

beboda [i.] 　　　mid wordum [k.] his foresette [g.] þam heard
mandata domini 　*verbis* 　　　*præponat.* 　　*duris vero*

heortan [d.] 　　bilehwitum mid his [c.] dædum [c.] þa godcundan
corde 　et *simplicioribus* 　*factis* 　　*suis* 　　*divina* 　5

beboda [b.] he geswuteliað ealle þinc. [b.] þe leorninccnihtum.
precepta 　*demonstret;* 　*Omnia* 　vero *que* 　*discipulis*

he læræð beon [h.] wiðræde on his dædum he gebicnige 　na
docuerit 　*esse* 　*contraria in suis* 　*factis* 　*indicet* 　*non*

to donne þæt oðrum bodiende [m.] he sylf [k.] wiðercora
agenda 　ne *aliis* 　*predicans* 　　*ipse* 　　*reprobus*

ne si gemett þæt ahwenne him na secge 　[c.] syngendum
inveniatur 　*nequando* 　*illi* 　*dicat* 　*deus* 　*peccanti.*

to hwi na ðu cyðst rihtwisnysea mine 7 þu underfæhst
Quare 　tu *enarras* 　*justitias* 　*meas.* et 　*assumis* 　10

gewitnysse mine þurh þinne muð þu 　　hatodest steore
testamentum meum per 　*os tuum* 　*Tu vero odisti disciplinam*

7 ðu awurpe spræca | mine *bestande 7 þa ge on breðer þines
a.) et *projecisti sermones* | *meos* 　*post te* et *qui* 　*in fratris tui*

ege 　mot gesawe on ðinon ege beam ne gesawe þu la
oculo festucam videbas. in 　*tuo* 　*trabem non* 　*vidisti;*

[a.] Na si [c.] fram him [b.] had on mynstre [d.] [a.] asyndrod
Non 　　ab 　eo *persona in* 　*monasterio* 　*discernatur.*

na si an swiðor gelufod mid godum dædum oððe gehyrsvm-
non unus plus ametur 　*bonis* 　*actibus aut* 　*oboedi-* 　15

nesse *ænne oðer butan þancþe he met beteran ne si
entia quam alius nisi 　*quem invenerit meliorem; Non*

forasett se æðelborenne þeowdome ge [c.] cyrrendum [e.] buton
preponatur 　*ingenuus* 　*ex servitio* 　*convertenti.* 　*nisi*

---

1. *leorn,* which belongs to *cnihtum,* has been put before *forebeon.* For
leorninccniht? 　12. *ðu* not quite clear, a stroke running through ð
and along the top of the *u,* making it look like *a.* *bestande,* read *beftan*
ðe. 　16. *ænne,* read *þænne.*

---

12. *meos,* MS. *meo. post te,* MS. *poste.* 　15. *bonis,* MS. *actionis;* clearly
the scribe's eye was caught by the next word.

wenunga   sum   gesceadwislic [f.] intinga [e.] wunige þæt [a.]
forte   *aliqua*   *rationabilis*   *causa*   *existat ;*   *Quod*

gif biÐ rihtwisnesse dihtendre [c.] þam [b.] abbude sewen ge. [a.]
si   ita   justitia   dictante   abbati   visum fuerit.

[g.] be   sumere   be æudebýrdnesse þæt [h.]   hedo elles
et   de   cujus libet   ordine   id   faciat; Sin alias ;

agenre [a.] higehealdan [b.] stowa forÐam swa þeowa [g.] [h.] swa
propria   teneant   loca.   quia sive servus   sive

fræc [h.] ealle [d.] on christe an. [e.] þe we sin [a.] 7 under anc
5 *liber ;   omnes   in christo unum   sumus.   et sub uno*

drihtene gelicue [b.] þeowdomes cam dom [b.] 7 we aberaÐ forÐam
domino   æqualem   servitutis   militiam   bajulamus. quia

þe *þe is mid gode   *bada   *anstangynnes [b.] þæt an [b.]
non   est apud deum personarum   acceptio;   Solum   modo

[a.] Ðisum dæle [c.]   mid him [d.] he tosyndraþ gif beteran
in   hac   parte apud ipsum discernimur. Si meliores

oÐram [h.] [h.] on godum weorcum [h.] 7 eadmodren we beoÐ
aliis   in   operibus   bonis   et humiliores inveni-

gemette   gelie [b.] [a.] si fram him [g.] eallum [d.] [k.] soÐlufu
10 *amur; Ergo equalis   sit   ab   eo   omnibus   karitas ;*

an sigegearcod on eallum æfter [b.] gearnunge steor [f.]
Una   prebeatur in omnibus secundum   merita disciplina; In

lare [h.] witodlice on his se abbod [e.] apostolice [a.] sceall
doctrina namque   sua   abbas   apostolicam   debet

þæt he æfre [f.]   hiwe   healdan on Ðam he sæigÐ. [g.]   þrea
illam semper formam servare in qua   dicit ;   Arguae.

halsa   cid   þæt [a.] is [a.] mængcende   tidum   tida [c.]
obsecra. increpa.   id   est   miscens temporibus tempora

ogum. egesum. geswæsnyssa 7 reÐe [e.] lareowas [b.] arfæst
15 *terroribus   blandimenta; Dirum   magistri.   pium*

fæderes [c.] heatiwe [a.] lufe [b.] þæt is [f.] þæt ungeþeawfæstan [i.]
patris   ostendat affectum.   idem   indisciplinatos

6. The glossator has once more written *servitutis* over the same word in
the text, and over that the gloss *þeowdomes.* 8. *ipsām*, sic in MS.
9. *operibus*, *p* has a line through the downstroke as a sign of contraction for *er*,
and yet *er* has been written. *humiliores*, MS. *humiliō.* Of the other texts AC
have *humiliores*, the others *humiles.* 13. *servare*, *rv* on erasure. It is
possibly to be regarded as an unsuccessful attempt to correct the *servire* of the
MS. into *servare.*

7 þa ungedefan he sceall stiðlicor þrean [h.] þa gehýrsuman
et   inquietos   debet   durius   arguere.   obedientes

soðlice | 7 þa [d.] liðan [c.] 7 paðildigan [e.] [r.] þæt hi [g.] beteron
b.) autem | et   mitæs   et patientes. ut in melius

geðeon debere ñhalsian [b.] þa gemeleasan [d.]   7 ða for-
proficiant obsecrare.   Neglegentes   autem et con-

hicgenden [d.] þæt he ðræge 7 þæt he gestande [c.] [c.]
tempnentes.   ut increpet et   corripiat

*þe myngiað ne he *bennðe hiwige sýnna agyldendra ahhe
ammonemus ;   Neque dissimulet peccata delinquentium. sed 5

sona *þonne hi onginnað upasprungan grundlunga hig beðam þe he
mox   ut ceperint   oriri   radicitus ea ut pre-

mæg ofadoceorfe .sit. freccdnýssa   sacerdes of silan 7 þa
valet amputet. memor periculi heli sacerdotis de silo; Et

arwurðan witodlice 7 þa andgýtfulran mod mid þære forman
honestiores quidem atque intellegibiles animos;   prima

oððe oþrasýðan mýnegunge mid wordum [a.] 7 hegeþrege
vel secunda ammonitione   verbis   corripiat

þa ðwýran   7 þa heardan 7 þa modigan oððe þa *ungehýr-
inprobos autem et duros ac superbos vel inobedi- 10

sumantes mid swinglan oððe lichaman oððe oððe preagunge
entes   verberum   vel corporis   castigatione ;

on ðam sýlfan angýnne sýnne he þreage witende awriten
in ipso initio peccati coherceat sciens scriptum;

se dýsiga mid wordum na bið geðread 7 eft sleg. slch.
Stultus verbis non corrigitur ; Et iterum ; Percute

þa bearn þine midgyrde 7 *þa alyst sawle his of deaðe
filium tuum virga et liberabis animam eius a morte ;

gemunan [a.] sceal æfre [a.] scabbod þæt þe he is cweden 7
Meminisse debet semper abba quod dicitur ; et 15

witan þæt bið þam ðe mara bið befæst mare fram him
scire quia cui plus committitur ; plus ab eo exitar ;

2. þæt, þ torn in two.   3. MS. deð, which Latin addendum is in
hand of glossator.   5. þe, read we. bennðe, read bemiðe, and see note. d of
-dra above the line.   6. þonne, sic in MS. Read ponne.   7. sit, Latin in
hand of glossator. silan or silon.   10. ungehýrsumantes, probably after
having written ungehýrsuman, which read, the scribe's eye was caught by
the -tes which must have been in the Latin original.   13. gðread, wrongly
glossed by original glossator, who must have read corripitur in his text.
14. þa, read þu.

10. inprobos, MS. inprobus. inobedientes, MS. inobeliendos.   16. cul, in
accordance with other texts and with the gloss, MS. cujus.

[a.] 7 he wite [b.] hu [b.] be earfoðe [b.] he underfeht 7 sticol
*Sciat*que   *quam   difficilem   rem   et   arduam*

[b.]   gewissian sawla   7 mænigra þcowan þeawum 7 sumne
suscepit   regere   animas. et multorum   servire moribus et alium

witodlice mid gcswæsnyssum oðerne   mid þræigum
quidem   blandimentis   alium vero incrcpationibus ; alium

mid   larum   7   æfter   ge æghwylces   hwylcnysse   oððe
suasionibus ;   Et   secundum   unius cujusque   qualitatem   vel

      andgit   hine sy!fne on callon þingan 7 he gehiwige 7
5 *intelligentiam.   ita se omnibus conformet   et*

he geþæslæce þæt he na þæt an nyðerunga. æfwyrðe heorde
    aptet   ut   non solum   detrimenta   gregis

hims ylfan befæstre | þolige cac swylce on [g.] geeacnunge
    sibi   commissi | non pat:atur.   verum   in   augmentatione (124 a.)

godre heorde he geblissige toforan callanþingan   behiwiende
boni gregis   gaudeat ;   Ante   cmnia   non dissimulans

oððe for * forht taliendre hæle   saule   him sylfan. bi. fæstra
aut   rarvi   pendcns salutem animarum   sibi commissarum.

swiðor he ne do hohfulnesse   be þingum gewitendlicum 7
10 *plus   gerat   sollicitudinem de   rebus   transitoriis.   et*

iordlicum   7   gcwitendlicum   ah   he þence þæt he
terrenis atque   caducis ;   sed semper cogitet   quia

saula underfænc togewissianne be ðam 7 gcscead þe he his
animas suscepit   regendas.   de quibus et rationem reddi-

to gyldenne [a.] 7 þæt he na cide he læssan færunga landare
turus est ;   Et   ne   causetur   de minori   forte   substantia

he gemuna   gcwrit   æræst   [q.] secað   godes   rice
meminerit   scriptum ;   Primum   querite   regnum   dei   et

rihtwisnesse 7 his 7 ealle þas þinc beoð hihte   7   eft
15 *justitiam   ejus et haec omnia   adicientur vobis ; Et iterum ;*

naht wana   nis ondrædendum hine [a.] 7 he wite [b.] þæt he
    *Nihil   deest timentibus eum ;   Sciat*que   *quia*

se ðc underfehð sawla to gewissianne iarcie hine to gescead
qui suscipit   animas   regendas   preparet   se   ad rationcm

---

6. *æfwyrðe*, read *æfwyrdle*?   7. *g* before *geeacnunge*: as there are no
'paving' letters in this passage, *g.* may be an anticipation of *geeacnunge.*
9. *forht*, *o* and *h* cor. from two other letters ; see note.   10. *ne*; but for
context, *u* might be read as *m.*   13. *na cide*, *a* and *cide* possibly on crasure.
14. [q.] Is this one of the 'paving' letters ?

---

7. *augmentatione*, MS. *aumentatione.*

ageldenne [a.] 7 swa micel undergẏmenne gebroðia hine
reddendam; Et quantum sub cura sua fratrum se
habban [a.] swa he wite [a.] getel he onenawe to soðan þæt he
habere scierit numerum; agnoscat pro certo. quia

sẏlfra ealra þara sawla sceall agẏldan
in die judicii ipsarum omnium animarum est redditurus

buton twẏn to gehiht his agenne sawle
domino rationem. sine dubio addita et sue animae;

[a.] [d.] [e.] [f.] [g.] þa toweardan smeagunge [h.] hẏrde
Et ita semper timens futuram discusionem pastoris 5

[i.] of befæstum sceapum mid ælfremedum sceadwisnyssum
de creditis oribus; cum de alienis ratiociniis

wærnað he si gewordan [c.] [b.] hohful [a.] þonne
cavet reddatur de suis sollicitus; Et cum

he mẏnegungum be his bote oðrum [a.] þenað he si
ammonitionibus suis emendationem aliis subministrat, ipse

geworden fram leahtrum rihtlæcð
efficiatur a vitiis emendatus.

be gegearnendum to ræde gebroðra.
DE ADHIBENDIS AD CONSILIUM FRATRIBUS. (CAP. III.) 10

swa oft swa sind [ð.] ænige healice þinc [a.] to donne
QUOTIENS ALIQUA PRECIPUA AGENDA

b.) [a.] on mẏnstre mẏnstre [d.] gelangige [e.] se abbod
SUNT IN Mo | nasterio; convocet abbas

[f.] ealle [f.] gegæderunge 7 he sẏlf secge [h.] hwanon
omnem congregationem. et dicat ipse unde

[h.] he beo astired [i.] [l.] gehẏrende [m.] gebeah gebroðra
agitur; et audiens consilium fratrum.

7 he smæge [k.] mid him sylfan [n.] þæt [o.] is nytwyrð-
tractet apud se; et quod (est) uti- 15

licor. [n.] 7 he deme forþig ealle to gepeahte
lius judicaverit [faciat] Ideo autem omnes ad consilium

gecian we secgat forþam oft þam gingran drihten þe unwryhð
vocari diximus; quia sepe juniori dominus revelat

---

10. *gebroðra*, both context and lemma make one expect *gebroðrum*.
14. *astired*, *i* of peculiar form below the line.

---

6. *ratiociniis*, MS. *rationem*. 7. *sollicitus*, MS. *sollicitur*. 15. *est* a
little erased. See note.

C

þæt betere is swa   syllan   geþeaht mid ealre
quod melius est; Sic autem dent fratres consilium cum omni

eadmodnesse. underþeodnesse þæt na gedýrstlæcan gemahlice.
humilitatis   subjectione   ut non presumant   procaciter

bewerian. þæt hieom heom gesawen bið ah furþor
tendere quod   eis   visum fuerit.   sed magis

on þæs abbodes hit stande kýre be þam *hwonlicor oððe
in   abbatis   pendeat arbitrio eo quod   salubrius

gesælicor þe he demð ealle gehýrsumian [a.] ah [c.] swa swa
5   *judicaverit   cuncti obediant.   Sed   sicut*

leorniccnihtum gedafenað [f.] þæt gehyrsumian [g.] lareowe
discipulis   convenit   obedire   magistro.

 [b.] 7 him foraglæwlice 7 rihtlice gedafenað [d.] ealle þinc
ita et ipsum provide   et juste condecet   cuncta

[c.] gedihtan [d.] on eallum þingum [b.] iornostlice ealle [c.]
disponere ;   In   omnibus   igitur   omnes

[c.] lareowlicum [a.] hi fýlian [c.] regole [f.] [h.] fram him
magistram   sequantur regulam ; ne   ab   ea

[i.] þristelice [f.] na na si gebogen fram ænigum [a.] na [b.] ænig
10   *temere   declinetur a quoquam ;   Nullus*

on minstre [a.] na fylige [c.] agenra heortan willan
in monasterio   sequatur   proprii cordis voluntatem.

[f.] ne ne gedýrstlæce [f.] [g.] ænig [n.] midhis abbude [n.]
neque presumat   quisquam   pro abbate   suo

[l.] wurðlice [h.] wið innan [h.] oððe wiðutan [m.] on mýnstre
proterve   intus   aut   foris   monasterium

[k.] flitan [a.] þæt gif gedýrstlæcð [b.] ænig [e.] regolicore
contendere ; Quod si presumpserit quisquam   disciplinae

---

3 *ealra* along with its lemma *omnium* is found in the text, after *heom*,
see Latin note to l. 4.   4. *hwonlicor*, see note.   Sign for *oððe* above
line.   6. *leorniccnihtum*, read *leornic*, i. e. *leorninc*.   7. *him*, last stroke
of *m* erased, by mistake, when the *g* of *sigut* was erased. *gedafenað*, *d*
corrected from some other letter.

---

1. Before *melius* the word *faciat* is erased ; it is found after *judicaverit* in
the other Latin texts. *dent*, *e* corrected from *i*.   3. *omnium* erased
before *visum*.   *visum* in margin in glossator's hand, by way of correction
for the misreading *omnium*.   4. *pendeat*, written by glossator over
gaudeat, which is erased.   5. *siqut*, corrected into *sicut*.   6. MS. *discipulus*. Some one, seeing that this word ought to be *discipulis*, began wrongly
to erase *s*, then stopped this, and indicated correction from *u* into *i* by putting
a dot over second stroke of *u*.   10. *quam* (other texts *que*) erased after *ne*.
12. *pro*, other texts have *cum*.   That this has been in original of our text
is probable, as the gloss has *mid*.

[e.] styre [c.] he underhnige [b.] sýlf swa ðcah. [b.] se abbod
regulari   *subjaceat ;*   *Ipse*   *tamen*   *abbas*

[c.] mid godes ege   [f.] 7 gehealdsumnesse regules [t.] ealle þinc
cum   *timore*   *dei* et   *observatione*   *regule*   *omnia*

[a.] do. witende hine buton twýn be eallum his domum þa riht-
faciat. *sciens* *se* *procul dubio* *de omnibus* *judiciis* *suis*

wisestan deman godc gescead to aiýldenne gyf [e.] hwýlce
equissimo *judici* *deo* *rationem redditurum;* *Si* *qua*

[b.] [f.] læssan þe inc syndon to done   [g.] on
vero *minora*   *agenda*   *sunt*   *in* 5

a.) [h.] mýnstres [g.] on nýtwýrdnýssum caldra [i.] þæt an
monasterii   *utilita | tibus*   *seniorum*   *tantum*

[a.] he bruce [o.] geþelhtc swa swa hit awriten is ealle [l.]
utatur   *consilio*   *sicut*   *scriptum* *est;* *Omnia*

[k.] do mid ræde [m.] 7 [n.] [o.] *æter dædum 7 hit þe ne ofrcow
fac *cum consilio.* et   *post* *factum non*   *penitebis;*

hwýlce beon   tol   godera   weorca.
Que Sint Instrumenta Bonorum Operum. (Cap. IIII.)

ealra æræst drihten god lufian calre heortan mid
In *primis* *dominum* *deum* *diligere ex toto* *corde* *tota* 10

eallra sawla mid calre mihte sýððan ncxtan ealswa þe sýlfne
anima *tota* *virtute ; Deinde proximum. tamquam se ipsum ;*

debemus ofslean   umihthæman na don þeofæ
Deinde *non occidere* *Non* *adulterare.* *non facere furtum.*

ne gewilnian na leas gcwitnesse secgan arwurðian
non concupiscere. *non falsum testimonium dicere;* *Honorare*

debemus calle men him sýlfan æni beon þæt ðæt nclc
omnes *homines* et *quod sibi quis fieri non vult.*

oðrum 7 þæt ne do wiðsacan. sic hinc sylfne   himsylfum þæt
Alii *ne faciat; Abnegare semet* *ipsum* *sibi ;* *ut* 15

3. *þa*, read *þam*. 7. [o.] perhaps *ō=on*. 8. *æter*, read *æfter*.
12. *debem'*, in glossator's hand, not in other Latin texts; cf. l. 15; p. 20,
l. 15, and passim. *þcofæ*, *þ* corr. from some other letter. 14. *debem'*,
cf. l. 13. 15. First *þæt* added later on by glossator. *sylfne*, *f* added
later on by glossator. *sic*, stands by the side of *wiðsacan*, not over *se*.

2. *timore*, MS. *timorem*. 5. The words *aut major* (read *majora*?) are
found after *ayenda*; they are probably originally a marginal note copied
into our text, and not in the other texts. 6. *seniorum* to *sicut* inclusive,
together with gloss, left out by copyist, and put in top margin. 10. *corde*,
MS. *corda*.

he fýlige　　crist　lichaman　þrean　estmettas　　befon.
sequatur christum.　Corpus castigare; Delicias non amplecti

fæsten debemus lufian þearfan　　fedan　　nacodne et scredan
Jejunium amare;　Pauperes recreare; Nudum　vestire.

untrume 7　geneosian　deadne　bebyrgian　on　gedrefednesse
Infirmum　visitare.　Mortuum sepelire.　In　tribulatione

gehelpan　sargenne　gefrefrian　fram　weorulde　[a.] dædum
subvenire. Dolentem consolari.　A　seculi　actibus

　don　ælfræmedne æniþincg cristes lufan na foresettan ýrre
5 *se facere alienum;　Nihil　amori christi　preponere.　Iram*

non debemus gefremman ýrsunge timan na　healdan　facn
non　perficere.　Iracundie tempus non reservare; Dolum

on heortan na healdan lease sibbe　cost　na　syllan þa soðe
in　corde　non tenere.　Pacem　falsum non dare.　Kari-

lufan　na　na forlætan　na　swerian þe he hine forswerige
tatem　non derelinquere.　Non　jurare　ne forte　perjuret.

* soðfæsten debet of heortan 7 of muðe forðbringan.　ýfel　for
Veritatem　ex corde　et　ore　proferre.　Malum pro

ýfele debemus agildan　tregan debemus　gedonne dæde
10 *malo　non reddere.　Injuriam non facere. sed et factam*

geþýldelice ah forþyldian * frýnd　lufian　þa awýrigendan
patienter　sufferre;　Inimicos diligere;　Maledicentes

[c.] non debemus agen wýrian ah swiðor bletsian　[d.] elnnesse
se non　remaledicere　sed magis benedicere.　Persecutionem

for rihtwisnesse þolian. beon　　ðe modig　na windrucen
pro　justitia　sustinere. Non esse superbum. non vinolentum;

na mycelæte |　　　　na*sia　　na *sceac mur-　(125 b.)
non multum |　ædacem; non somnolentum; non pigrum;　non

nigende naceriende　na * ælendne　　　hiht　his gode
15 *murmuriosum;　non detractorem; debet spem suam deo*

betæcan　god　æni þinc on him sylfan þonne he gesyhþ
committere; Bonum aliquid　in　se　　cum　viderit:

---

2. *debemus*, in glossator's hand, not in other Latin texts.　*et scredan*,
MS. *& scredan*; did the scribe find *ed-*, *æt scredan* or *7 scredan* in his
original?　　6. *non debemus* over *gefremman*.　　9. *soðfæstne*, read
soðfæstnesse.　　11. *frýnd*, read *fýnd*.　　12. *non debemus* in margin.
13. *ðe*, see note.　　14. *nasia*, read *slapol?* *sceac*, read *sleac*. *ælendne*,
read *telendne*.

---

1. *Delicias*, MS. *dulcias*; it would seem that an attempt was made to
correct it.　3. *risitare*, underlined in MS. repeated by mistake after
Mortuum.　10. *factam*, see note.　13. *superbum*, MS. *desuperbum*,
see note.　15. *detractorem*, *o* corr. from *a*.

gode ne betæce na him sylfan yfel him. sylfan æfre fram
deo applicet non sibi ; Malum vero semper a se

gedon he wite him. sylfan 7 getelle domes dæig
factum sciat ; et sibi reputet ; Diem debemus judicii

ondrædan helle aforhtian þæt ece lif mid ealre gast-
timere ; gehennam expavescere ; vitam æternam omni concu-

licere gewilnunge gewilnian [b.] deað [c.] dæghwamlice
piscentia spiritali desiderare ; Mortem cotidie

[c.]ætforan eagan [d.]gewenedne [a.]habban dæda lifes his
ante oculos suspectam habere ; actus vitæ sue 5

on ælcere tide gehealdan on ælcere stowa gode hine besceawian
omni hora custodire ; In omni loco deum se respicere

[a.] tosoðan [b.]witan geþohtas þa yfelan heortan his to becu-
pro certo scire : Cogitationes malas cordi suo adveni-

menne sona to christe *aslidan þam gastlican ealdre
entes ; mox ad christum allidere ; et seniori spiritali

7 gesutulian he his muð fram yfele fram yfcle oððe þwyrlice
patefacere. Debet os suum a malo vel pravo elo-

spræce gehealdan mycel swyðe [b.]spræcan na. [a.]lufian
quio custodire ; Multum loqui non amare. 10

idele word hlehtregamene. oððe lilic micelne leahtor oððe
Verba vana aut risui apta non loqui ; Risum multum aut

to sceacenne lufian halige rædinge lustlice lysta. oððe
excussum non amare ; Lectiones sanctas libenter audire ;

gehyra gebeda [c.]*frædlice 7 onsigan his forðgewitena yfela
orationi frequenter incumbere ; Mala sua preterita

mid tearum oððe geomorunge dæghwamlice on gebeda gode
cum lacrimis vel gemitu cotidie in oratione deo

anddettan of ðam sylfan yfelum þærto eacan betan.
confiteri ; de ipsis malis de cetero emendare; 15

gewilnunga lichaman [d.] gefremman willan agenne
Desideria carnis non perficere. voluntatem propriam

[d.]hatian bebodu on eallum þeh þe sylf do
odire ; preceptis abbatis in omnibus obedire ; Etiam si

---

1. *ne*, wrong gloss. 8. *aslidan*? Perhaps the scribe found *aslean* in his text, and his eye was caught by the *allidere* of the Latin. 13. *frædlice*, see note ; *yfela*, top part of *l* erased by erasure in *audire* (Latin notes on l. 1ᵌ). 15. *anddettan*, first *d* above line, and at the end of line, but probably belongs to the word.

---

1. *applicet*, MS. *amplicet*. 2. for *debemus*, see note to p. 20, l. 15. See infra, l. 9. 9. *Debet*, see note to l. 2. 12. *audire*, erasure of about two letters between *i* and *r*. 16. *propriam*, *i* above line.

he   elles þæt feor sig sýlf do gemýndige   þæs   drihtenlican
ipse aliter quod absit   agat ;   memor   illius   dominici

bebodas þa *sed gat   doð   þa ðinc   þe hi doþ   don
precepti. Que   dicunt facite ;   que   autem faciunt   facere

nelle   na   nellan beon gesæið halig   ærðamþe hesig
nolite ; Non velle   dici   s\nctum antequam sit ; sed

ær   ah beon þæt soðlicor þæt þæt he is gesæd godes beboda
prius esse.   quod verius | dicatur ;   Precepta   (126 a.)

    mid dædum dæihwamlice   gefyllan   clænnesse lufian
5 *dei   factis   cotidie   adimplere ; Castitatem amare ;*

uchne non æfest 7   andan   habban geflit. oððe ceaste
nullum odire ; zelum et invidiam non habere ; Contentionem non

                   upahofennesse   idelne *iyl forfleon 7   þa yldran
amare ;   elationem   rel jactantiam fugere ; Et   seniores

arwurðian þa iynran   on christes *lufian for feondum
venerari ; juniores   diligere. in christi amore pro inimicis

gebiddan mid þam ungeþwærum ær   nyðersige. oððe gange
orare ;   Cum discordantibus ante   solis   occasum

on sibbe gehwyrfan non be godes mildheortnesse debemus næfre
10 *in pace   redire ;   et de dei   misericordia   numquam*

geortruwian efne þas sind   tol   cræftis gastlices þæt þonne
desperare ; Ecce hec sunt instrumenta artis spiritalis que cum

beoð gefylde fram   us   unablinnendlice dægges 7 nihtes
fuerint   a   nobis   die noctuque   incessa-

unateoriendlice to gefyllanne   on domes dæge   7 betæhte
'   *biliter adimpleta ;   et in   die   judicii reconsignata.*

seo med us fram drihtne bið agolden þe he sylf   behet
illa merces nobis a domino reconpensabitur quam ipse promisit ;

    eage   þæt ðe ne geseah   earc ne ne gehýrde ne ne on
15 *Quod oculus   non   vidit. nec auris   audivit ;   nec in*

heortan mannes astah þa ðinc þe gearcode   þisum. þa ða
cor   hominis ascendit ; que   preparavit deus   his   qui

---

2. *sed gat*, *d* of unclear shape in MS., but no *c*: read *scegat*.   6. *non*
Latin, over *odire*? cf. infra, l. 10, perhaps to be taken to *neh ne*, and to be
read *mon*.   7. *iyl*, read *iylp*.   8. *lufian*, read *lufan*.   12. *unablinnendlice*, the fourth *n* corr. from some other letter, probably *a*.   Read *d. 7 n.
unabl. unateor. adimpleta*, glossed as if *ad implenda*.

---

1. *memor*, MS. *memoris*.   3. *dici*, MS. *dice*.   10. *dei*, MS. *dim*, *m*
misread from sign of contr. above *i*, for *e* of *dei*.   11. *n* in *cum* corr. from
some other letter.

lufiað hine [c.] smeðe [b.] *iþærwe [i.] calle þas ðin:e
diligunt deum; Officina vero ubi hæc omnia

[k.] geornlice [i.] wýrccan [d.] clýsunga [a.] [e.] mynstres 7
diligenter operemur. claustra sunt monasterii; et

staðolfæstnys [g.]
stabilitas in congregatione;

De Obedientia Discipulorum Qualis sit. (Cap. V.)

[c.]se for witodlice [f.] eadmodnes [e.] se forma stæpe ans [c.] gehýr-
Primus itaque humilitatis gradus est: obe- 5

sumnes [d.] butonýldinege [b.] þasðine [a.] gerist [c.] þisom [d.]
dientia sine mora; Haec convenit his qui

nuht [g.] himsýlfum [h.] criste [f.] leofre [c.] ænigþineg [d.] padene-
nihil sibi christo carius aliquid exis-

wenað [i.] forðam þeowdome haligan [k.] þe hi [k.] beheton
timant: propter servitium sanctum quod professi

[k.] [l.] oððe [l.] for [l.] hogan helle [m.] [o.] oððe [o.] forwuldre
sunt: seu propter metum gehenne: vel gloriam

(126 b.) [p.] lifes [p.] þæs ecan is sona [s.] ænig þine [r.] þonne biðbe-
vite aeterne; Mox ut | aliquid impera- 10

boden [d.] fram ealdre [r.] [a.] acswilcc [x.] godcundlice [a.] hitsibe
tum a maiore fuerit: ac si divinitus im-

boden [c.] ýldinege et þrowian hý niton on donlicum þinegum
peretur. moram pati nesciunt in faciendo;

[a.] be ðam [b.] [a.] swigð for [c.] hlýste [d.] earan
De quibus dominus dicit: ob auditu auris.

[a.] he gehýrsumede [b.] 7 [a.] cft he scigð [a.] [b.] lareowum
oboedivit mihi; Et iterum dicit doctoribus;

[e.] se ðe [f.] eow [e.] gehýrð me [c.] gehýrð þas oððe þillice
Qui vos audit: me audit; Ergo hi tales 15

[f.] forlætende [g.] þarrihte [h.] þe heora [h.] 7 [k.] willan
relinquentes statim que sua sunt; et voluntatem

[k.] agenne [i.] forlætende [m.] sona [n.] gebýsgodum [n.] handum
propriam deserentes; mox ex occupatis manibus

---

1. iþærwe, sic in MS.: probably i as 'paving' letter. þær as gloss to ubi, and
we belonging to wyrcean. 5. for, read forma. The MS. has csefor.-ans
over est, I cannot explain. 7. þadenewcnað, i.e. þa ðe ne wenað. 10. is.
Latin? the gloss above ut is illegible.

S. sanctum (sčm), MS. serundum (scdm). 12. Above the o of moram
there is written a z.

7 þæt hi didon [p.] unfulfremcd [i.] forlætende [e.] mid [h.]
et quod agebant inperfectum relinquentes : vici-

gehendum [g.] gehýrsumnesse [e.] fet bebeodendes [c.] stefne
no oboedientiæ pede jubentis vocem

[d.] middædum [a.] hi fýllian [a.] 7 swýlce [d.] onanre [d.] hand-
factis sequuntur ; Et velut uno mo-

hwile [b.] seoforesæda lareowas [b.] hæs [c.] 7 fulfremcd
mento predicta magistri jussio et perfecta

[f.] leorninccnihtas weorc [g.] onhrædnesse [h.] godes eges [h.]
5 discipuli opera in velocitate timoris dei

[k.] bute þa [k.] ðinc [l.] gemænlice [m.] hærdlicor 7 be ongefýl-
ambe res communiter citius explican-

lede þam [n.] to þam [a.] ecan life [q.] [p.] to gangenne
tur. Quibus ad vitam æternam gradiendi

[o.] lufu [n.] onsigð for þone neorwan weig hi gelettað þanon
amor incumbit. Ideo angustam riam arripiunt : unde

sæig se nearwa weig is se læd to life þæt heora
dominus dicit angusta via est que ducit ad vitam : ut non

agenre kýre na libbende heora gewilnungum 7 lustum
10 suo arbitrio viventes : vel desideriis suis et voluptatibus

gehýrsumiende ac gangende on ælfræmedum dome 7 on
obedientes sed ambulantes alieno judicio et im-

anwealde on mýnstrum drohgende abbod heom sýlfum fora
perio et in coenobiis degentes : abbatem sibi pre

beon hine gewilnian buton twýn þas. swilce þone [a.] ge-
esse desiderant ; Sine dubio hi tales illam domini imi-

efenlæcean cwude [c.] þam ic na com don minne willan
tantur sententiam ; qua dicit ; Non veni facere voluntatem

ac þæs se ðe ascnde me [a.] ah [b.] þeos sýlfe [b.]
15 meam ; sed ejus qui misit me : Sed hec ipsa

[b.] gehýrsumnesse [c.] þonne [d.] anfenge [b.] bið gode 7 wýnsum
oboedientia tunc | acceptabilis erit deo et dulcis (127 a.)

mannum gif hwæt bið beboden forhtlice ne lætlice ne
hominibus ; si quod jubetur ; non trepide ; non tarde ; non

---

2. bebeodendes, second e above line. 3. handhwile, the two h's above the
line. 5. hrædnesse, h above line.

---

3. momento, MS. monumento, nu crossed out. 7. gradiendi, MS. gra-
dienti. 13. desiderant, MS. desiderent. 16. acceptabilis, MS.
acceptabis.

erhlice   oððe mid ceorunge oððe oððc mid andswere [c.]
tepide ; aut   cum   murmurio.   vel   cum   responso

nellendes biðgeworden. [a.] forðam þe [b.] bið gehýrsumnes
nolentis   efficiatur :   Quia   oboedientia

  ealdran [d.] se ðe bið iarcod [c.] godc [a.] gegearcon hesýlf
que majoribus   prebetur :   dco   exibetur.   Ipse

  sæde se ðe eow þegehýrð [b.] * m. [a]gehýrð [a.] 7 [d.] mid
enim dixit ; Qui vos   audit   me   audit :   Et   cum

godum mode [c.] fram * leornincchintum [b.] beon gegearcod
bono   animo   a discipulis   preberi 5

[a.] hit gedafenað [e.] forðam þoneglædan sýllan [c.] þelufað
      oportet.   quia   hilarem   dutorem   diligit

gode [a.] soðes na bið [g.] mid ýfelum [g.] mode gif gehýrsumað
deus. Nam   cum   malo animo   si   obedit

leorninceniht 7 na þæt an   on muðc ac eac swýlce   on
discipulus : et non   solum   ore.   verum   ctiam in

heortan gif he ceorað   7 gif he gefýlle   hæse   [c.]
corde   si   murmuraverit. et si   impleat jussionem ; tamen

[b.] anfenge   [a.] [a.] [d.] se ðe heortan his besceawað ceori-
acceptum jam non erit dco ; qui   cor   ejus   respicit   mur- 10

endes   7 he for swýlcere dæde ænigne ne begitt   þanc
murantis ; Et   pro tali facto   nullam consequitur gratiam.

[b.] gif git swiðor [c.] wice [d.] ceorigendra [a.] onbecýmð gif
     Immo   penam   murmurantium   incurrit   si

[c.] he hit mid fulre dædbote [e.] na gebed
     non   cum satisfactione emendaverit.

DE TACITURNITATE.   (CAP. VI.)

utondon þæt ðe sæde se witega ic sæde ic gehealde wegas mine
FACIAMUS QUOD AJT PROPHETA. DIXI CUSTODIAM. *rias meas :* 15

þæt ic na gýlte   on minre tungan icsette muðc minon heord-
ut non delinquam in lingua mea ; Posui ori   meo   cus-

rædne ic adumbede 7 ic eom geeadmed   7 ic suwode
todiam :   obmutui   et humiliatus s m   et   silui

---

3. A letter (s?) erased before *gode*.   4. *m*, probably no ' paving' letter,
but for *me* (m̄).   5. *leorninechintum*, read *leornincenihtum.*   10. *his, i*
above line.

---
                     i
4. *Qui vos*, MS. *Quos.*   10. *murmurantis.* MS. *murmorantis.* *nullam,*
MS. *millam.*

fram godum [a.] her geswutulað [a.] [b.] gif [e.] fram godum
  a bonis :   Ilic ostendit   propheta ;   si   a   bonis

[c.] spræcum oðerhwile interdum for [g.] * salnesse beon gesuwod
    eloquiis propter   taciturnitatem

[c.] scel   beon gesuwod lahu micele swiðor fram ýfelum
  debet   interdum   tacere :   quantomagis   a malis

wordum   for   wite   sýnne   þeah sig be godum 7
verbis propter penam peccati ; Ergo quamvis de bonis | et ^(127 b.)

haligum   et   timbrunga   [d.] spræcum 7 fulfremedæ [b.]
5 *sanctis   et aedificationum   eloquiis   et   perfectis*

leorningccnihtum.   fore.   [f.] stilnesse stæððinesse * sýlfsýne
  *discipulis   propter taciturnitatis gravitat*em   *rara*

to specende [a.] geunnen [e.] leaf forðam þe hit is awriten on
loquendi   concedatur licentia ;   quia   scriptum est ;   In

manifealdre þu ne forflihst   sýnne   on oðerstowe deað 7
multiloquio   non effugies   peccatum. Et   alibi :   Mors et

lif on handum tungan soðes sprecan 7 læran lareowum
vita in manibus lingue ; Nam loqui   et docere magistrum

gedafenað suwian 7 heorenian leornicenihtum gedafenað
10 *condecet ; Tacere et audire   discipulo   convenit ; Et*

    gif wilce þineg sind to smeagenda fram dre mid ealre
ideo si   qua requirenda sunt   a priore cum omni

eadmodnesse 7 underþeodnesse 7 beon gesmeade befrinonne þæt
humilitate et   subjectione   reverentie   requirantur ;

ne si gesewen furður spræcan þonne hit gefremige   higlista
non videatur plus   loqui   quam   expedit   Scurilitates

  oðþe idelword   stirienda   eeer   clýsunga
vero vel   verba   otiosa et risum moventia ; aeterna clausura

on   ealle   stowum we ne fordemað   to hwýlcere   spræce
15 *in omnibus locis   dampnamus ; Et ad   talia   eloquia*

leornicceniht geopenodum muð 7   we ne ðafiað
discipulum   aperire   os   non permittimus.

---

2. *interdum* in glossator's hand. *oðerhwile*, as gloss to *interdum*, stands above it. *salnesse*, read *stilnesse*. *et*, MS. &.   6. *sýlfsýne*, see note.

---

2. *eloquiis*, MS. *eloquris*.   3. *quantomagis*, *n* above line. *malis*, *l* partially erased?   5. Second *et* above line. *perfectis*, MS. *perfectus*, but *i* written above *u*.   7. MS. *liquendi*, but changed into *loquendi*.   12. *reverentie* in margin.   13. *Scurilitates*, *li* above line in later hand.

De Humilitate. (Cap. VII.)

[b.] clẏpaðͧ c. vs. ẏ.　gewritt [d.]　þæt [d.] godcunda　cala [a.]
CLAMAT NOBIS　　SCRIPTURA　　DIVINA　　FRAT..ES

[e.] seccende [b.] ælc. [d.] se ðe [c.] hine [c.] upahefðͧ [a.] bið ge-
DICENS.　　omnis　　qui　se　exaltat　humilia-

eadmͧet [e.] 7 bið [f.] se ðe [f.] geeadmeðͧ upahafen þonne
bitur　et　　qui　se　humiliat exaltabitur:　Cum

þas þinc [o.] sæigð geswutulað [a.]　us　7 ælce upahafennesse
haec ergo　dicit;　　ostendit　nobis omnem exaltationem 5

cẏn　beon modinesse hine warnian　se witiga　þæt gebẏcniaþ
genus　esse　superbie　quod se cavere propheta　　indicat

la drihten　nis　upahafen　heorte mine nana upahafen
dicens;　Domine non est exaltatum　cor　meum neque　elati

sind eagan mine　　ne ic na ferde on mærlicum þingum na
sunt oculi mei;　Neque　ambulavi　in magnis;　neque　in

on wundorlicum ofor　me ah la hwæt sæig he gif ic ne ge- |
mirabilibus　super me.　Sed　quid sinon　humiliter |

(128 a.)

eadmodlice þwærlæhte ac ic upahof　mine sawle　swa swa is
sentiebam sed exaltavi　animam meam　　sicut 10

þæt *openodum cild puer [a.] ofor　his moder　þu forᵹẏldst
ablactatus　est　super　matrem suam ita　retribues

on　minre　sawle　[a.] wanon. [k.] gif healicere eadmod-
in animam meam;　Unde fratres　si　summe　humili-

nesse we wẏllað gepincðe [m.] hreppan　[o.] ad illam
talis　volumus　culmen　adtingere　et ad

[o.]　　[o.]　　[o.]　[p.] to þære þurh andweardes lifes
exaltationem illam celestem　ad quam　per　presentis vite

eadmodnesse [p.] bið astigen　　hrædlice becuman dædum
humilitatem　ascenditur　volumus velociter pervenire. actibus 15

---

2. c. vs. ẏ, sic in MS.; see note.　3. seccende, second c changed into c.
9. geeadmodlice, a letter between g and e? 　11. openodum, read awenode.
puer not in other texts, added by glossator, as the word to which ablactatus
refers.　13. ad illam in glossator's hand-writing.

---

3. qui, dot under u, as if it were meant to be expunged.　5. ergo, MS. ẏ.
11. ablactatus, MS. ablactatum.　retribues; of the other Latin texts (cf.
Schröer, W. V., p. 30, and see Schmidt, p. 17), S has retributio, T and U
have retribues, and G has bues erased. Our MS. had first retributio, then o
was erased, i lengthened into s, and t changed into e. With this newly-
fabricated retribues the gloss corresponds. 　15. ascenditur, some other
ending changed into itur.

urum   upastigendum   h dre   [b.] sco hlæðð. is up to aræranne
nostris   ascendentibus   scala   illa   erigenda   est

[c.] seo [c.] on swefne   [d.] þeatiwde [c.] [f.] þurhðage [g.] him
que   in sompnio   iacob   apparuit ;   per quam   ei

7 niðer astigende [h.] 7 upastigende   [f.] sutulodan
descendentes   et   ascendentes   angeli   monstrabantur ;

na bið ælles buton twýn se nýðerstigc se 7 upstige fram us
Non aliud sine   dubio   descensus   ille et ascensus   a   nobis

understandan   buton   mid   upahafennesse   nýðerastigan mid
5 *intellegitur   nisi   cum   exaltatione   descendere ;   et*

eadmodnesse   upastigan   [c.] seo sýlfe   [b.] uparærede
humilitate   ascendere ;   Scala   vero   ipsa

hlæddra   ure [d.] is [a.]   lif [d.]   on [e.]   worulde   [f.] seo bið
erecta   nostra   est   vita   in   seculo ;   Que

geeadmedre heortan [k.] [g.] uparærede to heofonum   [c.] sidan
humiliato   corde   a domino ; erigitur ad celum ;   Latera

[b.] sint þære [e.] dran [a.] we secgað urne [g.]   [f.] beon
enim   ejus   scale ;   dicimus   nostrum   esse

[g.] lichaman 7 sawle. [g.] on ðære sidan [a.] gesætt [d.] mistlice
10 *corpus   et animam ;   in   que   latera   diversos*

[d.] stapas eadmodnesse oððe [f.]   lare   gecigednýss [b.]
gradus   humilitatis   vel   discipline :   evocatio

[b.] seo godcund [c.] þa upastigændan   a an
divina   ascendendos   inseruit ;

[b.] se forma   [c.]   [d.] eadmodnesse [b.] stape is [a.] [e.] godes
PRIMUS   ITAQUE   HVMILITATIS   GRADUS   EST :   SITI-

ege him sýlfum [k.] aetforan [k.] eagan [i.] æfre [h.] secende
morem dei   sibi   ante   oculos   semper   ponens

[g.] foregýtelnýsse [f.] eallunga [e.] gif he flihð   he sig
15 *oblivionem   omnino   fugiat ;   et semper   sit*

gemýndig calraþinga þæt bebead god   [a.]   [d.] þa forhic-
memor   omnium   que precepit deus ; Qualiter   contemp-

genden [d.] gode [h.] on   helle   forsýnnum   [a.] hi on (128 b.)
nentes   deum ; | in   gehennam   pro peccatis   inci-

---

1. *hdre ; hlæðð*, probably both words are meant for *hlæddre*.   12. *a an*
over *inseruit*, see note.   14. *secende*, sic in MS.

---

2. *sompnio, p* corr. from *n*.   5. *cum* added in the margin ; *exaltatione*,
MS. *exaltationem*.   11. MS. *gradis*, marked in MS. to be changed into
gradus.   16. *contempneutes, p* below line.

befeollan [f.] 7 þæt ece lif þæt [k.] adrædendum god [k.] is
dunt; et vitam aeternam que timentibus deum pre-

gegearcod is [h]on his mode æfre [g.] [f.] 7 he wealce 7
parata est animo suo semper revolvat. Et

gehealdende hine fram synnum 7 leahtrum þæt is
custodiens se omni hora a peccatis et vitiis id est

geþohta tungan eagana handa fota oððe ageres
cogitationum lingue; oculorum manuum pedum, vel volun-

willan ah gewilnunga lichaman ofadon he ofeste wene
tatis proprie; sed et desideria carnis amputare festinet; Estimet 5

man of heofonum fram gode æfre beon behealdenre
se homo de celis a deo semper respici

on ælcere tida 7 his dæda on ælcere stowe fram gesyhðe
omni hora; et facta sua omni loco ab aspectu

godcundnysse 7 beon gesawen fram englum on ælcere
divinitatis videri; et ab angelis deo omni

tide 7 beon gekydde gesutulað us þæt witega on urum
hora renuntiari; Demonstrat nobis hoc propheta cum in

geþancum esse esse andweardne þonne he geswu-
cogitationibus nostris deum semper presentem ostendit 10

tulað asmaidan heortan 7 lendenu god
dicens; Scrutans corda et renes deus; et item

can geþohtas manna idel 7
Dominus novit cogitationes hominum quoniam vane sunt; Et

eft he sægð þu understode mine geþohtas forrane 7 þæt
item dicit Intellexisti cogitationes meas a longe; Et quia

geþanc mannes anded þe soðes þæt hohful sig
cogitatio hominis confitebitur tibi; Nam ut sollicitus sit circa

soðes oððe secge se nydwyrða
cogitationes suas perversas; dicat semper utilis 15

broðor on his heortan þonne ic beo *ungewemned toforan heom
frater in corde suo; Tunc ero inmaculatus coram eo;

gif ic gehealde me fram minre unrihtwisnesse willan
si observavero me ab iniquitate mea; Voluntatem vero

---

11. *asmaidan*, see note.   15. *soðes oððe secge*, see note.   16. *unge-*
wemned, read *ungewemmed*. *foran*, o crossed, as if corrected from e.

---

1. *aeternnam*. *a^e* MS., e added later.   3. *omni hora* added by glossator.
17. *observavero*, second o in MS. ō.   *mea*, MS. *me*.

agene   don   we forbeodað þonne sæigð gewrit   us
propriam   ita facere prohibemur   cum   dicit scriptura nobis

fram þinum willan 7 si ðu awend 7 eft 7 uton biddan god
Et a voluntatibus tuis   avertere ;   Et item roge | mus deum (129 a.)

on gebede 7 þæt gewýrðe his   willa   on   us   we beon
in oratione   ut   fiat   illius voluntas in nobis; Docemur

gelærede rihtlice urne   na don   willan   þonne we gewarniað
ergo merito nostram non facere voluntatem cum   cavemus

þæt   þæt   sæig þæt halige gewrit sýnt wegas þa beoð
5 *illud quod   dicit   sancta scriptura ;   Sunt   vie   que*

gesawene fram mannum rihtlice   þara enda   oð dýpan * helde
videntur   ab   ominibus recte   quarum finis usque ad profundum

besent   7   eft þonne we gewerniað þæt be þam
inferni demergit ; Et cum   item   cavemus   illud quod

gýmeleasum þæt ðc is gesæd   gewemmede sýnt 7 laðe
de neglegentibus   dictum   est ;   corrupti sunt et abo-

oððe andsæte 7 insint gewordene willum   on heora on
minabiles facti svnt   in   voluntatibus suis ;   In

gewilnungum soðlice lichaman swa   us   god semper we lýfað
10 *desideriis vero   carnis. ita nobis deum   credamus*

æfre beon andwýrde þonne sæið se witega ætforan þe is
semper esse presentem ; cum dicit propheta ; Ante te est

eal gewilnunc min   is to wearnienne   ýfel gewilnunc
omne desiderium meum ; Cavendum est ergo ideo malum desiderium ;

deað wið infereld gelustfullunc forðam þe is gesæd wanon
quia mors secus introitum delectationis   posita est ;   Unde

gewrit   * behýt secgende æfter þinum gewilnungum
scriptura precipit dicens ;   Post concupiscentias   tuas

ne farðu   gif besceawiað
15 *non eas ; Ergo si oculi domini speculantur bonos et malos*

          7 he beheal
et dominus de caelo semper respicit super filios hominum.

þæt he * osco gif he is to understandenne oððe secende god
ut videat si   est   intellegens   aut requirens deum ;

---

5. *sæig*, for *sæigð*.   6. *helde*, read *helle*.   7. *besent*, read *besenct*.
9. *insint*, see note.   10. *semper* added by glossator.   14. *behýt*, read
hebýt.   17. *he osco*, read *he seo*. See note.

---

1. *prohibemur*, MS. *prohibetur*, marked by glossator to be changed into
prohibemur.   4. *caremus*, MS. *canimus*.   6. *ominibus* (for *hominibus*),
MS. *omnibus*.   11. *est*, MS. *cos*.

7 gif fram englum * hetelicum dæghwamlice dæges 7 nihtes
et si ab angelis nobis deputatis cotidie die noctuque

drihtne urum scýppende ure weorc gif beoð gecýðce is to
domino factori nostro opera nostra enuntiantur: caven-

warnienne on ælcere tide swa swa sægð on * ða * scalmo
dum est ergo omni hora fratres. sicut dicit in psalmo

þæt us bugande to * ýfele 7 unnýtwýrðe 7 ge-
propheta ne nos declinantes in malum. et inutiles factos

(129 b.) wordene on ænigera tida þæt * ne * besceal 7 * aræriende us on
aliqua hora aspiciat deus et parcendo | nobis in 5

ðissere tide forðam þe is 7 he anbidað us gecýrran to
hoc tempore quia pius est; et expectat nos converti in

beteran us on toweardum þas þinc ðu dýdest
melius cotidie ne dicat nobis in futuro. Haec fecisti

7 ic suwude.
et tacui. II.

se oðer eadmodnesse stepe is gif ænig na
Secundus humilitatis gradus est: si propriam quis non

lufiende willan his gewilnunga ne gif gelustfulað gefýllan
amans voluntatem. desideria sua non delectetur implere 10

þas stefne drihtnes mid dædum ac he geefenlæce. secgendes.
sed vocem illam domini factis imitetur dicentis;

ic na com æfter
Non veni facere voluntatem meam sed ejus qui me misit. Item

lufe hæfð wite 7 neodþearfnes 7 akenð
dicit scriptura. Voluptas habet penam et necessitas paruit

cinehelm se ðridde stæpe is þæt under æni for
coronam. Tertius humilitatis gradus est: ut quis pro dei

godes lufan mid ealre gehýrsumnessa hine sýlfne þeowde ealdre
amore omni obedientia se subdat majori; 15

geefen læcende drihtnes be ðam þe he seið se apostolo wæs
immitans dominum de quo dicit apostolus;

he wæs geworden gehýrsum oð deað
Factus obediens usque ad mortem; IIII.

---

1. hetelicum, read betehtum. 3. ða, read ðam. sealmo, with Latin
ending, the scribe's eye being caught by the almo in psalmo under it.
4. ýfefle, read yfele. 5. ne besceal, read he be sceawie. aræriende, read
arieude. 14. under, see note. 16. þe, þ corr. from h ? apostolo, read
apostol.

2. factori, MS. facturi. cotidie. Not in any other text. 9. Secundus,
MS. secundum. propriam, MS. propria. 12. Item, sic in MS. 16. apostolus, MS. apostolis.

se feorða eadmodnessa stæpe is on ðære sylfra gehyrsumnessa
Quartus humilitatis gradus est; si in ipsa obœdientia

stiðum þingum. 7 wiðerweardum oððe eac swilce sumum
duris et *contrariis rebus; vel etiam quibuslibet*

on gebrohtum teonum mid stillum ingehyde   gif he
inrogatis injuriis; tacita conscientia patientiam am-

befehð   7 for þyldigende oððe aweig gewite
plectatur et *sustinens non lacescat vel discedat:*

secgendum gewrita seðe þurhwunað oð ænde   þæs
5 *Dicente scriptura : qui perseveraverit usque in finem ; hic*

hæle bið oft he seið dicit si ge strangod þin heorte 7 forþyldiga
salvus erit; Item   confortetur cor tuum ; et sustinet

drihten gesutuliende   swa swa
*dominum ; Et ostendens fidelem * pro * nos deus igne nos*

þu afandodes swa swa bið afandod scolfor þu ongelœddest
examinasti. sicut examinatur argentum. Induxisti

us on grin þu gesettest gedrefednessa on urum * hicce 7
nos in laqueum. posuisti tribulationes in dorso nostro; Et

þæt getiwe under ealdre | us scealan beon he fylige   (130 a.)
10 *ut ostendat sub priore* | *debere nos esse. subsequitur dicens;*

þu ongesettest men ofer urum heafdum ah ge bebed
Inposuisti homines super capita nostra. Sed et *preceptum*

drihtnes on * ðryrnyssum 7 on teonum þurh geþyld gefyl-
domini in adversis et *injuriis per patientiam adim-*

lende þa þe synd geslegene hleor *hiercian 7 oðer æthredendrum
plentes. qui percussi in maxillam. prebent et aliam : Auferenti

        7 forgifan 7 wrœfels genydde twamilan hi gan
tonicam. dimittunt et *pallium. Angarizati miliario. radunt*

---

6. *dicit*, in glossator's hand.   9. *hicce*, read *hricce.*   12. *ðryrnyssum,*
read *ðwyrnyssum.*   13. *hiercian,* read *hi iercian.*

---

3. *patientiam*, MS. *patientia.*   4. *lacescat*, MS. *lasescat.*   6. *confortetur*, MS. *confitetur.*   7. *pro nos*, a whole passage has been here
left out between *pro* and *nos* by the scribe, the Latin of which in S runs
as follows:—pro (Domino universa etiam contraria sustinere debere dicit ex
persona sufferentium: Propter te morte afficimur tota die, estimati sumus
ut oves occisionis, et securi de spe retributionis divine subsecuntur gaudentes
et dicentes. Sed in his omnibus superamus propter eum qui dilexit nos ;
et item alio loco scriptura Probasti) nos.   10. *nos*, MS. *non.*   14. *angarizati.* All other texts have *angariati.* But as our form occurs not only
here, but also twice in ‘Wright-Wülker's Anglo-Saxon and Old English
Vocabularies’ (353. 30; and 479. 17), I dare not change it, to which Wülker
apparently sees no objection ; cp. ib. J, p. 479, note 19.

þa leasa gebroðra
pergere unum et *duo* C*um* *paulo apostolo* *falsos* *fratres*
hi forðildian
    sustinent. et *persecutionem propter justitiam patiuntur* et
7 þa awýrgedan hig 7 hig blettian.
maledicentes. se benedicunt. V.

[b.]   [c.]   [b.] [a.] [d.] calle ýfele geþohtas [g.]
QUINTUS *humilitatis gradus est si omnes cogitationes malas*
[i.] [i.] [h.] cumende [k.] [k.] [m.] [l.] digellice
cordi suo advenientes vel mala a se absconse commissa 5
þurh eadmode andetnesse abbote gif ne bediℏ gað his tiht
per humilem confessionem abbati nm̄ celaverit suo hor-
[a.] [b.] be ðisum þince gewrit [d.] [e.] unwrigon drihtne
tatur nos de hac re scriptura dicens: revela domino
weig þine 7 liht on higne 7 eft he seið [a.] andetað
viam tuam et spera in eum et item dicit confitemini
drihtne [b.] forðam [c.] þe is [d.] god forðam þe is [g.] his
domino quoniam bonus, quoniam in seculum mise-
·mildheortnesse [f.] [f.]   [b.] gild mine [b.]
ricordia ejus Et item propheta delictum meum 10
cyð [c.] ne ðe [d.] ic [a.] dýde 7 rihtwisnýssa mine
cognitum tibi feci. et *injustitias meas non operui:*

Dixi: pronuntiabo adversum me injustitias meas domino. et *tu*
      arleasnessa minre heortan
30 b.) *remisisti im | pietatem cordis mei* VI.

          mid calre wacnisse æftergenc-
SEXTUS *humilitatis gradus est. si omni vilitate vel ex-*
nýsse. oððe endemestnesse hýlde gýf bið to eallum
tremitate contentus sit monachus et ad 15
þingum himsýlfan þa ðe beoð geðeodde swýlce ýfel wrýhta
omnia que sibi injunguntur velut operarium

---

6. *bediℏ gað, ℏ* corrected from other letter; then erasure. *gað,* lower down,
read *bedihligiað.* 11. Erasure before *cyð.*

---

1. The words *pergere unum* are not in the other texts. *twamilan* would
seem to be the gloss to *et duo.* 6, 7. *hortatur;* after this some letter only
faintly discernible. 14. *humilitatis,* MS. *nnmililatis.*

D

---

7 hedeme   unwurðne   to
malum   se   judicet   et   indignum   dicens   sibi   cum   propheta   Ad

nahte   ic eom agen gehwýrfæd 7 ic ne cuðe   swa swa nýten
nichilum   redactus sum   et   nescivi.   ut jumentum

ic eom
factus sum apud te. et ego semper tecum.   VII.

he eallum   7   læssan
SEPTIMUS HUMILITATIS GRADUS EST. SI OMNIBUS SE *inferiorem et*

wacran   na   þæt an   mid his tungan   gif hit   ahhe eac swýlce
5 *viliorem non   solum   sua lingua   pronuntiet   sed   etiam*

mid incundre   gelýfe   lufe   gceadmetende   hine sýlfne
intimo   cordis credat affectum   humilians   se et dicens

mid þam witegan ic eom   *wursan 7   na   man
cum propheta.   ego   autem   sum   vermis   et non homo.

manna   7 aworpones folces   sum upahafen   7 ic eom
obprobrium hominum et   abjectio   plebis Exaltatus autem et humi-

geeadmed   gescýnd   god   me   þæt þu geead-
liatus sum   et confusus. et itum.   bonum mihi   quod humi-

mettest þæt ic leornige   þine   beboda
10 *liasti me.   ut   discam   mandata tua.*   VIII.

gif nadeð naht se munuc buton
OCTAVUS HUMILITATIS GRADUS est. *si   nihil agat monachus nisi*

þæt þe se gemenlica   rego mýnstres oððe   ealdra tihtað
quod   communis monasterii   regula   vel   majorum cohor-

oððe lærað   býsna
tantur   exempla.   VIIII.

---

2. *gehwýrfied*, r corr. from another letter, probably *f*.   7. *wursan*, see
note.

---

5. *lingua*, MS. *linguet*.   13. After the word *exempla* there follows in our
MS. the following passage in Latin, which has been put in the note, as it is
unglossed, and as it is not contained in any of the other Latin texts used by
Schröer or Schmidt :—Sicut scriptum est. humiliatus sum usquequaque *domine*
vivifica me *secundum* verbum tuum.   Et *dominus* dixit : Discite ame quia
mitis sum *et* | humilis corde *et* invenietis requiem animabus *vestris* ; Et (131 a.
apostolus dixit petrus ; Humiliamini sub potenti manu dei.   ut vos exaltat in
tempore visitationis.   omnem vestram sollicitudinem proicientes in eum :
quoniam ipsi cura est de *vobis* Sobrii estote *et* vigilate : quia adversarius
vester diabolus tamquam leo rugiens circuit querens quem devoret ; Cui
resistite fortes infide, scientes eandem passionem ei.   que in mundo est *vestre*
fraternitati fieri ;

gif tungan to sprecanne gif
NONUS HUMILITATIS GRADUS EST. *si linguam ad loquendum pro-*
forbidde se munuc stilnesse habbende * oððe ax-
hibeat monachus et taciturnitatem habens usque ad interro-
unge 7 he ne spece swytelunge write þæt na on
gationem et non loquatur monstrante nobis scriptura quia in
mænifealdum spræce byð forflogen sinn 7 þæt na bið se
multiloquio non effugetur peccatum et quia vir
fealaspreocala wer gerihtlæhð
linguosus non dirigetur super terram X.   5

gif na bið eðhylde 7 * bræd.
DECIMUS HUMILITATIS GRADUS EST SI NON SIT FACILIS ac *promp-*
caf. on hlehtre forðam þe hit is awriten se dysega
tus in risu. quia scriptum est : stultus in risu
upahefð his stefne
exaltat vocem suam. XI.

þonne he sprece se munuc
UNDECIMUS HUMILITATIS GRADUS EST. SI. CUM LOQ*uitur monachus.*
liðelice 7 butan hlcahtre eadmodlice mid gedreoge oððe feawa
leniter et sine risu. humiliter cum gravitate vel pauca 10
word 7 gesceadwislice gif na sprycð 7 he na beo hlutclipol on
verba et rationabilia loquatur Et non sit clamosus in
stefne swa swa hit awriten is se wisa wordum gesutulað
(131 b.) *voce sicut scriptum est | sapiens verbis innotescit*
mid feawum
paucis XII.

gif na þæt an
DUODECIMUS GRADUS HUMILITATIS EST SI NON SOLUM *corpore sed* et
en heortan se munuc * eadmodnyssum geseondum æfre gif ne
corde monachus humilitatem videntibus se semper in- 15
gebicniað þæt is on weorce on gebedhuse on minstre on
dicet. id est : in opere. in oratorio. in monasterio. in

---

2. *oððe*, read *oð*. 5. *feala-*, first *a* above line. 6. *bræd*, *b* above line, read *hræd*. 11. *hlutclipol*. The MS. has *hut-*; the *l* is written over the *u*. 15. *eadmodnyssum* under the combined influences of (humilitate)*m* and *geseondum*.

---

3. *monstrante*, MS. *monastrante*. 8. *exaltat*, MS. *expectat*. 15. *semper* in glossator's hand. 16. *opere*, MS. *opore*.

---

orcerde on wege on æcere oððe swa hwar swa he bið fuerit
orto.   in via   in agro   vel   ubique

sittende gangende oððe standende ahyldum he sẏg æfre
sedens. ambulans vel   stans   inclinato   sit semper

heafde gefæstnodum on eorðan gesyhðum scẏldine hine on ælcere
capite defixis   in terram aspectibus.   reum   se   omni

tida be his synnum   wenende eallunga hine on ðam
hora de peccatis suis   exist'mans   jam   se tremendo

*gefullan dome beonge andwerded hewene secgende himsẏlfan on
5   *judicio dei representari   estimet. dicens   sibi   in*

heortan æfre þæt þæt he sæde publicanus ge godspellica
corde semper illud.   quod   publicanus   ille

manfulla gefæstnodum on eorðan gesyhðum sæde la ðu
evangelicus   fixis   in terram   oculis   dixit: Do-

drihten ic ne eom wurðe ic synfulla upahebban eagan mine to
mine non sum dignus ego peccator levare   oculos meos ad

heofonum   dicit mid þam witegan ic eom gebẏged 7
celum;   Et item cum   propheta: Incurvatus sum et

ic eom geeadmet   æghware oððe on ælcere stowe
10 *humiliatus sum usque   quaque: Ergo*

þingum eallum ðisum eadmodnẏsse   se munuc
his omnibus humilitatis   gradibus ascensis monachus

sona to ðære soðan lufan godes becẏmð to ðære fulfremed
mox ad   karitatem   dei perveniet   illam que perfecta

ut seo asend ege þurh þæt he ealle þinc   ær
foras mittit timorem: per quam   universa   que prius

buton forhte þe he geheold buton ænigum geswince
non sine formidine observabat.   absque ullo   labore

swilce gekẏndelice of gewunan anginne gehealde na
15 *velut naturaliter ex consuetudine incipiet custodire non jam*

mid ege helle ac mid cristes lufan 7 gewunan þa sẏlfan godu
timore gehenne. sed amore christi et consuetudine   ipsa   bona

7 gelustfullunge mihta   on his wẏrhtan
et delectatione virtutum. que dominus jam | in   operario (132 a.)

---

1. *fuerit* in glossator's hand. 5. *gefullan*, read *egefullan*. 6. *pub-licanus*, Latin repeated as gloss, whereas *manfulla* in l. 7 is the English gloss. *ge*, read *se*. 9. *dicit*, glossator's handwriting. 10. *stowe* or *stuwe*?

---

7. *flvis*, MS. *fixus*.

on middan earde fram lcahtrum 7 synnum mid þam haligan
suo   *mundo a vitiis* et   *peccatis*   *spiritu*   *sancto*
þa gemedemode geswutulian
   dignabit   *demonstrare.*

DE OFFICIIS DIVINIS IN NOCTIBUS. (CAP. VIII.)

Wintres [k.] on tide [i.] [i.] fram clỹpunge [m.] þæs nỹgcðan mon-
HÝEMIS TEMPORE   ID EST A   KALENDIS   *novem-*
ðes [m.] [n.] oð eastran [n.] æfter forasceawunga [o.]   [p.]   [b.] æt
bris   *usque inpasca.*   *juxta considerationem rationis.*   *oc-* 5
ðære ehtera tida [b.] [c.] is to arisan [a.] [a.] [d.] æt hwe lỹtle mare [e.]
tava   *hora noctis*   *surgendum est. ut*   *modice amplius*
[a.] þære [f.]   [f.]   [d.] þæt hi gerestan [n.]   [b.]   [i.]   hi
de media   *nocte*   *pausentur*   *etiam*   *digesti sur-*
arisan [g.] [a.] þæt to lafe [b.] is [a.] æfter uhtsange [c.]   [f.]
gant   *Quod vero restat*   *post*   *vigilias*   *a fratribus*
þa þa sealmsanges [i.] oððe rædinge [k.] sum ðinc beheofiað [g.]
   qui psalterii   *vel*   *lectionum*   *aliquid*   *indigent.*
smeagunge [e.] si geþeowod [d.] fram [e.] eastran   [f.] oðða
  meditationi   *inserviatur.*   *A*   *pasca autem usque ad* 10
forasædon. clỹpunga [f.] þæs nigcðan monþæs [f.] swa   [b.]
    supra dictas kalendas novembris   *sic*
si gemedemod [a.] [c.] tid uhtsanga [d.] seo atreogenlice [g.]
   temperetur   *hora vigiliarum*   *agenda. ut*
betwux þam læstan [n.] fæte [n.] [o.] [f.]   to neodbeheofe
   parvissimo   *intervallo quo*   *fratres ad necessaria*
gecỹndes onðam utgan [m.] gehealdenum sona merrigenlice
nature   *exeant*   *custodito.*   *mox matutini qui*
lofsang. þa sint [i.] onginnendum [l.] leohte [k.] todreogenne
    incipiente   *luce*   *agendi*   *sunt* 15
þæt æfter fỹlian
subsequantur.

QUANTI PSALMI DICENDI SUNT NOCTURNIS HORIS. (CAP. IX.)

[c.]   tide foresædon calra ærest mid ferse   fultum [g.]
Hiemis tempore premisso in primis   *versu*   *deus in adjutorium*

---

13. *fæte,* i. e. *fæce.*   14. *onðam?* indistinct.

---

4. *Hyemis,* MS. *hýems.*   5. *in,* MS. *an.*   6. *surgendum, d* corr. from *t,*
which is in the text, by writing a dot under it, and a *d* over it.   7. *de media,*
MS. *dimidia. pausentur,* MS. *pascuntur.*   13. *quo,* MS. *que.*   17. *Hiemis,*
MS. *hiems.*

mine [g.] begým oðer sidon þriwa is to [a.] singanne [a.]
meum *intende.* *in* *secundo* *ter* *dicendum est.*

[k.] mine [m.] weleras [m.] þu [l.] geopena [n.] 7 [o.]
domine *labia* *mea* *aperies* *et os*

min [o.] muð kýð [n.] þin lof [p.] þam isto under-
meum *adnuntiabit* *laudem* *tua*m *cui* *subjun-*

þeoddenne se ðridde sealm æfter [c.] þison [c.] [c.]
gendus est tertius psalmus et *gloria.   Post hanc psalmus*

se feower 7 hundnigon teoða sealm mid antemne
  5 *nonagesimus* | *quartus cum antiphona aut* (132 b.)

[b.] gewist [a.] is to singanne [a.] e*st* þam æfter fýlige godes
certe *decantandus.* *Inde sequatur am-*

leof sex * psealmas mid antiphonum þam
brosianus. Deinde sex psalmi cum antiphonis. Quibus

gesungenum [c.] gecwedenum [d.] [d.] [e.] [a.] gebletsige. [b.]
dictis ; *dicto versu benedicat abbas.*

[a.] [h.] [h.] [i.] 7 beon [a.] gerædde
Et sedentibus omnibus in scamnis legantur

stuntmælum [d.] [e.] ofor rædine scamol [f.] [g.]
10 *vicissim a fratribus in codice super analogium tres*

betwux [b.] þam [l.] [l.] [l.] æfter [n.]
lectiones inter quas. tria responsoria canantur. Post

þære [n.] þriddan [c.] rædinge [n.] se ðe singe he secce
tertiam vero lectionem qui cantat dicat gloriam.

[d.] [a.] þonne ongýnð se sangere singan sona [f.] ealle of
Quam dum incipit cantor dicere. mox omnes de

heora setlum hi arisan for wurðmýnte 7 arwurðnesse þære
sed'*libus suis surgant. ob honorem et reverentiam* sancte

halgan þrinnýsse [c.] [b.] [a.] beon geredde æt uhtsangum
15 *trinitatis. Codices autem legantur in vigiliis*

godcundlices ealderdomes geðære ealdan gecýðnýsse [f.] geþære
divine auctoritatis tam veteris testamenti quam

niwan [g.] ac eac swilce. forgesetnýssa heora þa fram þam
novi. *sed expositiones earum que a*

---

6. *est.* Latin in glossator's hand.   7. *psealmas,* read *sealmas.*
16. *cyðnýsse,* second *s* above the line.

---

4. *psalmus,* MS. *psalmis.*   12. *lectionem,* MS. *lectionum.*   14. *sedilibus,*
corr. in the MS. from *sedelibus* by writing a dot under the *e,* and the *i* over it.
15. *legantur,* MS. *leganter.*   17. *expositiones,* MS. *expositionis,* changed
into *expositiones.*

namcuðestan lareowum 7 rihtgelÿfendum   fæderum
nominatissimis   et   orthodoxis   catholicisque   patribus

wæron [k] gewordene [k.] æfter |a.] þisum [k.] ðrim [b.]
facte   sunt ;   Post   has   vero

rædingum [c.]   [c.| [d.] mid heora repsum [d.] fÿlian [a.]
tres   lectiones cum   responsoriis   suis sequuntur

oðre sex sealmas [e.] mid all*eluia*n [g.] to singanne [f.] æfter [b.]
reliqui sex psalmi   cum   alleluia   canendi ;   Post

þÿsum [b.] rædine [c.] þæs * ap*ostolos [d.] æfter fÿlige [a.]
hos   lectio   apostoli   sequatur   5

butan [f.] bec to receanne. to singanne [g.]   [h.] 7 halsung
ex corde recitanda et   versus et supplicatio

gebedu þæt [k.] is drihten gemildsa us [m.] 7 swa beonge endode
letanie.   id est   kyrieleison.   et sic   finiantur

nihtlice [n.] uhtsangas [n.]
*vigilie   nocturne ;   (C*AP*. X.)*

QUALITER ESTATIS TEMPORE AGATUR NOCTURNA LAUS.

[c.]   [b.] oðða [o.] clÿpunga þæs nigeþan monðæs [d.] es
A pascha autem   usque ad calendas   novembris 10

ælc [e.]   swa swa [a.] hit her bufan gesett sealmsangas [f.]
omnis   ut   supra   dictum   est   psalmodie

mÿcelnÿss [e.] [a.] sigehealden utasÿndredum [h.] þæt [k.] rædinga
(133 a.) *quantitas | teneatur   excepto   quod   lectiones*

[l.] on bec   for seeornesse [m.] nihta [n.] þæt nateshwonne [i.]
*in codice propter   brevitate*m *noctium   minime*

beonge [i.] [a.] ah si forðam sÿlfan ðrim   rædingum anre [b.]
legantur.   sed   pro   ipsis   tribus lectionibus   una

lectio [b.] of ðære ealdan gecÿðnysse gemÿndelice geræd. oððe
de   veteri testamento memoriter   dica- 15

sungen   scort [g.] [g.] * fers þam [f.] æfterfÿlige [a.] 7
tur   Quam   breve responsorium   subsequatur :   Et

---

5. *apostolos*, read *apostoles.*   10. *es*, cf. Introd., Ch. V, § 4.
11. *gesett*, read *gesegd.*   15. *lectio* added in glossator's hand.   16. *fers*,
read *reps.*

---

5. *apostoli*, corr. in the MS. from *apostolos* by putting *i* over *os.*
7. *finiantur*, MS. *firinantur.*   9. *estatis*, MS. *etatis.*   12. *quod, qu*
corr. from two other letters.   14. *una*, MS. *uno.*   15. *memoriter*, MS.
memoritur.   16. *responsorium*, MS. *responsorum.*

oðre [b.] ealle ða ealswa hit bufon is geseed beon [a.] gefÿllede
reliqua *omnia* *ut dictum est* *impleantur :*

[d.] [d.] [e.] þæt ne sig [e.] læs [g.] [g.] twelf sealma　　　[h.]
id *est* *ut* *numquam* *minus* *a duodecim* *psalmorum*

[g.] to micelnÿsse [f.] to nihtlicum uhtsangum gesungenne utaѕÿn
quantitate *ad* *vigilias nocturnas* *dicantur ex-*

dredum þam ðriddan [i.] 7 þan feower 7 hund nigoteðan
cepto *tertio* *et* *nonagesimo quarto*

sealme.
5 *psalmo ;*

Qualiter dominicis diebus vigiliae agantur.　　(Cap. XI.)

on ðam drihtenlicum dæge [c.] [b.] gemetlicor [a.] si arisan [a.]
Dominico　　　　die　　　　Temperius　　　surgatur

to nihtsangum [d.] on ðam uhtsangum si gehealden [a.]
ad　　vigilias ;　*In quibus*　*vigiliis*　　*teneatur*

gemet [b.]　　þæt [d.] is ge tɪÿmedum [f.] swa swa we bufan
mensura.　　*id*　*est*　*modulatis.*　　　*ut supra*

gedihton [f.]　[g.] sÿx sealmas [h.] 7 fers　[k.] sittendum
10 *disposuimus.*　*sex*　*psalmis.*　*et*　*versu.*　*residentibus*

[k.] eallum gedihte 7 [i.] be endebÿrdnÿsse on sceamolum [c.]
cunctis　*disposite* et　　*per ordinem*　*in*　*subselliis*

[i.] beon geræcde [m.]　on　bec　swa swa　we bufan [p.]
legantur　　*in*　*codice.*　*ut*　　*supra*

sædon [p.] feower [q.] rædinga [q.] mid repsum [r.]　þær [s.]
diximus.　*quattuor lectiones*　*cum*　*responsoriis suis. ubi*

þæt [t.] an [a.] on ðam feorðam repse [u.] gesungæn fram ðam
tantum　*in quarto*　*responsorio dicatur*　*a cantante*

singendum þane [f.] þonne [e.] onginð [e.] [b.] sona ealle [c.]
15 *Gloria ;*　*Quam*　*dum*　*incipit.*　*mox*　*omnes*

mid arwurðnessa [a.] arison [b.] æfter þisum rædingum [b.]
cum　*reverentia*　*surgant :*　*Post quas*　*lectiones*

fÿlian　[c.] be endebÿrdnesse [d.] oðre sÿx [e.] sealmas mid
sequantur　*exordine*　*alii*　*sex*　*psalmi cum*

---

3. First *to*, dittography in the wrong place.　　10. *fers*, *f* corrected
from *r*.

---

3. *quantitate*, MS. *quantitatem.*　　11. *disposite, dis-* corrected in the
MS. from *des-* by writing *i* over the *e.*　*subselliis*, MS. *subsellis.*

antiphonam [f.] swa swa [g.] þa æreran [g.] 7 mid ferse [h.]
antiphonis   sicut   anteriores   et   versu.

æfter [c.] þam [c.] [b.] eft [a.] beon geredde oðre [d.] feower [d.]
Post   quos   iterum   legantur   alie   quattuor

rædinga [d.] [e.] mid repsum be endebyrdnesse swa swa¯we her
lectiones.   cum responsoriis :   ordine quo

(133 b.)   bufon sædon. æfter [b.] þysum beon [a.] geþıy [c.] canticas be
supra ;   Post   quas | dicantur   tria   cantica. de

ðam [d.] witegendum þe [e.] ðe ge [e.] gesette [f.] þa *cantincas
prophetis.   que   instituerit   abbas. que   cantica 5

mid [h.]   [h.]   beon [g.] gesungenne gecwedenum [f.]
cum   alleluja   psallantur.   Dicto   etiam

[f.] verse [a.] 7 bletsiendum [g.] abbude [h.] þam beon [a.] ge-
versu   et   benedicente   abbate   legan-

rædde [b.]   [b.]   [b.] of ðæıe [c.] niwan gecyðnysse [c.]
tur.   alie quattuor lectiones de   novo testamento.

be endebyrdnesse. swa swa we bufon sædon [c.]   [e.]
ordine quo supra ;   Post   quartum autem

[e.]   onginne [a.]   [b.] lofsang   [d.]   [d.]
responsorium   incipiat   abbas   ymnum.   te deum laudamus; 10

[a.] þam gesungenum [a.]   ræde [b.]   [c.]   [d.]   of ðam god-
Quo   dicto ;   legat abbas lectionem de   evan-

spelle [f.] mid wurðmynte [f.] [g.] 7 mid ege   [h.]
gelio ;   cum   honore   et timore stantibus omnibus ;

þam geræddum andswarian ealle [c.]   [d.]   [a.] 7 þam æfter
Qua   perlecta   respondeant omnes   Amen.   Et   subse-

filige [a.] [b.] se abbod [d.]   [e.] [e.]   [e.] [f.] 7 for [f.] gifenre
quatur mox abbas   ymnum. Te decet laus. et data benedic-

bletsunge [g.] hi anginnan mergenlicelof þæt [a.] [b.] onænde [æ.]
tione.   incipiant   matutinos ;   Qui   ordo 15

uhtsanga [c.] [d.] ælceretide [d.]   [e.] swa sumeres [e.]   swa
vigiliarum   omni   tempore tam   aestatis   quam

3. The top of the two *b*'s partly erased.   4. After *b* con a piece of the MS.
is away.   5. *cantincas*, read *canticas.*   6. The gloss to *Alleluja* is
erased ; the *h* is probably a 'paving' letter.   7. *bletsiendum*, *u* corr.
from *ei.*   15. *þæt onænde*, as gloss to *qui ordo*, I do not know how to explain
the *þæt*, unless here the contraction *þ* stands for *þe* ; *onænde*, however, stands
for *on ændebyrdnesse.*

2. Erasure after *alie.*   3. *quo*, *o* corr. from *i*?   5. *instituerit*, MS.
instetuerit.   11. *de*, *e* above line ; *ad*, which was in the MS., has been corrected into *de* by underdotting the *a*, and adding the *e.*

wýntres gelice [g.] [h.] on ðam drihtenlicum dæge sigehealden [a.]
hiemis aequaliter   in   die dominico teneatur.

[i.] buton si [k.]   þæt næfre na   gewýrðe   lætlicor [l.] arisan
nisi forte.   quod absit tardius surgatur.

sum ðinc of rædingum [p.] is to scýrtanne [n.] oððe of repsum
aliquit   de lectionibus   breviandum est. aut responsoriis.

þæt [r.] sig þe ah hwæðere [s.] eallunga [t.] gewarnod [r.] þæt
Quod   tamen   omnino   caveatur   ne

hit ne [k.] belimpe [n.]   þæt [a.]   gif hit [a.] belimpð [a.]
5   *proveniat ;   Quodsi   contigerit.*

wýrðfullice þanon [b.] he gebete [b.] gode [d.] on cýrcean [e.]
digne   inde   satisfaciat   deo   in oratorio

[f.] þurh þæs gýmeleastum þe hit becýmð.
per cujus evenerit neglectum.

(Cap. XII.)

on mergenlicum
QUALITER MATUTINORUM SOLLEMPNITAS AGATUR. In MATUTINIS

[d.] lofsangum [c.] on sunnan [c.] dæge ealre æræst si gesungen se sýx
10   DOMINICO DIE   INPRIMIS   DICATUR   SEX-

7 sýxteogaða sealm se sýx 7 sýxtigoða scalm [e.] buton
agesimus sextus psalmus   sine

[f.] antempne forð rihte   [b.] þar æfter þam sigesungen
antiphona   in directum.   Post quem   dicatur

se fifteogaða sealm [e.]   [c.]   [b.] [b.]   [a.] se hun-
quinquagesimus   cum alleluja ;   Post quém dicatur cen-

teontigoða sealm. 7 se seofonteoða sealm 7 [d.] se twa 7 sýx-
tesimus septimus | decimus   et   sexagesimus (134 a.)

teogaða [d.] scalm [d.] þanon bletsunga [b.] 7 [c.] lofu [c.]
15   *secundus.   inde benedictiones   et   laudes.*

of unwrigednesse [f.] 7 an [d.] buton bec [e.] 7 reps [g.]
lectio de apocalipsi   una ex corde   et responsorium.

[h.] 7 godes lof [h.] 7 fers [i.] [k.] lofsanc [i.] of þam godspelle
et ambrosianus.   versus.   canticum   de evangelio.

gebedu 7 hit bið [n.] geendod [n.]
letania. et   completum est ;

---

14. The second word *sealm*, last stroke of *m* erased. *bletsunga*, *e* very
indistinct.

3. *de lectionibus*, MS. *dilectionibus.*   12. *antiphona*, MS. *antiphonam.*
15. *benedictiones*, the last *e* corr. from *i* in MS.

Qualiter privatis diebus matutini agantur.

(Cap. XIII.)

[c.]　[b.]　[c.] on sýndorlicum dagum æftersanga sýmbolnýs
Diebus autem　　　privatis　　　matutinorum　　　sol-

[d.]　　si gedon [a.] þæt [f.] is [g.] þæt sig　[h.]　　[h.]
lempnitas ita　　agatur.　id　　est　　ut sexagesimus sextus

[h.]　　[g.] sungen　[i.] buton antempne　[k.] teonde
psalmus　dicatur　　sine　antiphona.　　subtrahendo

æt hwega [l.] swa swa [m.] on ðam [m.] sunnan die dæge þæt [n.]
modice　　sicut　　　dominica.　　　ut　　5

ealle becuman [n.]　　[p.]　　toðan fiftugeðan sealme　se sige
omnes occurrant　ad psalmum　quinquagesimum.　qui cum

[r.]　　[q.] sungen æfter [b.]　þæm [b.]　[c.]　[c.]　[c.]
antiphona　dicatur;　Post　　quem　alii　duo　psalmi

beon gesungenne [a.]　æfter　　[d.] [d.]　[e.] on monan [f.] dæge
dicantur　secundum consuetudinem id est　secunda feria.

[f.] 7. se. y 7　þritteoga sealm 7 se fif þæs * tides dagæs [a.]
quintus.　et　trigessimus　quintus.　tertia　　feria

se twa 7 feowerteogaða sealm [b.]　7 se sýx 7 fifteogaða　[c.]
quadragesimus secundus.　et　quinquagesimus　sextus. 10

þæs [a.] wodnes dæges [a.]　seo þreo 7 sýxteogaða sealm [b.]
Quarta　feria.　　sexagesimus tertius

7 se feower 7 sýxteogaða sealm　se fifta　dæig　se seofon 7
et　sexagesimus quartus.　Quinta　feria　octogesimus

hundeahteoða　7 se nigoða 7 hund eahtoða sealm þæs frian dæges
septimus.　et　octogesimus nonus.　Sexta feria

se fif 7 sýxteogaða　　　7 sean 7 hund nigenteoða
septuagesimus　quintus.　et　nonagesimus primus.

sæternesdæge　　　7 hund teontigoða. 7 se twa 7 feower-
Sabbato　autem　　centesimus quadrage- 15

tigoða san.　　　7　cantic　　　se * deo todæled
simus　secundus.　et canticum deuteronomii　quod dividatur

---

5. die, Latin in glossator's hand.　9. y over first quintus; probably
originally = fifta, which must also be understood over the second quintus.
tides, read tiwes. 16. san, pro salm or sang? deo, read beo.

---

4. sine above the line.　7. antiphona, MS. atiphona.　12, 13. octogesi-
mum and octogesimus, MS. octuagesimus, -m.　14. primus is a correction
of the MS. from quintus, which was there first, and which is marked for
expunction by a line of dots over and under it; primus is then written
over it.

on twam glorian   soðes [a.]   [b.]   [b.]   an *cantinc
in   duas   Glorias ;   Nam   ceteris   diebus   canticum

anum anum [d.]   gehwýlcum   dæge [d.]   he   [c.]   *εw
     ununquodque die suo ex*   [*prophetis. sicut* (134 b.)

[f.] singað se romanisca laðung si gesungen [a.] æfter þisum
   psallit   aecclesia   romana   dicatur ;   Post   hec

filian [a.] lofu [c.]   capitul   gemimorlice
sequantur laudes :   Deinde   lectio   una   apostoli   memoriter

to secanne
5 *recitanda. responsorium. ambrosianus. versus. canticum de Evan-*
                   gewistlice [b.] is to donne [a.]
gelio. letania et completum est ;   Plane   agenda

meriendlice lofsang [c.] oððe [d.] on æfen [d.] sanc ne wite [e.]
   matutina.   vel   vespertina   non   transeat

æhwænne [f.] buton on ðære ýtemesta endebýrdnýsse [k.]
   aliquando.   nisi   in   ultimo ordine

[h.] bed þæt drihtenlicge [h.] eallum gehýrendum si gesun-
   oratio   dominica   omnibus audientibus   dica-

gen [g.] fram ealdre [h.] for [i.] aswicunga [k.] þornum [i.]
10 *tur   a priore   propter   scandalorum   spinas*

þam [l.] upasprungen [l.] gewuniæð [n.] gecýrde [r.] þurh ða sýlfan
   que   oriri   solent   ut   conversi   per   ipsius

gebedas behat [q.] on ðam [t.] sægað [e.]
orationis sponsionem   qua   dicunt. dimitte nobis sicut et nos

       þæt [u.] hi gefeormian [a.] fram þas [p.] geræ-
dimittimus   purgent se   ab   hujus-

dum [p.] leahtre [p.] [d.] oðrum [d.] tiṁam [b.] [d.] donlicum
   modi   vitio.   Coeteris vero   agendis :

[c.] se ýtemesta [c.] þæs gebedes [e.] sigesungen [a.] [f.] fram
15   *ultima   pars ejus   orationis   dicatur   ut   ab*

eallum [g.] þæt si [f.] geandswarod ah alýs us fram
   omnibus   respondeatur. sed   libera   nos   a

ýfele
malo.

---

1. *cantinc*, read *cantic.*   2. Erasure after *sw*, read *swa* ; even *sw* is barely visible.   8. *ýtemesta* ; it is possible that the *n* we expect here should be cut away ; first *e* is partly cut away.   14. *timam* in the MS. ; *m*, however, is underdotted, and a *d* written over it, and *a* seems to be changed into *u*, yielding for the whole, *tidum.*

---

4. *memoriter*, MS. *memoritur.*   5. The MS. reads *evangelico*, but the *c* is expunged.

QUALITER IN SANCTORUM NATALITIIS VIGILIE
AGANTUR. (CAP. XIV.)

[c.]   [d.]   [b.] [c.] on freolsungum [m.] oððe on eallum [e.]
IN SANCTORUM VERO   FESTIVITATIBUS   VEL   OMNIBUS

sȳmelnȳssum [e.] swa swa [f.] we sædon [f.] on ðam drihten-
sollempnitatibus.   sicut   diximus   dominico

licum [g.] is to donne [a.] [e.] [i.] sigedon [k.] utasȳndrodum
die   agendum.   ita agatur   excepto   5

þæt beon [i.] sealmas [m.] [n.] oððe antempnes [o.] rædinge [o.]
quod   psalmi   aut antiphone   vel lectiones

to þam [q.] sȳlfum [q.] dæge [p.] gebȳriende [l.] sungenne
ad ipsum   diem   pertinentes   dicantur.

gemed [c.] [b.] þæt foresæde sige healden
Modus   autem suprascriptus   teneatur

QUIBUS TEMPORIBUS ALLELUIA DICATUR. (CAP. XV.)

fram þam halgan [f.] eastran [f.] to [g.] pentecosten [g.]
A   SANCTO   PASCHA   USQUE PENTECOSTEN :   10

butan [e.] to forlætennesse si gesungen [a.] [b.] geon [c.]
SINE   INTERMISSIONE   dicatur   alleluia.   tam

a.) sealmsange [c.] ge [d.] on repsum [d.] [c.] [b.]
in psalmis | quam in responsoriis : A pentecosten autem

oð [d.] angin [d.] lænctenfæsten [d.] eallum [e.] nihtum [e.]
usque in caput quadragesime omnibus noctibus

mid sex [f.] æftrum sealm [g.] þæt an to uhtsangum sigesungen
cum sex posterioribus   tantum ad nocturnales dicatur :

ælcon [b.] sunnandæge [e.] [s.] butan lænctene [d.] canticas
Omni vero   dominico   die extra quadragesimam. cantica. 15

meriendlice lofsangas. prim undernsanc [g.] middæigsanc [i.]
matutini.   prima.   tertia.   sexta.

nonsangc mid [l.] beon sungenne [a.] æftersanc [c.] [b.]
nonaque cum Alleluia   dicantur ;   vespera   vero ;

næfre ne sigesungen sang mid alleluia butan fram eastran
numquam   dicantur cum Alleluia. nisi a pasca.

oððone fȳfteoða dæig
usque ad pentecosten.

---

3. [d.] Top part erased. · 11. æt in forlætennesse not clear; t may be d,
and æ probably corrected from a.   17. æfter sanc, probably a mistake for
æfen sanc.

---

10. Pascha, h above line. 15. die, later addition, which is in no other text.

QUALITER DIVINA OPERA PER DIEM AGANTUR. (CAP. XVI.)

swa swa se witega sæde seofonsiðon on   dæge   lof [a.]
UT   AIT   PROPHETA.   SEPTIES   IN   DIE   LAUDEM

ic sanc [b.] ðe þæt [a.] seofonfealde [a.] þæt halige [a.]
DIXI TIBI ;   Qui   septenarius   sacratus

getel [a.] fram us [b.] [a.] syge fylled gif meriendlice
numerus   a   nobis   sic impleatur.   si   matu-

lofsanges [i.] primsanges [k.] as [l.] as [m.] as efensang
5   tini.   primae   tertie   sexte   none   vespere

7 [o] nihtsanges [a.] on tide ures þeowdomes [g.] þenunga
   completoriique   tempore nostre servitutis   officia

we gelæston forðam [p.] be þisum [p.] tidum þe he sæde [p.]
persolvamus.   quia   de   his   oris   dixit :

[t.]   [a.] on dæge [s.] lof dixi sang þe [x.] [a.] soðes
septies   in   die laudem   tibi ;   Nam   de

benihtlicum [c.] [c.] uhtsangum se ilca [b.] se sylfe [b.] witega [b.]
nocturnis   vigiliis   idem   ipse   propheta

[a.] sæde [b.] to midderenihte [b.] [a.] ic aras to andedende [c.]
10 ait ;   media nocte   surgebam ad confitendum

þe [d.] [b.] on þisum [e.] tidum [e.] [a.] we gereccað lofu [c.]
tibi ; Ergo   his temporibus   referamus   laudes

urum [d.] sceppende [d.] [f.] ofor domes [f.] [g.] his riht-
creatori   nostro   super   judicia   justi-

wisnesse [g.] [h.] þæt is æfter sangum primsang undernsanc
tiae   sue.   id   est   matutino.   prima.   tertia.

middægsang nonsanc æfensanc nihtsang 7 on nihte 7 utan arisan
sexta.   nona.   vespera. completorio et nocte surgamus

to andedtenne him   .
15 ad confitendum ei.

---

2. Erasure after dæge?   4. bi = the glossator's correction of impleatur
into implebitur, which is in the other texts, is found over the a of impleatur.
5. as, three times, merely the termination of words, which are understood
to be known, showing that the Latin words are plural. efensang, or
æfensang.   8. dixi, omitted in Latin text, and supplied by glossator.
10. andedende, i. e. andettende ; the last d is corrected from n.   15. andedtenne, read andettenne.

---

4. impleatur, see supra, note to l. 4.   6. completoriique, MS. completorique.
9. ipse above line.   13. sue, MS. fue.

Quanti psalmi per easdem horas dicendi sunt. (Cap. XVII.)

nu soðes þe nihtlicum vigiliis uhtsangum oððe meriendlice
Jam   de nocturnis.   vel   matutinis

lofsangas æfter sanges endebýrdnesse [b.] [c.] sealmsanges [g.] [c.]
digessimus   ordinem   psalmodie.

nu [g.] þe æfterfýliendum tidum [h.] uton [f.] wearnian
(135 b.) nunc de sequentibus | horis videamus ;

on þære [c.] formantide *becna þreo sealmas [b.] sindorlipes [d.]
Prima   hora   dicantur   psalmi   tres   singillatim.   5

7 na under anum glorian lofsang þære ýlcan tide [g.] æfter [h.]
et non sub una gloria. ymnus ejusdem hore post

verse [h.] o [i.] mine [l.] fýlst [l.] beiým [k.] ærðam [m.]
versum. deus in adjutorium meum intende : Antequam

[n.] sealmas [m.]   æfter gefýllednesse þreora sealma [d.]
psalmi   incipiantur : Post expletionem trium psalmorum

[a.] si gereht [a.] kapitol [b.] [b.] an et 7 fers 7 drihten si mid us 7
recitetur lectio una   versus. et Kyrieleison et

hit bið geendod [g.] undernsanges. soðlice. middægisanges 7 non-
missa est : Tertie vero. sexte. et 10

sanges on ðære endebýrdnesse si gebremod [a.] gebed [b.] þæt is
none   eo ordine celebretur   oratio.   id est

[h.] fers lofsanges þæra ilcan [k.] tidana [k.] þreo sealmas capitol [m.]
versus. ymni earundem horarum terni psalmi. lectio.

7 vers [n.]   7 hit bið geendod gif [a.] mare [c.] gega-
et versus. ΚΥΡΙΕΛΕΙϹΟΝ. et missa est ; Si major con-

derunc [b.] bið [a.] mid antempnes soðlice læsse forðrihte beon
gregatio fuerit. cum antiphonis. si vero minor. in directum psal-

gesungene [c.] æfen [b.] [c.] tidsanc mid feower [d.] sealmas [d.]
lantur ; Vespertina autem sinaxis. quattuor psalmis 15

---

2. *vigiliis* supplied by glossator. It is only in S. (Schröer's Winteney Version). 3. The *es* over *psalmodie* stands much lower than *sealmsang*, making it look as if *es* were written first by one who only wished to indicate the ending. Then some one else put in *sealmsang*. All this appears to have been carefully copied by our scribe. 5. *becna*, probably read *beon a* (*sungenne*) or read *beeweden*? 7. *o* over *deus*, no 'paving' letter, but sign of vocative. 9. *et* after *an* by glossator. 10. *middægisanges*, *g* inserted by glossator himself, but probably in the wrong place, *middwigsanges* being the word which it was intended to produce. 14. *antempnes*, *s* corr. from *r* or *n*.

---

2. *Jam*, wrongly rubricated in the MS. *Nam*. 3. *psalmodie*, MS. *psalmodiet*. 12. *terni*, MS. *termi*; the first stroke of *m* perhaps erased. 14. *in directum*, MS. *in directu*. 15. *autem* here and passim indicated in MS. by hᶜ.

mid [e.] antempne [a.] si geendod æfter [b.] þisum [b.]
cum   antiphonis   terminetur: Post   quos

sealmum [b.] capitul [c.] is to reccanne [a.] is [a.] þanon [d.]
psalmos   lectio   recitanda   est.   inde

reps [e.] godes lof [f.] [g.] [h.] lofsang of ðam godspelle
responsorium. ambrosianus. versus   canticum de   evangelio.

gebedu [k.] [l.] 7 þæt drihtenlic gebed [l.] [m.] heo beon geen-
letania   et   oratio dominica. et   fiant.

dode [m.] [c.] nihtsanc soðlice þreora [c.] sealma [e.] * forð-
5 *misse ; Completorium   autem   trium   psalmorum   dic-*

rihtes [b.] si geendod [a.] þa sealmas [a.] [a.] forðrihtes [b.]
tione   terminetur ;   Qui   psalmi   directanei

butan antemne [c.] sint [a.] to singanne [a.] æfter [d.] þisum [d.]
sine antiphona   dicendi sunt.   Post   quos

lofsang [e.] þære ylcan tide [f.] capitol [g.] an [g.] 7 vers [h.]
ymnus   ejusdem   hore.   lectio   una.   versus.

   [i.] 7 bletsung [k.] 7 hi gebeon geendode
kirieleison.   benedictio   et   misse fiant ;

10   QUO ORDINE IPSI PSALMI DICENDI SUNT. (CAP. XVIII.) | (136 a.)

calra ærest [t.] æfre [b.] on dæghwamlicum [d.] tidum
  INPRIMIS   SEMPER DIURNIS HORIS

[a.] sigesungen   mine fultum   beiym [d.] eala þu
DICATUR VERSUS deus in adjutorium meum intende.   domine

drihten to gehelpanne me efest 7 gloria þanon lofsang
ad adjuvandum   me festina. et gloria: inde ymnus

anrehwylcre æghwilcre tide syððan on ðære forman tida
unius cuiusque hore.   deinde prima hora do-

on sunnan dæge die tosecgenne feower cwydas psalmi þæs
15 *minica   dicenda   quattuor capitula centissimi*

hundteontiga 7 cahtateoðan sealmas on oðrum soðlice tidum
      octavi decimi ;   Reliquis   vero   horis

þæt is undernsang   þry capitulas þæs foran
id est   tertia.   sexta. nona. terna capitula   supra

awritene sealmas   beon gesungenne
scripti psalmi centissimi octavi decimi.   dicantur ;

---

6. *forðrihtes*, evidently a mistake for a word that can be a gloss to *dictione* ;
for dihte? 15. *die* inserted by glossator. *psalmi* added by glossator, to
which the *sealmas* in l. 16 is the gloss.

---

11. *diurnis*, MS. *diurnus*.

æt primsange þæs monan dæges beon gesungenne
Ad primam autem secunde ferie dicantur

þreo sealmas þæt is se forma se oðer 7 se syxta 7 swa ion
tres psalmi. id est primus. secundus. et sextus. et ita per

ænlepige dæges æt primsange oððane drihtenlican dæg diem
singulos dies ad primam usque ad dominicam

beon gesconde be endebyrdnesse þry sealmas oððone nigon
dicantur per ordinem terni psalmi. usque ad

teoðan sealm swa gewislice þæt se nigoða sealm
nonum decimum psalmum. ita sane; ut nonus psalmus 5

7 se seofonteoða sealm beon todælede on twam glorian 7 swa
et septimus decimus dividantur in binas glorias. et sic

hit beo þæt si æt uhtsangum on sunnan dæge die æfre
fiat. ut ad vigilias dominico semper

fram þam twentigoðan sealme ongunnon to undernsange
a vigessimo. incipiatur. Ad tertiam vero;

þæs monan dæges *niwe genewidas þa þe
sextam et nonam secunde ferie. novem capitula que

to lafe synt of þan huntcontigoðan 7 eahtateoþan sealme
residua sunt de centessimo octavo decimo 10

þa sylfa þry sealmas geond þa ylcan tida beon gesun-
psalmo ipsa terna per easdem horas dican-

genne utasyndrodum [b.]
tur; Expenso ergo psalmo centessimo octavo decimo

on twam dagum þæt is asunnandæge 7 on monan dæg
duobus diebus. Id est dominico et secunda feria.

7 on tiwes dæg eallunga æt undernsange æt middægsange
tertia feria. jam ad tertiam sextam

oððe æt nonsange beon gesungenne þreo sealmas fram þam
136 b.) *vel nonam | psallantur terni psalmi a cen-* 15

hundteondtigoðan 7 nigonteoðan sealme *oððe þone hundteon-
tessimo nono decimo usque ad centesi-

teoðan 7 seofon 7 twentigoðan sealme *niwe 7 þa
mum rigessimum septimum. psalmi novem: Quique

---

2. *ion* for *iond*. 3. *diem* added by glossator. 4. *gesconde*, corrected in margine into *gesungenn*. 7. *die* added by glossator after *dominico*. 9. *niwe, novem* glossed, as if *novum*, cf. l. 17. 16. *oððe*, read *oð*. 17. *niwe*, cp. supra, note to l. 9.

---

1. *secunde*, MS. *sccundum*. 2. *tres*, MS. *te es*. 5. *decimum*, X^{mum} in MS., *mum* in glossator's handwriting?

E

sealmas   oððone drihtelican   dæig   iond þa ýlcan tida
psalmi semper   usque ad   dominicam per easdem horas
eftsonas gcedlchte lofsanga   eac eacswilce rædincga oððc   vers
itidem repetantur. ymnorum nihilo minus. lectionum vel versuum
gesetnýssa   anrædlice   eallum dagum gchealdcn 7 swa gewislice
dispositione uniformiter cunctis diebus   servata. et ita   scilicet
æftc   on ðam drihtelican dæge fram þam hundteontigoðan 7
semper   *dominica a centesimo octavo*
eahtateoðan sealme hit si agunnen æfensanc   dæghwamlice
5   *decimo incipiatur.   Vespera autem   cotidie*
mid feower * scalmorum mid drcamc si gesungen þa sealmas
quattuor psalmorum modulatione   canatur.   Qui psalmi
beon agunnenne fram þam hundteontigoðan 7 nigoðan sealme
incipiantur   a   centessimo nono.   usque ad

centessimum quadragesimum septimum. exceptis his qui in diversis

horis ex eis sequestrantur. id est a centessimo septimo decimo.

10 *usque centessimum vigesimum septimum* et *a centessimo triges-*
                                   ealle þa oðre
simo tertio. et centessimo quadragesimo secundo; Reliqui omnes
on   æfen sind to singanne 7 forðam læs þc cunnð þreo
in vespera   dicendi sunt. Et quia   minus veniunt tres
sealmas forði hig sýnd todælcnne þa þa gctclc on ðam
psalmi.   ideo dividendi sunt   qui in numero supra-
foresædan strengran beoð gemettc
scripto fortiores   inveniuntur.   id est centesimus trige-

15 *simus tertius et centesimus quadragesimus quartus. Centesimus*
                     forðam lýtcl þc he is
vero sextus decimus. quia parvus est cum centesimo
              si gcþeod gedihtcnrc   endebýrdnýsse
quinto decimo jungatur. | Digesto ergo   ordine (37 a.)
sealmsanga æfcnsanga   oðrc þæt is rædinga rcpsas
psalmorum vespertinorum reliqua. id est lectiones. responsoria.

---

6. *sealmorum,* read *scalma.*

---

2. *versuum,* MS. *rersum.*   13. *dividendi,* MS. *ridendi.*

* imnis versus [i.] oððe canticas swa swa we bufan scripsimus
ymni ;   *vel*   *cantica.*   *sicut*   *supra taxavi-*

awriten beon gefyllede   to nihtsange   þa ylcan sealmas
mus   impleantur ;   Ad completorium vero.   idem   psalmi

beon geedleehte   þæt is se feower 7 hundnigenteoða sealm
repetantur.   cotidie   id est   quartus.   nonagesimus.

                                            gedihtere [e.] [b.]
et *centesimus* et   *trigesimus tertius ;*   *Disposito ergo*

endebyrdnesse [c.] sealmsangas [e.] godcundlice [d.] calle [f.]
ordine   *psalmodie*   *divine.*   *reliqui* 5

ða oðre [f.] sealmas [f.] þa þa [g.] tolafe synt [g.] gelice [h.]
omnes   *psalmi*   *qui*   *supersunt*   *aequaliter*

beon *godælede [a.] ætforan nihta [m.] uhtsangum [l.] dælende [i.]
dividantur   *septem*   *noctium*   *vigiliis*   *parciendo*

gewistlice [k.] þa þa [n.] beotwux [p.] heom længran [o.]
scilicet   *qui*   *inter*   *eos*   *prolixiores*

synt [n.] *salmos [q.] 7 twelf [r.] iond [s.] æghwilce [s.] 7 beon ge-
sunt.   psalmi.   et   duodecim   per unamquamque   consti-

sette [q.] nihte þæt [b.] healicost [c.] myndigende [a.] þæt [d.]
tuantur noctem ;   Hoc   precipue   commonentes.   ut 10

gif [f.] wenunge [e.] [g.] þis todal [g.] sealma [b.] ænigum
si cui   forte   haec distributio   psalmorum   displi-

mislicað [f.] hegeendebyrde [d.] gif [l.] bett elles [k.] dem [i.]
cuerit   ordinet   si   melius   aliter · judicaverit.

þonne [m.] bid mid eallum [o.] ˙gemettum [o.] þæt [n.]
            dum omnibus   modis   id

be iymð [m.] þæt beon [p.] an ælcere [q.] wucan [q.] saltere [r.]
attendatur.   ut omni ebdomada   psalterium

of ansundan [s.] getele [s.] hunteontig [t.] 7 fiftig [t.]
ex integro numero   centum   quinquaginta 15

sealma [t.] gesungenne [r.] 7 [u.] on sunnandæge [y.] [y]
psalmorum   psallatur.   et   dominico   die

æfre [x.] fram [z.] aginne [x.] si geedleht to uhtsangum *et*
semper   a   capite   repetatur ad   vigilias.

---

1. *imnis.* Is the *s* of this Latin word perhaps a remnant of the plural
ending *-as* which may have originally stood over *ymni* ? See 54. 2. *versus*
supplied by glossator. *scripsimus* in glossator's hand, the gloss to which,
as well as to *taxavimus*, is *awriten* in l. 2. 7. *godælede*, read *gedælede*
or *todælede.* 9. *salmos*, scribe's eye caught by Latin ending. See note to
Latin, l. 9. 11. Erasure before *þis.* 13. *bid* or *bið* ? 15. *getele, te*
above line. 17. *et* added by glossator.

---

9. *psalmi*, MS. *psalmos.*

forðam [a.] swiðe [c.] cræftleasne * estfulnesses heora [d.] þeowdom
quia   nimis   iners   devotionis   sue   servitium

þe atiwað [a.] munecas [b.] þa þa [e.] læs [f.] sealmsanges [g.]
ostendunt   monachi   qui   minus   psalterio

[h.] mid lofsange [h.] mid gewunelicum [h.] iond [i.]
cum   canticis   consuetudinariis   per

þære [k.] uwucan emrene [i.] singað [l.] buton þonne [l.]
septimane   circulum   psallunt.   dum   quando

werædað [l.] ure halige [m.] fæderas [n.] [m.] on anum [q.]
5 *legamus   sanctos   patres   nostros uno*

dæge þæt [o.] hrædlice gefyllan [n.] þæt [r.] eala [r.] sleawe
die   hoc   strenue   implevisse.   quod   nos   tepidi.

gif ge | ucan [t.] on ansundre [t.] læstan [r.]
utinam | septimana   integra   persolvamus.

DE DISCIPLINA PSALLENDI. (CAP. XIX.)

æighwære [c.] we gelyfað [a.] godcundlice [d.] beon andweard-
UBIQUE   CREDIMUS   DIVINAM   ESSE PRE-

nysse [d.] [e.] eagan [f.] drihtnes [f.] on ælcere [g.] stowe [g.]
10 *SENtiam.   et   oculos   domini   in   omni   loco*

besceawian [e.] þagodan 7 þa yfelan [d.] swyðest [b.] þeah-
speculari   bonos   et   malos.   Maxime   tamen

hwæðere þæt [c.] butan ælcere [e.] twynung [e.] þa gelyfað [a.]
hoc   sine   aliqua   dubitatione   credamus.

þonne [f.] æt þam godcundlicum [g.] weorce [g.] we ætstandað
cum   ad opus divinum   assistimus.

forði [c.] æfre [b.] [d.] gemyndige we beon [a.] þæt sæde
Ideo   semper   memores   simus ;   quod ait propheta;

þeowiað   on æge 7 eft singað wislice [u.] 7 on
15 *Servite domino in timore ; Et iterum Psallite sapienter ; Et   in*

gesyhðc engla 7 ic singa [a.] þe [b.] [b.] utan foresceawian
conspectu angelorum   psallam   tibi. Ergo   consideremus

hu hit [c.] gedafenige [c.] [e.] on his gesihðe [c.] godcundnesse [f.]
qualiter   oporteat   in   conspectu.   divinitatis

---

1. *estfulnesses*, see note to Latin, l. 1.   4. *u* before *wucan* underdotted,
probably to be regarded as the wrong beginning of *ucan* instead of *wucan*.
11. [e.] not quite clear.

---

1. *devotionis*, MS. *devotioni*. An *s*, which is wanting here, is superfluous
in the gloss *estfulnesses*. May we suppose that an *s* written above the line was
wrongly transcribed as belonging to the gloss instead of to the lemma?
7. *septimana* in MS.   8. DE above line. PSALLENDI, I is cut away.

7 [g.] on ængla his [g.] beon [d.] 7 [h.] uton standan to
et   *angelorum*   *ejus*   *esse*   et *sic*   *stemus*   *ad*

singanne þæt [k.] ure [l.] mod [l.] geþwærlice [k.] ure [m.]
psallendum.   *ut*   *mens*   *nostra*   *concordet*   *voci*

stefne [m.]
nostre.

DE REVERENTIA ORATIONIS. (CAP. XX.)

gif   mid rican mannan   we wýllað sum þinc
SI   CUM   HOMINIBUS POTENTIBUS   VOLUMUS   *aliqua*   5

tihtan we na [a.] gedýrstlæcan [a.] buton mid eadmodnesse
suggerere.   *non*   *presumimus*   *nisi*   *cum*   *humilitate*

7 arwurðnessa 7 hu micele swiðor   gode ealra þingan
et *reverentia.*   *quantomagis*   *domino* *deo* *universorum.*

mid ealre ead   7 clænnesse mid estfulnesse is to halsi-
cum omni humilitate et puritatis   devotione   supplicandum

genne 7 na on mænifealdre spræce ac on clænnesse
est. Et non in   multiloquio   sed in puritate   *cordis*

7 on biyrdnesse   teara we ne beon gehýrede witon 7 forði
et *conjunctione lacrimarum. nos   exaudiri   sciamus. Et ideo* 10

scort sceal   7 clæna gebed buton wenunge of lufe
brevis debet esse et *pura oratio. nisi   forte   ex affectu*

eþunge godcundlicere gife hit beo gelend on gegaderunge
(138 a.) *inspirationis   divine gratie | protendatur; In   conventu*

eallunga * sescýrð gebed 7 gewordenre tacne fram
tamen omnino brevietur oratio; Et   facto   signo   a

þam caldran ealle ætgædere hi arisan.
priore.   omnes pariter surgant.

DE DECANIS MONASTERII. (CAP. XXI.)   15

gif mare bið   gegæderung beon gecorene of ðam sýlfan
SI MAJOR FUERIT CONGREGATIO ELIGANTUR   DE   IPSIS

gebroðran goddra gecýðnesse 7 haligre 7 * liredrohtnunge 7 beon
fratribus boni testimonii. et *sancte conversationis.* et *con-*

---

7. *swiðor*, *w* nearly effaced.   12. *gelend* for *gelengd*.   13. *sescýrð*, read
si gescyrð?   17. 7 *haligre* 7 *liredrohtnunge.* I think *lire* must be a
remnant of (*ha*)*ligre*, as gloss to *sancte*, and afterwards *haligre* has been
again put in.

---

6. *suggererc*, MS. *suggerc*.   8. *humilitatc*, an *c* over first *i*.

gesette hohfolnesse þa don ofor heora wican
stituantur decani ; qui sollicitudinem gerant super deca-

heora decanhades on eallum þingum *efter* godes bebodum godes
nias suas in omnibus secundum mandata dei

7 bebodu abbodes hcores *þu *decanis þyllice beon gecorene
et precepta. abbatis sui. Qui decani tales eligantur

on ðam he todælð orsorh se abbod swyrige hys byrðena 7 hi na beon
in quibus securus abba partiat honera sua. Et non eli-

gecorene endebyrdnesse ·ac æfter earnungum lifes 7
5 *gantur. per ordinem. sed secundum vite meritum* et

wisdomes 7 lare þæt ænig of ðam on sumere færunga
sapientiae doctrinam. Quod si quisque ex eis aliqua forte

to *bræd modignesse gif go bið met teallic geþreat ære
inflatus superbia repertus fuerit reprehensibilis. correptus semel.

7 eft 7 þriddan siðc gif he nele gebetan he si ut-
et *iterum. Atque tertio. si non emendare voluerit dei-*

adræfed on his styde se ðe is wyrðe
ciatur. et alter in loco cius qui dignus est

7 efterfilige beðam ut pravoste þæt ylce 7 we gesettað
10 *succedat ; Et de preposito eadem constituimus.*

QUOMODO DORMIUNT MONACHI. (CAP. XXII.)

ænlepige geond ænlepige bedd hi slapan beddreaf
SINGULI PER SINGULA LECTA DORMIANT; LECTI*sternia*

for gemede drohtnunge æfter gesetnesse. oððe dihtinge abbodes
pro modo conversationis secundum dispositionem abbatis

heora under hig gif hit mæg ealle on anre stowe hi slapan
sui accipiant. si potest fieri. omnes in uno loco dormiant ;

gif meniu ne geþafeð tynfealdum oððe twentifealdum
15 *Si autem multitudo non sinit deni aut viceni*

mid ealdrum þa ofer hig hohfulle beon hi gerestan candel
cum | senioribus qui super eos solliciti sint pausent ; Candela (138 b.)

æfre on ðam ylcan husc byrne oð merien gescridde
jugiter in eadem cella ardeat usque mane ; Vestiti

hi slapan 7 begyrde gyrdelsum oððe strængum 7 scax
dormiant. et cincti cingulis aut funibus et cultellos

---

3. *þu,* read *þa. decanis,* see note to 51. 1. 4. *swyrige,* see note.
7. *tobræd,* read *tobræd. gif ge bið met,* read *gif bið ge met.* 12. *ænlepige*
(twice) and in line 13. *forgemede;* in these three cases *e* seems to be corrected
from *i.*

heora æt sidan 7 hi nabban þonnc hi slapað   þurh
suos   ad latus   non habeant.   dum   dormiunt   ne forte per

swefn þelæs þe hi wyrðan oððe gewundode
somnium   .   vulnerentur   dormientes ; Et

    ah þæt hi beon   gewordenem tacne
ut   parati   sint monachi semper.   et   *facto signo*

buton ýldinge 7 a hi arisænde 7 hi efstæn heom betwýna fora-
absque mora   surgentes.   festinent   se   invicem pre-

hradian godes weorce mid calre swa ðeah * stæfnýsse 7 mid
venire ad opus dei. Cum omni   tamen   gravitate   et mo- 5

metfæstnýsse   þaginran gebroðra wýð hi sýlfe hi   nabban
destia.   Adolescentiores fratres   juxta se   non habeant

bed ah gemengede mid caldrum   arisende soðlice to godes
lecta. sed permixti cum senioribus ; Surgentes vero ad opus

weorce   gemedlice tihtan oððe laran   slac-
dei.   invicem se moderate   cohortent   propter somnolen-

fulran for beladunge
torum excusationes ;

DE EXCOMMUNICATIONE CULPARUM. (CAP. XXIII.)   :o

            to þunden
Si quis frater contumax aut inobediens. *aut superbus. aut*

cýrigende oððe on ænigan þingan wiðerweard [ý] wunigende
murmurans. vel   in   aliquo   contrarius   existens

þam haligon regole 7 bebodu heora ealdra forhicgend 7
sancte   regule. et preceptis seniorum suorum contemptor et

gif bið gemed   þes æfter bebode
repertus   fuerit. hic secundam   domini nostri preceptum

sý gemýlegod æne 7 oðersiðan dihlice fram his ealdrum
ammoneatur semel et secundo   secrete a   senioribus suis; 15

gif he hit na gebet he si geþread openlice toforan callum
Si non   emendaverit. objurgetur. publice coram omnibus ;

        gif he hit swa he bið geþread gýf he understent
Si vero   neque sic se correxerit.   si   intelligit

---

2. oððe, see note.   4. *a*, gloss to *semper* in l. 3 ?   5. *stæfnýsse*, read
stæpinýsse.   12. [*ý*.] not clear.

---

3. *sint* corrected in the MS. from *sunt* by underdotting the *u*, and writing an
i over it.   13. *et* not in other texts ; redundant.

hwýlc wite sig   amansumunge   he underhnigc elles
qualis pena sit. excommunicationi   subjaceat ; | Sin autem (139 a.)
wiðercoren he is lichamlicere   wrace 7 he sig underþeod
improbus est.   vindicte   corporali et   *subdatur ;*

QUALIS DEBEAT ESSE MODUS EXCOMMUNICATIONIS.
(CAP. XXIIII.)

æfter gemete   gyltas   amansumunge   oððe lare. stýre
5 SECUNDUM MODUM. CULPE. EXCOMMUNICATIONIS *vel discipline*
sceal beon aþenod gemet þæt gylta
debet   extendi   mensura ; Qui culparum modus in abbatis
hangige oððe stande on dome   þeahhwæðere   on
pendeat judicio ;   si quis   tamen   frater in
leohtum gyltum gif bið *gemedemod fram *heode dælnimunge
levioribus culpis   invenitur.   a   mense participatione
si gesýndrod * asýndrodest   fram meosan oððe fram gesceræ-
privetur ;   Privati   autem a   mense   consortio. ista
dene þis beo gescead on cýrican   sealm oððe antemp
10   *erit   ratio. ut in oratorio psalmum aut antiphonam*
þæt he na onginne na he na nuræðinge recce oððe fulre dæd-
non imponat   neque   lectionem recitet. usque ad satisfac-
bode gereordunge   æfter   gereordunge ana
tionem ; Refectionem autem cibi post fratrum refectionem solus
he under þæt swilce hic swacweðe   hegereordige to middæges
accipiat ut. si verbi gratia fratres reficiant sexta hora
se broðor to nonas   he on æfen oððæt he be mid
ille frater nona, si fratres nona. ille vespera. usque   dum
dædbote fulre þæslicere forgifennesse   gite
15 *satisfactione congrua   veniam   consequatur ;*

DE GRAVIORIBUS CULPIS. (CAP.) XXV.

se   broðer   hefolices gýltes mid dara   si
IS AUTEM FRATER QUI GRAVIORIS CULPE NOXA *teneatur. sus-*

---

2. *wiðercoren*, second e above the line; probably to be read *wiðercora*.
8. *gemedimod*, read *gemet*; see note. *heode*, read *brode*. 9. *asýndrodest*,
read *asýndrodes*. 11. *nu*, wrongly transcribed for *na*? *dædbode*, the third
d has been corrected either from or into t, probably the latter. 13. *he*
under, fill up *-fo. hic* for *ic*; the h has afterwards been underdotted.

---

2. *et*, cf. p. 55, l. 13 (note). 3. MODUS, MS. MODUM. EXCOMMUNICATIONIS,
MS. EXCOMMUNICATIONE. 5. EXCOMMUNICATIONIS, MS. EXCOMMUNICATIONES.
14. *vespora*, corr. into *vespera*.

framadon fram beode samod 7 fram cýrcean ænig him gebroðra
pendatur a mensa. simul et ab oratorio; Nullus ei fratrum
on ænigre na si geþeod gcferrædene ne on spræce ana
in ullo jungatur consortio neque in colloquio; Solus
   to weorce   to betæhtum þurhwunigende behreowsunge
sit ad . opus sibi injunctum.   persistens in poenitentie
on heofunge witende þonc egeslican   cwide   secgendes
luctu. sciens illam   terribilem apostoli sententiam dicentis.

betæhtne   þýllicne   manna þam sceoccan on feorwýrde
(139 b.) *tradi | tum hujusmodi hominem   satane in interitu*m 5
lichaman   þæt he halsie   on drihtnes dæge metes
carnis. ut spiritus   salvus sit in die domini; Cibi
   gereordung ana he underfo gemet oððe on tida on
autem refectionem solus percipiat. mensura vel hora. qua
ðære þe forsceawiað   him feccan ne he ne sige fram
previderit abba ei competere; Nec a
ænigum farendum bletsod   men na mete se þe bið him
quoquam   benedicatur transeunte. nec cibus qui ei
geseald   10
datur;

DE IS QUI SINE IUSSIONE ABBATIS JUNGUNTUR EXCOMMUNICATIS.

(CAP. XXVI.)

gif hwýlc broðer gedýrstlæcð butan hæse abbotes þam
Si QUIS FRATER PRESUMPSERIT sine jussione abbatis. fratri
amansumedan breðer mid ænigum gemete geþeondan gelice
excommunicato quolibet modo se jungere. similem
he gehleote amansumunge wrace
sortiatur excommunicationis vindictam.   15

QUALITER DEBEAT ABBA ESSE SOLLICITUS ET CIRCA
EXCOMMUNICATIONES. (CAP. XXVII.)

ealre hohfolnesse gýmene do   abutan þa agiltendan
OMNI SOLLICITUDINE CURAM GERAT ABBAS circa delinquentes
broðra forþam þe nis neode þam halum læce ah þam
fratres. quia non est opus sanis medicus. sed

---

2. *sprœcc, œ* or *a*?   5. *feorwyrdc, y* of peculiar form   8, 9. *na he sige
fram œnigum farendum bletsod men,* understand *na he si. f. œ. f. men
gebletsod.*   9. *farendum, u* indistinct.   14. *gepeondun,* i. e. *gepeodan.*

untruman oððe ẏfel habbendum 7 forþi he brucan he sceal
    male   habentibus ;   Et   ideo uti   debet

mid eallum gemete swa swa wis   læce onasændan swilce
  omni modo   ut   sapiens medicus. immittere quasi

dihle   frofra   þa ealdan   swẏlce
occultos ; Senpectas. id est seniores sapientes fratres. qui quasi

digelice þa gefrefran gesewene   broðor   7 hi tihta
 *secrete consolentur fratrem fluctuant*em. et provocent   eum

to fuleadmodnesse   dædbote   7 hi gefrefrian hine mid
5 *ad   humilitatis   satisfactionem.* et consolentur   eum   ne

   maran   unrotnessa þæt he ne si fornumen ac swa swa
habundantiori   tristitia   absorbeatur.   sed. sicut

sæde   si getrimed on him soð lufe 7 si gebeden
ait idem apostolus ; confirmetur in eo karitas ; et   *oretur*

* fram heom fram eallum gebroðrum   þearle swiðe   scel
pro   eo   ab   omnibus.   Magno | pere enim debet (140 a.)

mid hohfulnesse   don   se abbod 7 mid calre glæwnesse mid
sollicitudinem gerere abbas. et omni   sagacitate et

forwitolnesse 7 gelacnian   ænig of befæstum sceapum him
10 *industria curare.   ne aliquam de ovibus   sibi creditis*

sẏlfum þæt he na forlure   he   cunne   * untruwa
  perdat ;   Noverit enim se infirmarum curam

underfon   sawla   na ofor þa halan   wælreow oððe reðe
suscepisse animarum.   non super   sanas   tirannidem ;

7 heondræde   egesunge   þurh þone he sæigð
Et   metuat   prophete comminationem per quem   dicit

    þæt þæt ge   fæt   sawon   ge underfengon 7
deus ;   Quod   crassum videbatis   assumebatis ;   et

þæt wanhal wæs 7 gewiðsocan 7 he geafæn godes hẏrdas
15 *quod debile erat proicebatis ; Et   pastoris boni*

ærfæste læce bẏsene   forlætenum nẏgon 7 hundnigonti
pium imitetur exemplum qui .   relictis nonaginta

sceapum on dunum se ðe gode   þæt þe dwelede
novem in montibus abiit   unam ovem   que   erraverat

---

1. *uti* in glossator's hand.   4. *gesewene*, see note.   5. *fuleadmodnesse*
dædbote, for eadmodnesse ful(re)dædbote. 8. *fram*, read *fore*. 11. *untruwa*,
read *untrumra*.   15. *geafæn* belongs to *læce* in line 16.   16. Erasure after
hundnigonti ?   17. *gode* for *geode*.

---

3. *Senpectas*, MS. *senpecta*.   7. *oretur*, MS. *orietur*.   9. *gerere*, MS.
gegere.   MS. *sagacizate*.   17. Most of the other texts have *novem ovibus*,
which may have been in ours, as the gloss *sceapum* is there.

secan   untrumnesse swa midlum he besargode oððe mænde
querere ; Cujus infirmitate in tantum   compassus est.

hit on his halgum eaxlum   þæt he gemedemode
ut eam in   sacris humeris   suis   dignaretur

onasettan 7 ægen bringan *to* heorde
imponere. et sic reportare ad gregem.

DE IS QUI SEPIUS CORREPTI NON EMENDAVERINT.

(CAP. XXVIII.)

                                                    forgehwilcum gilte
SI QUIS FRATER FREQUENTER CORREPTUS PRO *qualibet   culpa.* 5
þeah þe he   amansumad   hit ne gebet   teartere
etiam   si excommunicatus non emendaverit acrior   ei

genealæce præiungan þæt is   swincla   wrace on him þæt
accedat   correptio   id est ut verberum vindicta in eum

forð stepð þæt gif he   he swang bið geþrend oððe
procedat ;   Quod   si nec   ita correxit   aut

wenunge þæt næfre ne gewyrðe on modinyssa oððe upahafan
forte   quod absit   in superbiam   elatus

bewerian oððe gif he wile his weorc þonne   swa swa
defendere voluerit   opera sua. tunc abba faciet   quod 10

wis   læce gif he gegearcað swoðunga smyrunga oððe
(140 b.) *sapiens medicus ; Si   exhibuit   fomenta. si unguenta ad-*

lara   læcedomas   gewrita   godcundra æt nextan
hortationum. si medicamina scripturarum divinarum si ad ultimum

berned   amansumunge oððe wita   girda
ustionem excommunicationis. vel plagas virgarum : etiam si

his * foran nahtswyrian glæwnesse he gearcie soðlice
viderit nihil   suam prevalere   industriam. adhibeat etiam

þæt mare is his gebed 7 ealra gebroðra   for him
quod majus est   suam   et omnium   fratrum pro eo 15

se ðe ealle þinc mæig þæt wyrce
orationem : ut dominus qui omnia potest. operetur salutem

embe þone untruman breðer   þæt gif he na forðam mid þisum
circa infirmum   fratrem ; Quod si   nec isto modo

---

3. *to* ; *t* corr. from *g.*   14. *foran nahtswyrian, naht,* gloss to *nihil* ;
see note.

---

2. *dignaretur,* MS. *dignretur.*   4. EMENDAVERINT, MS. EMENDAVERIT.
10. *defendere,* MS. *defende. volucrit,* MS. *volucre.*

gemete biÐ gehæled þonne eallunga se abbod bruce isene
sanatus fuerit.   *tunc   jam   abba   utatur   ferro*

ofkẏrfes eal swa sæde   afẏrsiaÐ þone ẏfelan fram
abscisionis   ut   ait   apostolus ; Auferte   malum   ex

eow 7   eft   swa ungelcafulla gif he aweig aweg gewite
vobis ; Et iterum.   Infidelis   si   discedit   discedat.

þæt na anadli sceap   ealle heorde   besmite
ne una ovis morbida. omnem gregem contaminet.

5 SI DEBEANT ITERUM RECEPI FRATRES EXEUNTES DE MONASTERIO.

(CAP. XXVIIII.)

          for agenum leahtrum qui seÐe utgæÐ oÐÐe biÐ uta-
FRATER QUI   PROPRIO VITIO EGREDITUR   AUT PROICI-

dræfæd   gecẏrran gif he wile behate   *œr*
 TUR   *de monasterio. si reverti   voluerit.   spondeat. prius*

      ealle bote   forÐam þe he utferde   on Ðære
omnem emendationem   vitii   pro quo egressus   est.   et   sic

ẏtemestan stæpe   hi si underfangen þæt of þam his
in ultimo   gradu   recipiatur.   ut   ex hoc ejus

10 eadmodnẏsse si gefandod þæt gif he oÐer siÐan utfærÐ oÐÐe
  humilitas comprobetur ;   Quod si   denuo exierit.   us-

þriddan siÐe he si underfangen soÐlice sẏÐÐan he wite ælcne
  que   tertio ita recipiatur.   Jam vero postea ; sciat omnem

him sẏlfum gecẏrrednẏsse færeld beon forwẏrned
  sibi   reversionis   aditum   denegari.

DE PUERIS MINORI AETATE QUOMODO CORRIPIANTUR. (CAP. XXX.)

ælc   * ẏÐ   andgit *agenge* met sceal habban
15 OMNIS AETAS VEL INTELLECTUS *proprias   debet habere mensuras:*

forþig swa oft cildra   oÐÐe ginran   ẏlde oÐÐe þa þe
Ideoque quoties pueri. vel adolescentiores aetate aut   qui

læs understandan swa magun humicel þæt wita is   amansu-
minus intellegere   possunt   quanta pena sit   excommuni-

munge þas þẏlice þonne hi agiltaÐ oÐÐe mid swiÐlicum
ca | tionis. hi   tales   dum delinquunt.   aut   jejuniis   (141 a.)

---

2. *kẏrfes*, *r* corrected from *f*.   7. *qui* repeated by glossator.   8. *œr*
indistinct, might be *ier*.   15. *ẏÐ*, read *ẏld.   agenge* nearly erased.   It
was probably the intention to erase *gemet* so as to put it over *mensuram.*

---

8. *spondeat*, MS. *sponde.*   11. *humilitas*, two letters erased between *a*
and *s.   denuo, o* above line.   14. PUERIS, MS. PUEROS. QUOMODO, q̆ in the
MS.   15. MS. *mensuram.*

fæstenum hi beon geswencte oððe mid * tearum swinglum hi
nimiis   affligantur   aut   acribus   verberibus co-
beon geþreade þæt hi beon gehealdenne
erceantur ;   ut sanentur.

DE CELLARARIO MONASTERII QUALIS DEBEAT ESSE. (CAP. XXXI.)

hordere   si gecoren of   gegæderunge   wis
CELLARIUS MONASTERII ELIGATUR DE CONGREGATIONE. *sapiens.*

on geripedum * wea   sifre   na   mycel   æte na upahafen
maturis   moribus. sobrius. non multum aedax: non elatus. 5

drefende   teonful.   sæne   na   cystig   ac
non turbulentus non injuriosus. non tardus. non prodigus sed

atodrædenne   se ealra gegaderunga si swa swa
timens   deum : Qui omni congregationi sit   sicut   pater ;

gimene hedo be eallon þingan butan   hæse   naht
curam gerat de   omnibus :   Sine jussione   abbatis nihil

he nado þa þinc þe beoð bebodene he gehealde   he na
faciat ;   Que   jubentur custodiat ;   fratres non

dræfa   gif hwilc broðor fram him færunga æni þing
contristet ; Si quis frater ab eo   forte   aliqua 10

ongesceadwislice   bitt   forsconde hine he ne gedrefe
inrationabiliter   postulat. non spernendo eum   contristet.

gesceadwislice   mid eadmodnesse ýfel biddendum ac he
sed rationabiliter   cum   humilitate   male   petenti   dene-

forwýrne   his lif   he gehealde gemýndig æfre þæs apostolican
get ; Animam suam custodiat : memor semper illius apostolici

bebodes forðam seðc wel   þenað   stepe godne him sylfum
precepti quia   qui bene ministraverit. gradum bonum   sibi

he begit   untruma   cildra   cumena   7 þearfena   mid
adquirit ; Infirmorum, infantium. ospitum.   pauperumque cum 15

ealre hohfulnesse   he do   buton twýn þæt he
omni sollicitudine curam gerat. sciens sine dubio. quia pro

foreallum þisum   sceall agýldan ealle
his omnibus   in die judicii rationem redditurus est; Omnia

---

1. *tearum,* read *teartum.*   2. *gehealdenne,* see note.   5. *wea,* read
pea, for *piawum.*   7. *atodrædenne* in the MS., but *o* looks like *d.*
This points to a gloss : *god drædenne,* which the lemma would make us
suspect.   13. *lif, f* corrected from *w,* and indistinct.

---

1. *acribus,* MS. *acris.*   3. MONASTERII, MS. MONASTERIO.   6. MS.
juriosus.   13. *apostolici,* MS. *apostoli.*   15. *ospitum,* MS. *inospitum.*

andluman 7 ealle æhte swýlce weouedes
vasa monasterii. cunctamque substantiam. ac si altaris

halige fatu he besceawige naht he ne getelle * gunlæslices ne
vasa sacrata conspiciat; Nihil ducat neglegendum. nec

gitsung he ne hogige na he na si cýstig oððe mýrrent
avaritie studeat. neque prodigus sit ; aut stirpator

æhte ac ealle þinc gemetlice 7
substan | tie monasterii : sed omnia mensurate faciat : et (141 b.)

efter hæse ætforan eallum
5 *secundum jussionem abbatis ; Humilitatem ante omnia*

* þinga he hæbbe þær þær þam neuýs scðe foregifen
habeat et cui substantia non est que tribuatur.

spræc andsweras 7 si gereht god seo gode
sermo responsionis ⦁porrigatur bonus. ut scriptum est ; Sermo

spræce ofor þa selestan sýlene ealle þinc þe þe him betæht
bonus : super datum optimum ; Omnia que ei injunxerit

þa sýlfan he hæbbe under his gimena fram þam him
abbas ipsa habeat sub cura sua ; A quibus eum

þe beoð beboden he ne gedýrstlæce forasetne * bitleofan
10 *proibuerit. non presumat; Fratribus constitutam annonam*

buton ænigre * or hiunge oððe ýldinga he sýlle þæt hinc beon
sine aliquo typo vel mora offerat ; ut non scan-

geaswicode sit godcundre spræce hwæt gegearnige se þe
delizentur memor divini eloquii. quid mereatur qui

geaswicað ænne of ðisum lýtlingum gif gaderung mare
scandalizaverit unum de pusillis. Si congregatio major

bið frofras him beon gesealde fram þam he sýlf gefultumiað
fuerit ; solacia ei dentur. a quibus adjutus et

mid efnum mode gefýlle þenunge him sýlfan betæhte
15 *ipse aequo animo impleat officium sibi commissum ; Horis*

ongedafenlicum tidum beon gesealde þa þinc þe sint to sillanne
competentibus dentur que danda sunt

7 beon gebedene þa þinc þe sin tobiddanne þæt nan ne sig.
et *petantur que petenda sunt. ut nemo*

todræfd ne ne sig geunrotsaded on drihtnes huse
perturbetur. neque contristetur in domo domini.

---

2. *gunlæslic s,* read *gimlæslices.* 6. *þinga,* read *þingum.* 10. *bitleofan,*
read *bigleofan.* 11. *or,* read *on.* 12. *sit,* Latin added by glossator.

---

4. *mensurate, u* corr. from *m* by erasure. 13. *scandalizaverit,* MS.
scandalizare.

De ferramentis vel rebus monasterii. (Cap. XXXII.)

æhta   oððe reafum oððe mid-
Substantia monasterii in ferramentis vel *vestilus seu quibus-*
sumum þingum foresceawige   · be life þara   7
licet rebus prevideat abba fratres de quorum vita et
þeawum orsorh he sig 7 heom ænlepige be ðam nitwyrðlice þe
moribus securus sit et eis singula ut   utila ju-
he demð betæce þa gehealdennelicun 7 þa gelohgenlican of
dicaverit consignet custodienda atque recolligenda; Ex 5
þam [b.] gewrit [a.] tohealde þæt [e.] æfter þonne him
(142 a.) *quibus | abbas brevem teneat   ut dum   sibi*
sylfan   betahtum þingum [e.] stundmælum fylian
in ipsa assignata fratres vicissim succedunt.
[e.] he wite hwæt he sylle 7 hwæt he underfo [b.] gyf hwylc
sciat quid dat. et   quid recipit. Si quis
fullice [c.] oððe gimleslice þinc mynstres hrepað si ge-
autem sordide aut negligenter res monasterii tractaverit cor-
þread gif hit [f.] na gebett steore regolicere he under-
ripiatur. si non emendaverit discipline regulari sub- 10
þeodde
jaceat;

Si quid debead monachus proprium habere.

(Cap. XXXIII.)

healicost þes leahter grundlungæ is of todonne is
Precipue hoc vitium radicitus amputandum est. de monas-
þæt ne gedyrstlæce æni þinc syllan oððe underfon buton
terio. ne quis presumat aliquid dare aut accipere sine 15
hæse þæs abbotes ne   nabban sinderlice   ne
jussione abbatis; Neque aliquid habere proprium; neque
nan þinc calles na boc   na weaxbredu ne græf
nullam omnino rem; neque codicem. neque tabulas. neque gravium
ah na þinc   witodlice forþam ne habban his agenne
sed nihil omnino; Quippe quibus nec corpora sua

---

5. *gehealdennelicun*, read *gehcaldenlican.*   14. Not clear whether *healicost* or *healicost*; *grundlungæ*, or *grundlunga*.

---

5. *recolligenda*, *lig* above line, in glossator's hand?

---

lichaman willan alýfed habban   agenum anwealde   ealle
nec voluntates.   licet   habere in propria voluntate; Omnia vero

neodbchæfnýssa   hihtan   ne ne si æni þinc
necessaria;   a patre sperare monasterii;   Nec quicquam

gelýfed habban þæt þæt   ne scalde oððe ne geþafað
liceat habere quod   abbas non dederit aut non permis-

he ealle þinc eallum beon genæne swa swa hit is awriten
erit; Omniaque omnibus sint communia;   ut scriptum est;

ne ne secge ænig his   æni þinc   oððe gedyrstlæce þæt
5 *nec quisquam suum aliquid dicat vel presumat; Quod*

gif bið þisum wýrstan leahtre   arasod   beon gelust-
si quisquam huic nequissimo vitio deprehensus fuerit   delec-

fullod sý he gemýnegod æne 7   eft   gif hit   na gebett
tari.   ammonitus semel. et iterum; Si non emendaverit;

þræiunge he underrhige
correptioni subjaceat;

SI OMNES AEQUALITER DEBENT NECESSARIA ACCIPERE. | (142 b.)

10   (CAP. XXXIIII.)

                    wæs todæled ænlepigum þam þe wæs
SICUT SCRIPTUM EST DIVIDEBATUR   SINGULIS   *pro ut*

gehwýlcum neod þe wæs þær we na secað   hada   þæt
cuique opus erat;   Ubi non dicimus ut personarum quod

forsig onfangennisse   untrumnýssa ah forasceawung þær
absit acceptio sit. sed infirmitatum consideratio; Ubi

hedo se ðc læs hofað he do   7 he na si gecadmod
qui minus indiget agad deo gratias et non contristetur;

mare   he si gcadmet for untrumnesse 7
15 *qui vero plus et non indiget.   humilietur pro infirmitate;* et

he na si upahafen for mildheortnessa   ealle liman 7 beon
non extollatur pro misericordia; et ita omnia membra erunt

on sibbe ætforan eallum þingum   murcnuncge ýfel for
in pace. Ante omnia ammonemus ne murmurationis malum. pro

---

1. *anwealde*, see note.   8. *underrhige*, first *r* corrected from *n*, second *r* corrected by erasure into *n*, the whole evidently meant for *underhnige*.   14. *na si*, *na* above the line; *n* before and *a* after the *s*.

---

7. MS. *emendarerint.*   8. *correptioni*, MS. *correptionem.*   14. *agad*, MS. *aga.*   15. *indiget*, corr. from *indigetus* by underdotting the *us.*

gehwýlcum　intingan　on　ænigum　gehwilcum　worde　intingan
qualicumque　　　　　　*causa*　*in*　*aliquo*　*qualicumque*

on ænigum gehwilcum worde　　　oððe to getacnunge þæt he
causa in aliquo qualicumque　verbo　vel　significatione　ap-

na ætiwe　þæt　gif bið arasod ænig　　　hefelicor steore
pareat : Quod　si　deprehensus　qui　fuerit :　districtiori

stýðlicor stire he　si underþeod
discipline　　subdatur.

DE SEPTIMANARIIS COQUINE.　(CAP. XXXV.)　　5

　　　heom betwýnan　þenian　þæt nan ne si belaðod fram
FRATRES SIBI INVICEM SERVIANT ET NULLUS EXCU*setur*　*a*

cicene þenunge [b.] oððe mettrumnesse oððe on intingan hefigran
coquine officio nisi aut egritudine　aut in　causa　gravis

　　　ænig buton he si gebisgod [b.]　for þanon
utilitatis quis　　occupatus fuerit.　　quia exinde major

mede 7 soðlufu þam þe bið beiýten　þam wacmodum
*merces. et caritas　　adquiritur.　　Inbecillibus　aute*m

*þe onforsceawunge helpas　　　　mid unrotnessa þæt
procurentur　solacia ; ut　non cum　tristitia　hoc 10

he nado ahhi habban ealle frofras　æfter　gemete gegæder-
faciant : sed habeant omnes solacia. secundum modum congre-

unge　oððe gesetnýssa stowe gif mare gegaderung bið
gationis aut positionem loci ; Si major congregatio fuerit.

hordere　si belaðod fram　　　　oððe gif hwýlce swa swa
cellararius excusetur　a　coquina　vel　si　qui　ut

we sædon mid marum nýtwýrdnýssum býð gebýsgode oðre him
diximus　majoribus　utilitatibus　occupantur :　ceteri

sýlfan undre soðre lufe heom betwýnan *þeniant se ðe is ut to-
143 a.)	*sibi | sub　karitate　invicem　serviant ;　Egres-* 15

foranne　on　ðære ucan　on sæternes dæg clænsunga　do
surus de　septimana ;　sabbato　munditias faciat ;

---

1. *worde, intingan,* both in very black ink.　10. *onforsceawunge, unge*
has been corrected into *ode,* by underdotting *unge,* and writing *ode* over it,
in the same hand, read *beon forsceawode.*　15. *þeniant, t* owing to the
scribe's eye being caught by the ending of *serviant.*

---

1. *causa in aliquo qualicumque,* with its gloss, is repeated in the MS.
5. MS. SEPTIMANARIS.

[b.] wæterclað mid [c.] þam þe heom sylfan [u.]   handa
Linthea   cum   quibus   sibi   fratres manus.

oððe fet *clipiað [a.] he þwca [c.] fett soðlice ge se   se ðe
aut pedes tergunt.   lavet ;   Pedes   vero   tum   ipse   qui

utgæð   ge se   se þe is in tofarenne [e.]   eallum
egreditur   quam   ille   qui intraturus   est ; omnibus

hi þwean fata þenunge his clæna 7 hale [eb.] hordere he
lavent ; Vasa ministerii sui munda et sana cellarario re-

5 betæce   [a.] betæce se hordere   eft   into farenne dum he
consignet ;   Qui cellararius   iterum   intranti   con-

betæce þæt he wite hwæt he sylð oððe hwæt he underfo [c.] þa
signet.   ut   sciat   quid   dat aut   quid   recipit ; sep-

wucan þegnas [b.]   ær   anre [d.] tide gereordunge *mman
timanarii autem   ante   unam horam refectionis.   accipiant

[d.] forgesetne bilcofan [d.] ænlepige [c.] drencas [e.]   [f.]
super statutam annonam   singulos   biberes   et panem ;

on tide gereordunge buton   ge 7 hefigum geswince
ut hora refectionis sine murmuratione   et   gravi   labore

[g.] þæt hi þenian heora gebroðrum on simbel swa þeah
10   *serviant   fratribus suis ; In diebus   tamen*

dagum   *oððe   mæssan hi þolian. abidan [b.] þa in-
solemnibus ;   usque ad missas   sustineant ;   In-

farendan   [c.] 7 þa utfarendan [b.] ucuþena on gebedhuse
trantes autem   et   exeuntes   ebdomodarii in   oratorio

þærihtes merigenlicum geendedum on sunnandæge betyridum
mox   matutinis   finitis   dominica   provolutis

cneowum ætforan þam weofode   [f.]   [a.] biddan for hi beon
genibus   coram   altare   ab omnibus postulent   pro se

gebedene þa utgangendum   on þære ucan secgan þis
15 *orari ;   Egredientes   autem de septimana : dicant hunc*

fers   gebletsod þu eart eala þu drihten god þu fultumodest
versum ; Benedictus   es   domine deus qui   adjuvasti

7 þu gefrefredest me þam [c.] gecwedenum þriddan siðan.
me ; et consolatus es me ;   Quod dicto tertio.

---

2. *clipiað,* read *wipiað* ?   4. *þwean,* there is possibly an *i* between *w* and *e,* although this is probably part of the *g* of *egreditur* just above it. 5. *ce* of second *betæce* indistinct. *dum,* Latin in glossator's hand.   7. *mman,* read *niman.*   11. *oððe,* read *oð.*

3. *quam,* MS. *quo.*   4. *lavent,* MS. *avet.*   8. *statutam,* MS. *sta-turam.*

hi [a.] underfon [b.] bletsunge utgangende æfter fylian
accipiant benedictionem egredientes; Subsequantur autem

þa ingangende 7 hi secgan god mine fultum be·ym
ingredientes et dicant; Deus in adjutorium meum intende

eala þu drihten to gehelpanne efesð þæt sylf þriddan siðe
(143 b.) *domine ad adjuvandum me festina; | Et hoc idem tertio*

7 si geedleht fram eallum afangenre bletsunge 7 he
repetatur ab omnibus et accepta benedictione ingredi-
ingan :
antur;   5

DE INFIRMIS FRATRIBUS. (CAP. XXXVI.)

[c.] untruma[b.] gimen[d.] ætfcran callon þingan. 7 ofer ealle þinc
INFIRMORUM CURA ANTE OMNIA ET SUPER OMNIA

is to gearcienna soðlice swa þæt sigeþenod
adhibenda est. ut sicut revera christo ita ei serviatur.

forþam þe hesylf sæde untruman ic wæs 7 gegeneosodan me
Quia ipse dixit; infirmus fui; et visitastis me;

þæt þæt gedydon~ anum me hit gedydon
Et quod fecistis uni de is minimis meis mihi fecistis; 10

ah þa sylfan untruman sccawien on wurðmente godes heom
Sed et ipsi infirmi considerent in honorem dei

sylfum beon geþenod 7 mid heora oferflowednesse 7 hine ge-
sibi serviri; et non superfluitate sua contris-

drefan. heora gebroðra þeowiende heom sylfan þa swa þeah
tent fratres suos; servientes sibi; Qui tamen

geþyldelice sind to cepanne forþam swylcum genihtsumere
patienter portandi sunt: quia de talibus copiosior

med [d.] he bið beiyten [b.] seo mæsta gimen *sit
merces adquiritur; Ergo cura maxima sit 15

þam abbode ænigre gimcleaste þæt hi na þolian þa untru-
abbati; ne aliquam neglegentiam patiantur; Quibus

man gebroðra sig hus. cyte ofer hi betæht 7 þen
fratribus infirmis sit cella super se deputata; et servitor

---

11. *untruman*, first stroke of second *u* probably corr. from *e*.   15. *sit, t* copied from Latin, read *sig*.

---

4. *repetatur*, MS. *reperetur*. *benedictione*, MS. *benedictio*.   7. INFIRMORUM. I is forgotten by rubricator. *super*, MS. *supe*. 9. *visitastis*, MS. *visitatis*. 11. Erasure before *ipsi*. 14. *quia, i* above line. 17. *infirmis*, corr. from *infirmus* by erasure. *sit*, corr. from *scit*.

adrædende   7 lufiænde ac he fulfremed   baða bricc
timens   deum. et diligens ac   sollicitus.   Balnearum usus ;

þa untruman swa oft swa hit fremcð sigeboden þam halum 7
infirmis   quoties expedit offeratur ;   Sanis autem et

swýðest 7 geonclicum lætlicor si geunnen   [a.]   flæsca
maxime   juvenilus   tardius   concedatur ; Sed et carnium

*bæt þam untruman eallunga   þam wanhalum forhæle   ac si
esus   infirmis   omnino debilibusque pro reparatione con-*

geseald *þæt onne hi beoð *gebeorode fram flæsclicum midgewune-
5 cedatur : Ac ubi mel'orati fuerint ;   a   carnibus more solido*

lic þeaw ealle 7 hi forhabban [c.] þa mæsta [b.] gimene habbe
omnes abstineant ;   Curam autem maximam habeat

se abbod fram þam horderum oððe fram þenum þæt ne beo for-
abbas   ne a cellarariis   aut a servitoribus neglegantur

gimeleaste þam untruman forþam to him þehitlocað swa swa
infirmi | quia ad ipsum respicit.   quic- (144 a.)

hwæt fram leornincnihtum swa bið agýld.
quid   a   discipulis   delinquitur.

10   DE SENIBUS VEL INFANTIBUS. (CAP. XXXVII.)

þeah þesig þa sýlfe mænnisnesse gecind [c.]   [e.]
LICET   IPSA   HUMANA   NATURA   TRAHATUR

[f.] to mildheortnesse on þisum ýldum ealdra   7
AD MISEricordiam ;   in   is aetatibus   senum   videlicet et

cildra þeahhwæðere [c.]   regules ealldordomlicnýss heom
infantum ;   tamen   et regule   auctoritas eis

besceawige si foresceawod æfre wacmodnýss nateshwon
prospiciad ; Consideretur semper inbecillitas. et nullatenus

heom stiðnis regoles 7 na si gehealdan on fotum ac sig
15 *eis districtio regule   teneatur   in alimentis ; sed sit*

on heom arfæst foresceawung 7 hi forahrædian minsterlice
in   eis   pia   consideratio : et   preveniant horas

tide.
canonicas.

---

4. *bæt*, probably *b* is a 'paving' letter.   5. MS. *þonne* = *þæt* onne ; read
þonne. gebeorode, read *gebetrode*.   11. *mænnisnesse*, cf. Introd., Ch. V,
§ 67.   15. *fotum*, cf. ib., § 54.

3. *juvenilus*, MS. *invenilus*.   4. *infirmis*, corr. from —*us*.   12. *actatibus*,
MS. *eatatibus*.   15. *teneatur*, MS. *teneat*.   17. MS. *canonicis*.

De ebdomedario lectore. (Cap. XXXVIII.)

meosan　etenda　*gebroðrum　rædinc　wana　beon　na　scell　ne
MENSIS　FRATRUM　EDENTIUM　LECT:O　DEESSE　NON debet; ne

he　on　færlicum　gelimpe　se　ðe　gelæcð　bec　rædan
fortuitu　casu　　qui　arripuerit　codicem　legere

negedyrstlæce þæra seðe rædan sceall ealra þæra wucan on þam
audeat　ibi.　sed　lecturus tota ebdomada dominico

drihtenlicandæge ah inga　se　bidde　ingangende　æfter　mæssan
die ingrediatur;　　Qui　ingrediens;　post　missas 5

7　gemænsumunge oððe　huselgange　fram　'eallum　for　hi
et　communionem　petat　　ab　omnibus　pro　se

beon gebeden þæt awende fra him　g　　　modignisse　7
orari;　ut　avertat　ab ipso deus spiritum　elationis;　Et

sigesæd þis　færs　on　cyrican　þriddan　siðe　fram　eallum
dicatur　hic　versus　in　oratorio　tertio　　ab　omnibus.

him　sylf　swa　þeah　frum　anginne　　　　mine　lippan
ipso　tamen　incipiente.　　　Domine　labia　mea

þu geopena 7　min muð　7　kyð　lof　þin　[a.]　[b.]
aperies:　et　os meum　adnuntiabit　laudem　tuam　Et　sic 10

afangenre　bletsunge　7　he　inga　to　rædenne healic *smegen
accepta　benedictione. ingrediatur ad legendum;　Summumque

7　beo　[b.]　[c.]　æt　meosan　þæt　na　æniges　*drenc
fiat　silentium　ad　mensam　ut　nullius　musitatio

oððe　stefn　[h.]　buton　þæs　anes　ræderes　þær　si gehired. |
(144 b.)　*vel　vox:　　nisi　solius　legentis　　ibi audiatur* |

[f.]　þa þinc [b.]　neodbeheofe sind　etendum　7　drincendum
Que　vero　necessaria　sunt comedentibus et　bibentibus;

heom sylf stundmælum þenian　[c.]　ænig þæt ne behofige
sic sibi　vicissim　ministrent fratres ut nullus　indigeat 15

biddan ænig þinc gif hwile　neod beoð mid bycnunge
petere　aliquid.　Si quid　tamen opus fuerit　sonitu

sumes tacnes　swiðor sigebeden þonne mid stefne na he ne
cujuscumque signi otius petatur　quam voce: Nec pre-

---

2. *gebroðrum*, through influence of Latin ending for *gebroðra*. 7. *g =
god*? 9. *frum anginne*, see note. first *n* of *anginne* above the line.
11. *smegen*, read *swigen*. 12. *drenc*, see note. 13. *stefn, e* corr. from some
other letter. 16. *bycnunge, g* corr. from some other letter, *c*?

---

3. *casu*, MS. *causu*. 4. *lecturus*, MS. *lecturis*. 8. *versus*, MS. *vers.*
oratorio, MS. *oratorii*. 12. *musitatio*, corr. in MS. from *musitatione* by
the underdotting of *ne*. 13. *legentis*, MS. *legentes*, the *e* of *es* being
changed in the MS. from *i*.

gedȳrstlǽce þara ǽnig be þǽre sylfan　　　oðõe elles hwanonc
sumat　　ibi　aliquis de　　ipsa　　lectione aut　　aliunde
ǽnig þing smǽigan þǽt ne si geseald intingan buton wenunge
quicquam requirere :　　ne　　detur　occasio ; nisi　forte
se ealdor fore larc oðõe fram trimminge wylle　ǽnig þing
prior　pro　　　aedificatione　　voluerit　aliquid
scortlice secgan broðor　　　　seo wuca þeh nime　snǽdinge
breviter dicere ; Frater autem ebdomedarius accipiat mixtum
ǽr þan þe he aginne rǽdan forþam halgum gesumunge　[f.]
5 *priusquam incipiat legere. propter　　communionem sanctam :*
7 þǽt na sig　　healic　　him fǽsten forþyldian sȳðõan
et　ne　　forte grave sit ei jejunium sustinere ; Postea
　　　　　　　　cicenen. mid þam wucuþenum 7　þenum
autem　cum　coquine　ebdomedariis ;　　et　servitoribus.
hi gereordiað　[c.]　　　　na be endebyrdnesse rǽdan oðõe
reficiat ; Fratres autem　non per ordinem leyant　aut
singan ac þa getrimman þa gehyrandan
cantent sed　qui edificent　audientes ;

10　　　DE MENSURA CIBORUM.　(CAP. XXXVIIII.)

genihtsumian we gelȳfað to dægþerlicere reordunge [c.] gemid
SUFFICERE　CREDIMUS AD REFECTIONEM COTIDIAn*am :　tam*
dǽges　ge　nones eallum monðum twa gesodene syflian
*sexte　quam　none omnibus mensib*us　cocta　duo
sanda [g.]　for　mistlicora untrumnessa wenunge
pulmentaria. propter diversorum infirmitates. ut forte　qui
of anum seðe mǽg etan of oðrum þǽt he si gereord þonne
ex uno non potuerit edere ex alio　reficiatur ;　Ergo
twa sanda [i.]　　　　[h.]　　　[n.]　genihtsumiað 7 gif
15 *duo pulmentaria cocta omnibus fratribus sufficiant. Et si*
beoð ac hwanone ǽpla oðõe acennedlicu ofetu [g.] asigeglið
fuerint　unde　poma aut nascentia leguminum addatur
swilce þǽt þridde.　an pund　awegen genihtsumige on
et tertium ; Panis libera una propensa　sufficiat | in (145 a.)
dege swa hwǽðer [g.] swa [f.] [f.] ðu sig on gereordunge oðõe
die.　　sive　　una sit　　　refectio.　sive

──────────

4. *sco wuca þen*, see note.　16. *asigeglið*, I do not understand this gloss.

──────────

4. *ebdomedarius*, MS. *ebdomedariis*.　6. *eĩ*, sic in MS.; in glossator's
handwriting.　14. *potuerit*, *u* above line.　16. *poma*, MS. *pomi*.

gereordunge 7 æfenþenunge þæt gif hi sceolan on æfen
prandii et *cene ;*   *Quod si cenaturi*

gereordian of þam sylfan punde se þridda [c.] fram þam hordere
sunt. de eadem libra tertia. pars a cellarario

si gehealden to agifenne on æfenþenuungum [f.] geswinc   [f.]
reservetur. reddanda cenaturis Quod si labor forte factus

[f.] [g.] mare oncýre [d.]   de [e.] hitbeo gif hit fremað
fuerit major. in arbitrio et *potestate abbatis erit si expediat*

[k.] ýcan asýndrode toforan eallum þingum oferfýlle
aliquid augere remota pre   *omnibus crapula* ₅

þæt næfre ne undersmæge [m.] þam munece oferæt forþam
ut numquam subripiat monacho indigeries. quia nihil

swa wiðerweard þen is   swa swa oferfýlle   [s.]
sic contrarium est omni christiano quomodo crapula :

swa swa sæde ure drihten warniað þæt ne beon geheofogode
sicut ait dominus noster. Videte ne graventur

[c.] [c.] on oforfull cildum [g.] onginran ýlde [h.] seo ýlce
corda vestra in crapula. Pueris vero minore aetate. non eadem

ne si gehealdan micelness ah læsse þonne þam ýldrum
servetur quantitas.   *sed minor quam majoribus* 10

gehealdaura [m.] [l.] * fiðer * feteflæsð
servata in omnibus parcitate. Carnium vero quadrupedum omnino

[c.] si * forhæmed butan warhalum 7
ab omnibus abstineatur commestio. preter omnino debiles et

þa * metrunian
aegrotos ;

DE MENSURA POTUS. (CAP. XL.)

anra gehwýlc [b.] synderlice [a.] hæfð sýlene of gode sume
UNUS QUISQUE   PROPRIUM   HABET   DONUM EX DEO   alius 15

---

3. *æfenþenungum*, corrected from *æfenþenunge*, probably not contemporary.
10. *ne*, the *n* has a stroke through it.   11. *fiðer* over *carnium*, and *fetefæsð*
over *quadrupedum*, probably ought to be partially transposed. Read *flæsca*
(instead of *flæsð*) over *carnium*, and *fiðer fete* over *quadrupedum*.   12. *forhæmed*, read *forhæbben*.   13. *þa metrunian*, read *metruman* (for *med-
truman*).

---

1. *cenaturi*, MS. *cenatur*.   5. *remota*, MS. *premota*.   *omnibus crapula*, *ibus cra* on erasure, MS. *crapuli*.   15. DONUM, a letter erased
between D and O; E?

soðlice   [a.] [n.] mid sumum   ingehýda
summe sic alius vero   sic. Et ideo cum aliqua scrupulositate.

fram us   7 gemett bigleofa côra   7 is gesett swa þeah
a   nobis mensura   victus   aliorum constituitur : Tamen

untrumera   [g.]   wacmodnesse wegelýfað [d.]   gemet
infirmorum contuentes imbecillitatem :   credimus   eminam

wines geonden ænlepige genihtsumian geon dæg þam þe sÿ̂lð
vini   per sin.gulos   sufficere   per diem;   Quibus

          [f.] geþýld [h.] forhæfednesse   agene   he
5 *autem   donat | deus   tolerantiam abstinentie   propriam   se* (145 b.)

  silfe   mede   hi witan þæt gif   stowe neodþearfnesse
habituros mercedem sciant; Quod si aut loci   necessitas

oððe geswinc   [h.]   sumeres oððe swiðlic hæte þæt gif
aut   labor   aut ardor aestatis   amplius   popos-

bitt [d.] [b.]   on dome ealdres oððe hi wunige   [i.]   on
cerit   in   arbitrio prioris consistans. considerans in

callum þingum na þæt undersmege oferfýlle oððe drunccnnesse
omnibus   ne   subrepat   satietas aut ebrietas licet

þe we radan eallunga *windred   muneca   beon getiht
10 *legamus   omnino   vinum   monachorum persuaderi   non*

[a.] huru þinga huru þinga [g.] þæt   [f.]   þæt   þena
potest : saltem vel   hoc consentiamus. ut non usque

oð oferfýlle   drincan [k.] ac hwonlicor forþam *windrend
ad satietatem libamus sed   parcius.   quia   vinum

wiðersacan þedeð   þa witen þar þar   neodþearfnessa
apostatare facit etiam sapientes. Ubi   autem necessitas

stowe   bitt   [d.] þæt forasædegemed oððe forawritene beon
loci exposcit ut   ne   suprascripta mensura in-

gemett þæt fur ðonne mage ah micel   [h.] mid calle
15 *veniri   possit. sed   multo minus : aut ex toto*

naht bletsian god þara   eardiað 7   hi na cýrian
nihil benedicant deum qui ibi habitant et non murmurarent ;

---

7. *hæte* is gloss to *ardor*.   10. *windred*, read *windrenc*, i. e. *windrēc.*
11. *þena*, read *we na*, or more probably read *þe* as belonging to the preceding *þæt*.   12. *windrend*, read *windrenc*.

---

2. *victus*, MS. *victis*.   6. MS. *mercedam*. MS. *necessitate*, corrected into *necessitas*.   7. MS. *aestas*.   9. *aerietas* in the MS. for *ebrietas*.
10. Before *persuaderi*, the words *non esse, sed quia nostris temporibus id monachis*, found in the other texts, are omitted.   13. MS. *sapientis*.
16. *deum*, MS. evidently by mistake has *dominum* (*dū̄m*, for *dm̄*).

þæt   minigende   buton ceorunge þæt hi na
Hoc ante omnia ammonentes. ut   absque murmuratione
beon
sint ;

QUIBUS HORIS REFICIUNT FRATRES. (CAP. XLI.)

fram þære haligan castran [d.]   [d.]   to middæges
A SANCTO PASCHA USQUE AD PENTECOSTEN AD SEXtam
hi gereordian   to æfenne 7 hi gereordian fram pente-
reficiant   fratres. et ad seram   cenent ;   A   pente- 5
costen   on callum sumera geswinc   felda   gif hi nabbaðˇ
costen autem   tota estate : si labores   agrorum   non habent
munecas swiðlicnesse sumeras oððe ne gedefðˇ on wodness [c.]
monachi. aut nimietas estatis   non perturbat.   quarta.   et
[b.] dæg [a.] hi fæsten   oð non   on odrum dagum
(146 a.) *sexta feria   jejunent   usque ad nonam :   reliquis |*
dagum to middæge hi gereordian þa gereordunga to mid
diebus ad   sextum   prandeant ;   Que prandii sexta :
weorcum on æcerum gif hi habbað   sumeres   swiðlic hæte
si opera in   agris   haluerint.   aut aestatis   fervor 10
            bið to *belippendan bið þæs abbotes hit si on fora-
nimius fuerit :   continuanda   erit. et in abbatis   sit   provi-
scawunga   7 he gemetige ealle þinc and he gedihte
dentia.   Et sic   temperet   omnia   atque disponat
          saula   þæt þæt [c.] hi doð [c.] gebroðra
qualiter et anime salventur ; Et   quod   faciunt   fratres.
butan [d.] [d.] ælcere ceorunge 7 don fram anginnum [d.]
absque   ulla   murmuratione faciant ; Ab   idibus
          [e.]   oð   andgin fæstenes [f.]   to   nonas
autem septembris usque ad capud quadragesime   ad   nonam 15
[b.] hi gereordian on længtene fæsten [b.]   oð   castran
semper   reficiant.   In   quadragesima vero usque (in) pasca :

---

4. *midda* nearly quite erased.   7. *gedefð, ð* very pale ink, read *gedrefð.*
11. *lelippendan*, see note.

---

1. MS. *murmurationis.*   5. *fratres, fr* erased, then added at the top,
where it is again partially erased.   7. *nimietas, e* add. later, in very pale
ink.   9. *prandii, ii* above line, by way of correction to *-eant.* The MS. had
originally *prandeant.*   12. MS. *temperit ; atque ; disponit.*   16. *reficient*
in MS. There is an erasure before *pasca* in the MS. ; of *in* ?

on   æfæn   hi gereordian se sýlfa   æfen   si gedon
ad vesperam   reficiant;   Ipsa   autem vespera sic agatur:

   leoht   leohtfætes þæt hine behofian gereordgende mid leohte
ut lumen   lucerne   non indigeant reficientes.   sed luce

þagit dæges ealle þine ah beon gefyllede ac on ælcere   tide
adhuc diei   omnia   consummentur;   sed et omni tempore

swa æfen þenunge   oððe on tide swa þus gemedemod [g.]
sive sit cene sive refectionis   hora. sic   temperatur.   ut

mid dæg þæt gewyrdan ealle þing.
5 *cum luce   fiant   omnia.*

UT POST COMPLETORIUM NEMO LOQUATUR. (CAP. XLII.)

on ælcere tide   swigen   sceolan healdan   munecas swyðost
Omni tempore   silentium   debent studere   monachi.   maxime

þehhwæðere   on nihtlicum tidum   7 forði on ælcere tide sit
tamen   nocturnis   horis. Et ideo omni tempore sive

fæstenes sit gereordung g tima   gif hit bið gereordunge sona
jejunii. sive   prandii: si tempus   fuerit   prandii.   mox

þæt hi arisað fram æfen þenunge 7 hi sittan ealle togædere
10 *ut surrexerint a   cena.   sedeant   omnes in unum.*

7 ræde   an   *þurhtogenes race oððe on ealdfædera lifa oððe
et *legat unus   collationes.   vel   vitas patrum.   aut*

soðes sum ðine þæt getrymme þa gehyrendum
certe   aliquid   quod   edificet   audientes; Non autem epta-

       forðam untrumum andgitum þena bið
ticum aut   regum. | quia   infirmis   intellectibus   non   erit (146 b.)

nytwyrðlic on ðære tida   þis   gewrit gehyran on oðrum
utile   illa   hora hanc   scripturam audire. aliis vero

tidum [c.] beon geredde gif beoð fæstenes dagas   [a.]
15 *horis   legantur; Si   autem jejunii   dies   fuerint.*

gesungenum æfensanga betwux lytlum fæce sona hi gan to
dicta   vespera.   parvo   intervallo   mox accedant ad

rædinge   race oððe recednesse swa swa we bufon sædon 7
lectionem.   collationum   ut diximus.   et

8, 9. *sit, sit,* read *sig?* *sig?* *g tima,* very slight traces of erasure between
g and *tima*; read *gif?*   11. *þurhtogenes, s* owing to the influence of Latin
ending? read *þurhtogenc.*

---

12. *autem,* corr. from *auvero* by writing *tem* over *vero,* and *o* (=*idem*)
over *au.*   15. *legantur, a* corr. from *u.*

geræddum feower oððe fif leafum   [p.]   [p.]
lectis quattuor.   aut quinque foliis vel quantum hora

[q.]   eallum becumen togædere   [q.] þurh þas
permittit ;   omnibus in unum   occurrentibus per hanc

ýldinge rædinc gif ænig wenunge on ðam sýlfum
moram lectionis ; Si quis forte   in assignato

betæhtum him sýlfum þingum beon ænig bið gebisgod he
sibi commisso   fuerit   occupatus oc-

becume ealle   togædere gesette hi gefýllan 7 utgan-
currat ; Omnes ergo in unum positi compleant ; Et ex- 5

gende fram nihtsangum ænig 7 nasi leaf sýððan ænigum
euntes a completoriis nulla sit licentia denuo cuiquam

spræcon ænig þing þæt gif býð gemett funden   [a.]   ænig
loqui aliquid ; Quod si   inventus fuerit quisquam

þisne forgæian stilnesse   mid þearfnesse cumena
hanc prevaricari taciturnitatis regulam. si necessitas hospidum

gif ofor becimð wenunga   ænigum ænig þinc oððe hate
supervenerit : aut forte abba alicui aliquid jusseret

þæt [a.] beon 7 swýlce mid healicum gedreoge 7 gemetegunge
Quod tamen et ipsum cum summa gravitate et moderatione 10

arwurðlicor þæt beo
honestissime fiat.

DE HIS QUI AD OPUS DEI ET ADMENSAM TARDE

VENIUNT. (CAP. XLIII.)

to tide godcundre þenunge sona þonne bið gehýred swa
AD HORAM DIVINI OFFICII MOX UT AUDITUM   FUER*it*

beoð tacen eallum forlætenum [h.] swa hwýlce þinc
signum :   relictis omnibus   que libet fuerint 15

on handum mid hælicum ofoste [b.] si becumen mid
in manibus summa cum festinatione curratur : cum

gedreoge þeahhwæðere þæt ne ge higeleas mete tender
gravitate tamen.   ut non scurilitas inveniat fomitem ;

---

2. *becumen,* gloss to *occurrentibus* : read *becumendum.*   17. *higeleas,* probably the subst. *higeleast* was originally there.

---

3. *lectionis,* second *i* erased. *in assignato,* MS. *in* has *signato.*   8. *regulam,* not in the MS. ; *sine cessitas* in MS. Before these words a line (*regulam graviori vindicte subjaceat excepto*) has been left out. 9. *aut forte,* MS. *autferte* in one word, and *t* added above line in the MS. 12. QUI not in the MS.

naht godes weorce na si forasett þæt gif bið   to
Ergo nihil opcri dei preponatur; | *Quod si quis ad* (147 a.)

nihtlicum uhtsangum [o.] [q.]   [p.]   þas feower and hund-
*nocturnas rigilias post gloria*m *psalmi nonagesimi*

nigenteoðan sealmas þane forþi   callunga teonde
     quarti quem propter hoc omnino protrahendo et

latlice we wyllað beon gesæd begimð na stande on ændebyrd-
morose rolumus dici occurrerit. non stet in ordine

nesse [b.] on choro ac hæftemæst calra stande oððe on
5   *suo in choro. sed ultimus omnium stet; aut in*

stowe þe þe swylcum gimelesum   [k.]   asundran geset
loco quem talibus neglegentibus seorsum con-

se abbod þæt he sigewarnod fram him oððe fram
stituerit abba. ut videatur ab ipso: vel ab

callum oððe [o.] gefylledum weorce   mid fulre
omnibus usque du:n completo opere dei publica eatis-

dædbote he behreowsige for þi   [b.]   hi on ðam ytemestan stýde
factione peniteat; Ideo autem eos in ultimo aut

on sundran we demdon scylan standan þæt gesawene fram
10   *seorsum judicarimus. debere stare ut risi ab*

callum oððe for ðære sylfan seame   he beon gebette [a.]
omnibus. vel pro ipsa rerecundia sua emendentur; Nam

wið utan on cyrican gif hi beoð lifað býð færunga þýle
si foris oratorio remaneant: erit forte talis qui

     7 he slape oððe gewislice hi sette him sylfan
se aut collocet et *dormiat: aut certe sedeat sibi foris:*

þærute spellungum * gæænigtigað 7 beon geseald intinga þam
vel fabulis racet; et *detur oceasio*

awýridan deofle ah inga wið innan þæt he forþam
15   *maligno; Sed ingrediatur intro. ut nec totum*

ne forleose 7 be ðam oðrum hi si gebet on dægðerlicum
perdat et *de reliquo cmendctur; Diurnis*

---

2. [o.] [q.] [p.] are partly pasted over.   3. *teonde, eo* quite indistinct.
4. *latlicē,* sic in MS., but the stroke may be the remnant of a letter
erased after *quarti. begimð,* i. e. *becimð.*   6. *gimelesum, le* not quite
clear, probably *gimeæsum* was in the MS. first, then *l* was added through
the *æ,* making it into *gimelesum.*   14. *geænigtigað* or *geæmgtigað* ; read
gewmtigað.

---

2. *rigiliis* in MS.   3. *i* erased after *quarti.*   4. *morose, r* corr. from
another letter.   6. *talibus,* MS. *alibus.*   8. MS. *ominibus. satis-,*
MS. *sitis-.*   11. *sua,* put in later.   15. *intro, t* added above line.
16. *relinquo, ēē* (= *esse*) *mendetur* in the MS.

tidum [o.] [d.] [c.]
autem horis qui ad opus dei post versum et gloriam

þæs forman sealmas þe   bið gesungen se ðe na
primi psalmi qui post versum dicitur non occur-

becymð [d.] on æ onðære þe we bufan sædon   on
rerit. lege   qua supra   diximus in

ðære ÿtemestan stowe he stande ne he negedÿrstlæce beon
ultimo stet :   nec   presumat

gefærlæht   sin   oð fulre dædbote   ·   buton
sociari choro psallentium   usque ad   satisfactionem. nisi 5

        leafe   sÿlle be his þafunge [x.] [y.] [z.]
forte abbas licentiam dederit permissionem suam : ita tamen :

(147 b.) þæt he gebete scÿldig þanonforð
ut satisfaciat   reus ex hoc ;   Ad mensam | autem qui ante

        se de ne becÿmð þæt he sette   singan 7
versum non ocurrerit :   ut simul omnes dicant versum et

hi gebiddan 7 hi under anum calle genealæcan to meosan þurh
orent.   et sub uno omnes accedant ad mensam : qui

his gÿmeleaste   oððe leahtor se ðe ne becÿmð oð
per neglegentiam suam aut vitium non occurrerit : usque 10

oþre siðe [c.]   for þisum leahtre he si geþread [a.] eft
ad secundam vicem pro hoc corripiatur ; Si denuo

gif he hit na gebet   [c.]   gemenelicere meosan
non emendaverit   non permittatur ad mense communis

to dælnimiuge ac he geasindrod [h.] fram geferi ædene   [k.]
participationem :   sed sequestratus   a consortio   omnium

reordige ana ætbrodenum his dæle [n.] of wine [p.]
reficiat solus : sublata ei portione sua de vino : usque ad

oð fulre   dædbote   swa gelice [b.] he þolie se ðe na
satisfactionem et emendationem ; Similiter autem patiatur. qui 15

    ættan ferse [d.] bið andwerd þæt bið æfter mete
ad illum versum non fuerit presens : qui   post cibum

gesungen ne ne gedÿrst quam læce þare forasetan tide
dicitur ; Nec quis presumat ante statutam horam :

---

1. [d.] not quite clear.   16. *ættan* for *æt þam*.   17. *ne ne gedÿrst quam læce*; read *ne ne gedÿrstlæce*; *quam*, though belonging to *quis*, is in the hand of our glossator.

---

14. *de vino*, MS. *divino*.   16. *ad*, MS. *et*.

oððe æfter syððan ænig þing metes ge sægde drencg underfon
aut   postea   quicquam   cibi   ait   potus presumere ;

ahhe gif enignm bið bebedum æui þing fram þam ealdre
Sed   si   cui   offertur   aliquid   a   priore

7 underfon 7 he wið sæcð on tide þæt on þare þe he gewilnað
et accipere   renuntierit.   hora   qua   desideraverit.

[d.] þæt he þæt æfte þæt þæt he wið soc oððe   eallunga
hoc   quod   prius   recusavit.   aut aliud omnino

naht na underfon   æt fulre dædbote gecwemlice
5 *nihil accipiat :   usque ad emendationem congruam ;*

DE HIS QUI EXCOMMUNICANTUR QUOMODO SATIS FACIANT.

(CAP. XLIIII.)

for healicum gylte fram gebedhuse 7 *fram* beode se þe býð
QUI PROGRAVI CULPA AB ORATORIO *et   mensa   excom-*

amansumad on tide on þæt godes weorc on cýrcean þær bið wurðod
municatur : hora   qua   opus   dei   in oratorio percelebratur :

ætforan dýran   aþreht alinge naht secgende buton þæt an
10 *ante foras oratorii prostratus jaceat nihil dicens : nisi tantum*

ahýldum on eorðan heafde pro ascred eadmod ealra   of
posito   in   terram   capite :   Stratus   pronus omnium de

cýrcean utgangendre mid fotum 7 þæt swa lange   do
oratorio exeuntium   pedilus   Et hoc tam diu   faciat :

cððæt [s.]   deme   fullice gebed   se þonne
usque   dum abbas | judicaverit satisfactum esse ; Qui dum (148 a.)

he gehaten fram   cýmð abetyrne þam sýlfan
jussus   ab abbate. venerit :   volvat   se ipsius abbatis

fotum syððan eallra fotswaþum broðra þæt hi gebiddan.
15 *pedibus. deinde omnium vestigiis fratrum :   ut   orent*

for him 7 þonne gif hæt   he si underfangen on chore
pro ipso : Et tunc si jusserit abba ;   recipiatur   in choro

oððe on eddebýrdnýsse þar þar   gement swa vel plane
vel in   ordine :   quo   abba decreverit : ita   sane

---

1. *underfon, f* corr. from *r.*   2. *bebedum, bo* above the line ; read *beboden.*   8. *fram* (second). The MS. has *fra.*   10. *ælforan, ran* seems to be blotted. *aþreht,* for *astreht. alinge,* originally *alincge,* for *alicge.*   11. *pro* in glossator's hand.   14. *abetyrne, a* ' paving' letter?

1. *cibi,* MS. *ubi. ait* must be a very old mistake for *aut,* since a glossator, meaningless, has provided it with the gloss *sægde.*   11. *pronus* added by glossator. *de* corrected from two other letters.   13. *satisfactum, t* corr. from another letter by erasure.   14. *ab* omitted in the MS.   16. *si, i* corrected from *e.*

sealm　oðða　antemn　oððe　rædinge　oððe hwæt æni þing
ut psalmum.　ut antiphonam seu lectionem vel　aliud　quid

ne gedýrstlæce on gebedhuse aginnan　buton eft se *abbod*
non presumat in oratorio imponere : nisi　iterum　abba :

hate　7　on eallon tid*um*　þænne　þe　bið gefylled godes weorc
jubeat Et omnibus oris　dum　completur　opus dei

niðer　alenge hine sýlfne on eorþan on stowe on þam ðe
proiciat　se　in terram in　loco　quo

stýnd 7　swaful gebete 7 *hihtt oððæt　him hate　eft
stat. et sic　satisfaciat　usque　dum　ei jubeat iterum 5

þæt he geswice eallunga fulredædbote fram þissere
abba ; ut　quiescat jam　ab hac satisfactione ;　Qui

fram leohtum gýltum þa ðe beoð amansumode þæt an fram
vero pro levibus culpis　excommunicantur　tantum a

meosan on cýrican hit gebeta oðhige　hæse þæt abbotes
mensa : in oratorio satisfaciant : usque ad jussionem　habbatis

þæt fremman　oððe　bletsige 7 he secge genohhit is.
Hoc perficiant usquedum beneficiat et　dicat　sufficit ;

DE HIS QUI FALLUNTUR IN MONASTERIO. (CAP. XLV.)　10

gif ænig þonne　he aginð　sealm　repse　oððe an-
SI QUIS　DUM PRONUNTIAT *psalmum responsorium. aut anti-*

temp　leogð　rædinge butan þurh fulre dædbote
phonam. vel *fallitur lectionem nisi　per　satisfactionem*

þara toforan　eallum　geadmet　he beo mare wrace
ibi coram　omnibus humiliatus　fuerit : majori vindicte

he underhnige witodlice se ðe nolde mid eadmodnesse þreagian
subjaceat :　quippe qui noluit　humilitate　corrigere :

þæt þæt *he* agelte mid gimeleaste　cildra
quod　neglegentia　deliquid ; Infantes autem 15

for swilcum gýlta * beimbeswugen.
pro tali culpa　vapulent ;

---

4. *alenge*, cf. 78. 10; originally *alencye*, for *ale ge.*　5. *7 hihtt*, quid?
13. *ge admet*, erasure of one letter (*e*?) after *ge-.*　15. *he* above line.
16. *be imbeswugen*, or *beon beswugen*? Indistinct. Understand: *beon beswungen.*

---

9. *Hoc*, corrected from *non* in the MS.　10. MONASTERIO. All the
other texts have ORATORIO (cf. Schröer, W. V., p. 94; Schmidt, p. 49).
12. *fallitur.* Above *ll* there is the sign of contraction for *ur.* It has
been torn asunder by the stretching of the MS. consequent upon and
necessitated by the MS. being pasted up after the fire.

DE HIS QUI IN LEVIBUS REBUS DELINQUUNTUR.   (CAP. XLVI.)

gif   * spinð on ænigum geswince innon cicena on hederne |
SI QUIS DUM IN LABORE   QUOVIS IN COQUINA IN   CELLARIO. |(148 b.)

on þenunge on bæcerne   on orcerde on ænigum cræfte
in ministerio, in pistrino; in orto   *in arte aliqua.*   *dum*

          côðe on swa hwilcere stowe æni þing he agild oðŏe
*laborat.   vel   in   quocum*que   *loco   aliquid   deliquerit ut aut*

tobrýt   ænig þinc   oðŏe   forlýsð   gif
5 *regerit   quippiam.   aut   perdiderit sive aliud quid excesserit*

þær ubi 7   hesýlf cumende   þærrihte   toforan   þam abbode
  ibi   et   *non veniens   continuo   ante   abbatem.*

oðŏe to gegaderunge hit na sýlf willes gebete 7 he gefremmað
vel congregationem   ipse ultro satisfecerit   et   prodiderit

his gilt   þonne he þurh oðerne   cuð   hit bið
delictum   suum: dum per alium   cognitum   fuerit

maran bote underhnige   saule [m.] sýnne
  majori   subjaceat   emendationi; Si anime   vero peccati

intinga gif beoð lettinge þæt an þam abbude oðŏe gastlicum
10 *causa   fuerit   latens.   tantum   abbati   aut spiritalibus*

ealdrum   he geswutelige   þa   cunnan gelacnian heora
senioribus   patefaciat.   qui   sciant   curare   sua:

ælfremeda wunda   na abarian   7 geswutelian
et *aliena   vulnera non   detegere   aut   publicare;*

(DE SIGNIFICANDA HORA OPERIS DEI.) (CAP. XLVII.)

             godes   dæges 7 nihtes sig caru þæs
NUNTIANDA HORA OPERIS DEI DIE NOCTUQUE SIT *cura*

abbotes oðŏe hesýlf cýðan oðrum   holifullum breðer
15 *abbatis: aut   ipse   nuntiare: aut   tali   solicito fratri*

oðŏe betæce þas gimene þæt þæt   ongedafenlicum timan
injungat hanc curam: ut   omnia   horis competentibus

----

2. *spinð*, read *swinð*, for *swincð*, and take it as gloss to *laborat* in l. 4.
3. *in orto* in glossator's hand.   6. *ubi* written by glossator.   11. Erasure
after *geswutelige.*

----

2. COUINA in MS.   3. *aliqua*, MS. *aliquo.*   6. *veniens*, MS. *invens.*
7. *prodiderit*, MS. *perdiderit.*   10. MS. *fuerint. tantum. tantem*
in MS., but the correction is indicated by writing *u* over *e.*   12. After
aliena, rulnera is written above the line, possibly by glossator.   *detegerw* in
MS. *et* instead of *aut.*   13. The title of Chapter XLVII not being found
in our MS., it has been supplied from the other MSS.   16. *injungat*, MS.
injngat.

beon gefýllede sealmas soðlice oððe antiphonas æfter þam abbode
compleantur; Psalmos autem vel *antiphonas post   abba*tem
be heora ændebýrdnesse þam þe b.ð gehaten hi aginnan singan
  *ordine suo quib*us *jussum fuerit   inponant; Cantare*
  7 rædan ne ne gedýrstlæce buton se ðe mæg þa sýlfan
autem et *legere   non   presumat: nisi   qui   potest   ipsum*
þenunge welgefullan þæt beon getimbrode þa gehýrendum þæt
officium bene implere. ut   aedificentur   audientes;   Quod
                  7 mid ege beo 7 þam þe hæt.
cum humilitate: et gravitate: et   *tremore   fiat :   cui   jusserit* 5

abbas;

De opere manuum cotidiano. (Cap. XLVIII.)

  idelnes feond is sawle 7 forþi orgewissum tidum
Otiositas inimica est anime; et ideo   certis   *temporibus*
beon gebisgode scealan   on geswince handa   onge-
(149 a.)   *occupari   debent   fratres in   labore   manuum:* | *certis*
wissum eft tidum on godgundre rædinge 7 forþi þissere
    iterum   horis   in   lectione divina.   Ideoque   hac 10
        we gelýað æiwheþera tida   beon geendebýrde
*dispositione credimus   utraq*ue *tempora   ordinari.   id est*
        oðclýpunge þæs nigeþan monþas on ærne utgangende
a pascha   usque ad kalendas octobris   mane   exeuntes
fram primsange oððe fullan feorðan tida   hi swican
a   prima: usque   ad horam pene   quartam: laborent
þæt þæt beoð nýdbehefe   fram tide   þære feorðan
quod   necessarium   fuerit;   ab   hora autem   quarta
oðða sýxtan tide   hi æmtian æfter þære sýxtan
usque ad horam   sextam lectioni vacent;   Post sextam 15
tida arisende   hi geresten on heora beddum mid
autem surgentes a mensa   pausent   in lectis   suis   cum
eallum swige oððe wenunga se ðe wýle him sýlfan rædan
omni   silentio: aut   forte   qui voluerit   sibi   legere.
swa ræde þæt oðer he ne gedrefe sigedon   gemetlicor
sic   legat   ut alium non inquietet;   Agatur   nona temperius

---

10. *godgundre,* second *g* corr. from *t.*   13. *fullan,* gloss as if the lemma
were *plene.*

---

1. *Psalmus* in MS.   2. *jussum, jussus* in the MS., and the first *u*
added later.

G

midwengendum þære ehta tide   þæt þæt eis towyrcanne
    mediante   octava hora: et *iterum   quod faciendum*

  hi wýrcan oððe æfan   [a.] [b.] neodbehefnes
est operentur usque ad vesperum; Si autem   necessitas

stowe oððe *pearflices giforcrafað   wæsmas togegaderigenne
loci aut paupertas   exegerit ut ad fruges   colligendas

þurh hi þæt hi beon gebisgode hi na beon gedre°ede forþam
per   se occupentur   non contristentur :   quia

þonne soðan munecas   þurh *gespinð heora handa
5 *tunc veri   monachi sunt; si   labore manuum suar*um

gif hi libbað swa swa   ure fæderes
  vivunt.   sicut et patres nostri et apostoli ; Omnia tamen

gemetelice beon forþam wac modum fram clýpunge
*mensurate fiant : propter pusillanimes ; A   calendis aute*m

         oð anginn lænctenfæsten on þa oðran fulran tide
octobribus usque ad caput quadragesime : usque   in horam

          rædinge hi æmtian se oðer tida on ðære ucan s'gedon
secundam plenam lectioni vacent ; Hora   secunda   agatur

undern   on heora weorc 7 hi geswican
10 *tertia ; et usque ad nonam omnes in opus suum   laborent*

þæt bið   betæht gewordenum   forecnýll þære
  quod   eis injungitur ;   Facto   autem primo signo hore

nontide hi geðeodan fram *heora weorce ænlepie 7 hi beon
none : disjungant se ab opere suo   singuli. et sint

gearwe þor.ne þone oðerne cnýll   cnýlð æfter gereordunge
parati : dum secundum signum | pulsaverit ; Post refectionem (149 b.)

  hi æmtian heora rædingum   oððe on sealmum
autem   vacent   lectionibus suis aut psalmis ; In

lænctenes fæstenes   on dagum fram ærne merien oð ðære
15 *quadragesime vero diebus a   mane usque   ad*

þriddan tide   emtian *heorædingum   oðða
   tertiam plenam vacent lectionilus suis. et usque ad

---

1. *midwengendum*? *n* may be *r*; perhaps read *midligendum*. *eis*, Latin,
or *e* ' paving letter '? 3. *pearflices*, i. e. *pearflicnes*. *giforcrafað*, see note.
5. *gespinð*, read *geswinð*. 7. *clýpunge*, *l* above line. 8. *on*, *n* corr. from
other letter: *ð*? 11. *forecnýll*, read probably *forme cnýll*. 12. *heora*, *h*
indistinct. 15. *lænctenes*, *lænc* not quite clear. 16. *horædingum*, read
heora rædingum.

---

1. MS. *faciendam*.   3. *exierit* in the MS.   4. MS. *occupaentur*.
5. *labore*, MS. *labores*.   6. MS. *viant*.   9. *secundam*, MS. *secundum*.
16. *lectionibus*, MS. *lectiones*.

fullan teoðan tida   hi wýrcan þæt heom beoð   betæht
decimam horam plenam operentur quod eis injungitur.

on þam   dagum   lænctenfæsten   * hiderfan   ealle ænlepige
In quibus diebus quadragesime. accipiant omnes singulos

bec   of boc cýstan þa hi be   endebýrdnesse eall abutan
codices de bibliotheca quos per ordinem ex integro

rædan þa bec sýnd to sýllanne on anginne   fæsten
legant; Qui codices : in caput quadragesime dandi

     toforan eallum þingan   wislice si betæht an oððe
sunt ; Ante omnia autem sane deputetur unus aut 5

twegen ealdres þa   emfaran   mýnster   on tidum þam hi
duo seniores: qui cýrcumeant monasterium horis quibus

geæmtian   ræding 7 hi gewarnian þe læs þe si gemet
vacant fratres lectioni. et videant. ne forte inveniatur

    asolcen   se ge emtige idelnesse oððe spellingum 7
frater accidiosus : qui vacet otioso aut fabulis et

he nis   geornfull   7 he nis þæt an him unnýt wurðe
non est intentus lectioni : et non solum sibi inutilis est.

ac he   oðre upahefð þes þýllice   þæt feorsi gif he bið
sed etiam alios extollit : hic talis si quod absit reper- 10

gemet   si gebread æne 7   oðre side þæt an gif he hit
tus fuerit. corripiatur semel et secundo ; si non emen-

na gebett regollicere þreaiunge   be þam elles swa
daverit correptioni regulari subjaceat : et taliter

þæt oðre þæt ondrædað ne ne   to breðer
ut ceteri timeant ; Neque frater ad fratrem jungatur :

on ungedafenlicum tidum on þam drihtelicum dæge rædinge
horis incompetentibus: Dominico die lectioni

hi emtian ealle asindrodum þisum   mislicum þenungum
vacent omnes exceptis his qui variis officiis 15

þa þe sýnd betæhte gif ænig soðlice   gimeleas oððe asolcen
deputati sunt : Si quis vero ita neglegens et desidiosus

bið   þæt nele   oððe ne mage smægan oððe an
fuerit : ut non velit ; aut non possit meditari aut legere.

---

2. *hiderfan*, read *hi underfan*.   9. *þæt*, þ corrected from or into ð.
14. *on*, indistinct.   17. *an*, merely ending of (*ræd*)*an* to denote infinitive.

---

1. *injungitur*, MS. *ingungitur*. 3. *quos*, MS. *quas*.   4. *Qui*, MS. *quia*.
7. *inveniatur*, MS. *inveniat*. 13. *timeant*, MS. *timeat*.   15. *vacent*,
MS. *reacent*.   17. *velit*, MS. *fuelit*.

si betæht　him　weorc　þæt　he do　þæt he ne ge æmtige
injungatur　ei　opus　quod　faciat :　ut non vacet. |　　(150 a.)

þa [c.]　untruman [b.]　gebroðran [c.]　oððe [d.]　estfullum
Fratribus autem.　　　infirmis.　　　aut　　delicatis :

swylcum [c.]　weorca oððe … æft oððe si geþeoda þæt [f.] hi
talis　　opera　aut　ars　injungatur :　　ut nec

forðanne idele　　na hina mid stiðnessa geswing beon [i.] of-
otiosi　　sint.　nec　violentia　laboris　oppri-

sette　þæt [f.] hi beon aflingede　þara　* wacmodes fram
5 *mantur :　　ut effugentur ;　　Quorum　inbecillitas　ab*

þam abbote is to forsceawiende
abbate　　consideranda　　est ;

DE QUADRAGESIME OBSERVATIONE. (CAP. XLVIIII.)

[l.] þeh þe on ælcere [q.]　　　lif [m.] munecas lænctenfæstenes
LICET　　OMNI　TEMPORE VITA MONACHI QUADRAGESIME

sceale 7 gehealdsumnesse [p.] [o.]　forþam þe is forþam feawera
debeat　observationem　habere.　tamen　quia　paucorum

þe is þeos miht [a.]　we atihtað on [b.] þisum dagum læncten-
10 *est ista virtus.　ideo suademus　istis diebus　quadra-*

fæstenes [c.] [f.] on ælcere clænnesse heora lif [e.]
gesime.　omni　puritate　vitam　suam

[d.]　[h.] 7　ealra　heora gimeleasnesse [c.] [h.]
custodire :　et omnes pariter　negligentias　suas

oðra tida on þisum halgum dagum adlian þæt [a.]
aliorum temporum　his　diebus sanctis diluere ; Quod

[b.] wyrðlice bið [a.] gif fram eallum leahtrum [e.] [d.]
tunc　digne sit :　si ab　omnibus　vitiis temperemus ;

7 gebede [d.] mid wopum [f.] 7 onbryrdnesse [g.] [h.]
15 *Orationi　cum fletibus lectioni et compunctioni cordis*

7 [a.] forhæfednesse [g.] gimene uton [a.] syllan　on þisum
atque　abstinentie　operam demus ; Ergo his diebus

uton don　　sum þinc [d.] gewunelicne [c.] gafol
augeamus　nobis　aliquid　ad solitum　pensum

---

3. … æft, nearly illegible, read cræft.　5. aflingede, n under the line ;
cf. Introd., V. § 70. wacmodes, read wacmodnes.　9. forþam þe, dittography.
11. [c.] or [i.] ?　17. [c.] not quite clear ; may be part of d (of adsolitum).

5. effugentur, MS. effugatur.　7. The title in the MS. is DE XL^a
OBSERVATIONE.　9. paucorum, MS. parcorum.　13. sanctis, possibly in
glossator's hand. diluere, MS. defluere.　16. operam, MS. operum.　his
added by glossator.　17. augeamus in glossator's hand ; its gloss, uton don,
would make us think that the glossator has read agamus.

ures þeowdomes [f.]   sinderlices gebedu [g.]   [g.]
servitutis   *nostre.*   *Orationes*   *peculiares.*

metta 7 drencas [h.] for hæfednesse [i.] 7 anra gehwylc
ciborum et *potus*   *abstinentiam;*   *Et*   *unusquisque super*

      him sylfum on þam foresædan gemette sum þinc
mensuram   *sibi indictam :*   *aliquid*

mid agenum [s.] willa [r.] mid gefean [o.] þæs halgan gastes
propria   *voluntate cum gaudio*   *sancti spiritus*

ofrige gode   he ætbrede his lichaman of mette 7 of
offerat deo; id est *subtrahat corpori suo de cibo : de 5*

drencu of slæpe 7 of spræce 7 of higeleaste 7 [a.] he and [c.]
potu: de somno. de loquacitate: de scurilitate : et *cum*

gastlicere gewilnunge mid gefean [c.] mid blisse haligum [b.]
spiritalis desiderii   *gaudio*   *sanctum*

eastran bidige [a.] [b.] þæt sylfe [b.] peahwære [c.] þæt [d.]
pascha exspectat;   *Hoc ipsum*   *tamen*   *quod*

anra [e.] beode his [f.] abbode [f.] he tihte 7 hit beo [g.]
unusquisque offert;   *abbati suo suggeret;* et *cum*

mid his gebede [g.] bene [g.] 7 [i.] [i.] forþam þæt [m.]
eius   *fiat oratione* et *voluntate; quia | quod* 10

buton [n.] willan [e.] buton gastlices fæderes þe he bið [n.]
sine   *patris spiritalis fiat voluntate.*

dyrstignesse þe biþ geteald 7 na ideles [p.] wuldres [q.] buton
presumtioni deputabitur: et *vane gloria non*

wið [p.] meten mid willan þæs abbodes calle þinc
mercedi; Ergo cum voluntate abbatis omnia

sind to donne
agenda sunt;

DE FRATRIBUS QUI LONGE AB ORATORIO LABORANT AUT 15

IN VIA SUNT. (CAP. L.)

[b.] [i.] þa eallunga [k.] feor synd on geswince [m.] 7 hi na
FRATRES QUI OMNINO LONGE SUNT IN LABORE et *non*

magon ongenbecuman [p.] ongedafenlicere [q.] tide to [p.] myustre
possunt occurrere hora competenti ad

6. *he and, and* belongs to the *bidige* of l. 8. 8. *bidige*; see note to l. 6. *di* above the line. 13. *meten*, a mistake for *mede*?

2. *potus*, MS. *potius*, but *i* underdotted. 5. *de cibo*, MS. *decimo*. 7. *desiderii*, MS. *desiderio.* 15. MS. GONGE, AD.

[r.] se abbod [s.] þæt [r.] andgit þæt þæt swa is
oratorium   *et*   *abbas*   *hoc*   *perpendit*   *quia*   *ita est:*

[a.] don þærrihte godes [d.] weorc [d.] [e.] þar þar hi [n.]
agant   *ibidem*   *opus*   *dei*   *ubi ope-*

wýrcan [e.] [f.] ege mid godcundum bigænge [g.] [h.] * cwuwa
rantur   *cum tremore*   *divino*   *flectentes*   *genua ;*

[a.] swa gelice [b.] þa þa on [b.] gange [c.] sýnd [b.] asende [b.]
Similiter   *qui*   *in*   *itinere*   *sunt*   *directi ;*

* hid hi [e.] na for gimcleasian [p.] on gesettere tide [c.] ahbi [h.]
5 *non eos*   *pretereant*   *hore*   *constitute :*   *sed*

swa swa hi [k.] magon don [h.] heom sýlfum [l.] 7 [o.] þeow-
ut   *possunt*   *agant*   *sibi*   *et*   *servi-*

domes [o.] gafol [n.] hi na forgimelcasað agýldan.
tutis   *pensum*   *non neglegant*   *reddere ;*

DE FRATRIBUS QUI NON LONGE SATIS PROFICISCENTUR. (CAP. LI.)

[b.] þa for ænigre andsware þa beoð afarenne
FRATRES   QUI   PRO   QUOVIS   RESPONSO   PROFICISCUNTUR

7 on þam sýlfan dæge hi hihton gecýrran to mýnstre
10 ET   EA   *die*   *sperant*   *reverti*   *ad monasterium ;*

hina gedýrstlæcan wið utan [d.] etan [e.] [e.] þeah þe
Non presumant   *foris*   *manducare :*   *etiam*

[e.] beon fram ænigum [f.] men gecedene buton hit sig beboden
si   *a*   *quovis rogentur :*   *nisi*

wununga [i.] fram heora [k.] abbude [k.] heom [g.]
forte   *ab*   *abbate*   *suo*   *eis*   *precipiatur ;*

þæt [b.] gif hi elles doð [b.] hi beon * amsumude.
Quod   *si*   *aliter*   *fecerint :*   *excommunicentur ;*

15   DE ORATORIO MONASTERII. (CAP. LII.)

gebedhus [c.] [b.] þæt sig [a.] þæt hit is [d.] gecweden [d.] ne ne
Oratorium   *hoc*   *sit*   *quod*   *dicitur :*   *nec*

þær ænig þincg ælles si ge don [d.] oððe [e] gelod
ibi   *quicquam*   *aliud*   *geratur*   *aut*   *condatur*

---

3. *bigænge*, see note. *cwuwa*, read *cnuwa*. 5. *hid*, probably *d* is a
paving letter and *hi* dittography. 14. *amsumude*, read *amansumude*.
16. *gebedhus*, *h* above line. 17. *egelod*, see note.

---

gefylledum weorce [c.]   mid healicum [d.] swige   [b.]
Expleto   opere   dei: cum   summo   silentio

hi utgan 7 si gesungen mid arwyrðnysse [f.] þæt [g.]   [b.]
exeant: et   *agatur   reverentia   deo   ut   frater*

[l.] færunga heom sylfan [n.] synderlice [m.] se þe wile   [m.]
(151 a.) *qui   forte   sibi   peculialiter   vult | orare:*

[g.] na si gele*d*t oðres   mid onhrope [a.] 7   gif wile [a.]
non impediatur alterius   inprobitate;   Sed et *si   aliter*

him [g.] sylfum wenunga [k.] digelicor gebiddan [i.] andfealdlice
*vult   sibi   forte   secretius   orare: simplicit*er 5

ah he inga 7 he gebidde [b.]   na mid hludre [d.] stefne [d.]
intret et   *oret.   non in   clamosa   voce:*

ac on tearum   7 onbryrdnesse [f.] heortan [g.]   [b.]   se þe
sed in lacrimis et   *intentione   cordis;   Ergo   qui*

gelice weorc na   deþ he na si gepafod gefylledum [f.] weorce [f.]
simile opus non facit: non permittatur   explicito   opere

bæftan belifan   [c.]   eallswa hit is ge*r*æd   oðer
dei   remorari   in oratorio   sicut dictum   est. ne alius

lettinege þæt he na þolige.
*impedimentu*m   *patiatur;*   10

DE HOSPITIBUS SUSCIPIENDIS. (CAP. LIII.)

[b] ealle ofer becumendlicum [b.] cuman [b.]   swa swa crist [c.]
OMNES   SUPERVENIENTES   HOSPITES: TAMQUAM

[c.]   forþam [d.] þe his to cweðenne [d.] [e.]
christus suscipiantur.   quia ipse   dicturus   est:

cuma [b.] ic wæs 7 geunderfangenne [c.] [d.] [a.] 7 callum
hospes   fui: et   *suscepistis   me; Et   omnibus*

þæslic [b.] wurð menð [b.]   7 si gegearcod [a.] swyþest [c.]
congruus   honor   exibeatur: maxime 15

hiwcuðum [d.] geleafan 7 ælþeodigum [f.] [g.]   þonne bið
domesticis   fidei et *peregrinis;   Ut ergo   nun-*

gecyged [g.]   cu*m*a [h.] [a.] si becumen [b.] fram þam ealdre
tiatus   fuerit hospes: occurratur   ei   a   priore

---

4. *geledt, d* corr. from other letter, *o*? *onhrope, e* indistinct.   17. *gecyged.*
In the MS. *ged* is crossed out, and *dd* written over it.

---

7. *lacrimis*, MS. *lacrimo*; but *o* underdotted, and *is* written over it.
13. *suscipiantur*, MS. *suspiciantur*.   14. *hospes*, MS. *hos spes*.   *suscepistis*,
MS. *suscepistist*, but the latter *t* underdotted.   16. *peregrinis*, MS. *peregrinus*.

oððe fram [d.] gebroðrum [d.] mid ealre [e.] þenunga [e.]   soðre
vel   a   fratribus :   cum omni   officio kari-
lufe [a.] 7 ærest [b.] hi gebidan [a.] eac samod[c.] 7 swa hi beon[d.]
tatis ; Et primitus   horent   pariter :   et   sic sibi
gefærlæhtc [d.] on sibbe þæt [a.] na sig geboden sibbe   cost
socientur   in pace ;   Quod   pacis   osculum
[a.]   buton þam foresædan gebeda   for deoflum [f.]
non offeratur ;   nisi   oratione   premissa.   propter
swicuncgum [f.]   [f.]   [c.] on ðære sylfan gretinge [c.]
5 *illusiones   diabolicas ; In ipsa   autem   salutatione :*
ælc [b.] si [a.] gegearcod ei him   mæð   eallum [e.] aweg
omnis   exibeatur.   humanitas ;   Omnibus
oððe cumende [e.] [f.] gewitendum [f.] cuman sit [g.] ahyltum
venientibus   sive discedentibus hospitibus.   inclinato
heafde [g.] [h.]   [h.]   eallum lichaman on corðan [k.]
capite.   vel prostrato omni   corpore ;   in   terram
[b.] crist on [c.] heom si gebeden [a.] se ðe bið underfangen
christus in   eis   adoretur :   Qui et suscipitur ;
underfangenum [b.] [i.] cuman [g.] beon [a.] gelædde [c.]
10 *Susceptis   hospites   ducantur   ad*
to gebede 7 siððan [h.] 7 sitte [c.]   ealdor   [h.]
orationem. et   postea   sedeat   cum eis prior aut cui
[h.]   [h.] si geræd [a.] ætforan þam cuman sco [c.]
jusserit ipse ; | legatur   coram   ospite   lex (151 b.)
godcunde lage [c.] þæt [d.] beon getrymede   [e.] 7 æfter þisan
divina   ut edificetur   et post
     ælc [f.] him gearcod   mæð [f.]   [h.] fæsten fram ealdre
hec omnis   ei exhibeatur humanitas ; jejunium   a   priore
si tobroden for [d.] cuman [d.] buton wenunga [f.] healic [g.]
15 *frangatur propter hospitem :   nisi   forte   preci-*
dæg [c.] sig [g.] fæstenes se na mage beon * gewæmned [c.]
puus   sit dies jejunii qui non possit   violari ; Fratres
[b.]   [d.] gewunan fæstena [e.]   fylian   wæter [c.]
autem : consuetudinibus jejuniorum prosequantur ; Aquam in

---

6. *ei*, Latin in glossator's hand, under *him. mað*, see note. *aweg* belongs
to *gewitendum* in l. 7.   7. *sit*, Latin, or a misreading for *siy*, belonging
to *si gebeden* (l. 9).   10. [c.] or [e.]?   12. [c.] not clear.   14. [h.]?
or [k.]? or *hc*=*autem*?   16. *gewæmned*, read *gewæmmed.*

---

9. *adoretur*, MS. *adorietur. suscipitur*, MS. *suspicitur.*   10. *Susceptis*
in the MS. (read *suscepti*); a very old mistake, which has been glossed
accordingly.   14. *jejunium*, MS. *junium.*   15, 16. *precipuus*, MS. *precipius.*

on handum [d.] [b.] [a.]   cumum   sýlle [a.]   fete [g.]   [f.]
manibus   *abba*   *hospitibus*   *det ;*   *Pedes*   *vero*

[h.]   eallum cuman ge se abbod ge eall seo gæderunga [k.]
hospitibus   *omnibus*   *tam abba*   *quam*   *cuncta*

[k.]   þwea [e.]   þam geþwagenum [c.]   þis fers   [b.]
congregatio   *lavet ;*   *Quibus lotis :*   *hunc*   *versum*

hi seccan we underfengan   on midewcardan
dicant.   *suscepimus*   *deus misericordiam tuam in*   *medio*

[f.] þearfena 7 * eall þeodscipa swýðest underfangenia
templi tui ; Pauperum et *peregrinorum maxime susceptionum* 5

giman [h.]   hohfullice [a.]   si gegearcod forðam   on heom
cura   *sollicitate*   *exhibeatur.*   *quia in*   *ipsis*

swiðor [k.]   [g.]   sodes [a.]   bið   [h.]
magis   *christus suscipitur ;*   *Nam*   *divitum terror :*

[b.] him sýlfan [n.]   [a.]   wurðment ciceua [b.] þæs abbodes 7
ipse   *sibi*   *exigit honorem ; coquina*   *abbatis*   et

cuman [d.] ofer [c.] hig [e.] sig [a.]   7 ongewissum tidum ofer
ospitum   *super*   *se sit :*   *ut*   *incertis*   *horis*

[h.] becumenlice [h.]   [h.]   þam þe næfre ne ateriað   [k.]
supervenientes   *hospites*   *qui numquam*   *desunt* 10

[l.] minstre þæt hina gedræsan gebroðra on þa cicenan [c.]
monasterio :   *non*   *inquietent*   *fratres ; In*   *quam*

[c.]   to eare [d.]   ingan [a.]   twegen [b.]   gebroðra
coquinam   *ad*   *annum*   *ingrediantur*   *duo*   *fratres :*

þa [c.] sýlfum þenunge [g.]   [g.]   [f.] bene   [e.]
qui   *ipsum*   *officium*   *bene*   *impleant.*

þam [k.] behofiað þæt hi helpan [k.]   beon [h.] geþenode [l.]
quibus   *ut*   *indigent solacia*   *ministrentur.*   *ut*

buton ælcere [m.] ceorunge [m.] þæt hi [l.] þeowian. [n.] [o.]
absque murmuratione   *serviant ;*   et *iterum* 15

þonne hi habbað læssan * gemýsgunge [t.]   [t.]   [s.]
quando   *occupationem*   *minorem*   *habent :*

7 hi utgan [n.] þar [p.] þar [q.] bið [p.] beboden on
exeant   *ubi*   *eis*   *imperatur*   *in*

---

5. *eall þeodscipa = eallþeodscipa*, glossed as if the lemma were *peregrina-tionum.*   7. Over *suscipitur* there is a ' paving' letter, which is either two *f*'s above each other, or *f* over *x*.   10. *ateriað*, a dot or a small *c* over *er* ; possibly an *o*, making it into *ateoriað.*   13. *bene*, copied from the Latin. 16. *gemýsgunge*, read *gebýsgunge.*

---

7. *suscipitur*, MS. *suspicitur.*   9. *horis*, MS. *horet*, but *et* underdotted, and *is* written over it.

---

weorce 7 na þæt an [c.]   [c.]   on heom [e.] ah on eallum [c.]
opera ;   Et   non solum   in ipsis: sed in omni-

þenungum   [e.]   mýnstres [b.]   sig [a.] þeos foresceawunga [b.]
bus   officiis mona | sterii ista   sit   considerat'o.   (152 a.)

þæt þonne hi behofiað   [i.]   helpas   beon befæste
ut   quando   indigent :   solacia   accommodentur eis :

[k.]   [l.]   þonne hi [n.] æmtiað   [n.]   7 hi hirsumiað bebo-
et iterum   quando   vacant   obediant   imper-

denum   [c.]   [d.]   [e.]   cumena [f.]   habbe betælht hus   [b.]
5 *anti; Item et cellam   hospitum   abeat   asignatam   frater.*

þæs   sawle   godes [h.]   ege [h.]   he geahnige   þar beon
cuius   anima   timor   dei   possidet ;   ubi sint

bedreaf   genihtsumlice [m.]   [n.]   [n.] fram wissum mannum
lecti strati   sufficienter.   et domus dei   a   sapientibus

wislice   7 si geþenode [m.]   cuman   [b.] ' þam þe na bið
sapienter   amministretur ;   Hospitibus autem cui non pre-

bebeden   nateshwon na sigefærlæht ne ne sig   gesprecan
cipitur :   nullatenus   societur   neque   conloquatur.

7 gif he agen   cýmð   oððc he gesihð gegrettum [l.] swa
10 *sed et si   obviaverit   aut   viderit :   salutatis   humi-*

swa hit [m.] is   her bufan gesæd [m.]   gebedenra [k.]
liter   quod dictum   est :   et petita

bletsunga [k.]   ah he ga [i.]   [n.]   [p.]   na beon alifæd
benedictione   pertranseat   dicens sibi   non   licere

samod spræcon mid cuman
conloqui   cum hospite.

VT NON DEBEAT MONACHUS LITTERAS VEL ELOGIAS

15   SUSCIPERE.   (CAP. LIV.)

naht   na si alifed þam   nafram his magum
Nullatenus   liceat   monacho neque   a parentibus suis:

nafrom ænigum   mannan   heom betweona
neque quoquam hominum : nec sibi   invicem litteras. eulogias :

oððc ænige   lac   underfon oððe sýllan buton bebode
vel quelibet munuscula accipere   aut   dare   sine precepto

---

3. *accommodentur,* MS. *accommedentur.*   6. *anima,* MS. *animor.*
sint, added by glossator.   8. *sapienter,* MS. *sipicnter.   hospitibus,* MS.
hospotibus.   10. *obviaverit, ve* above line.   15. *suscipere,* MS. *suscipe.*
18. *munuscula,* MS. *munusculpa.*

þæs abbodes þæt gif biö eac swýlce fram his 　magum
　abbatis.　　　Quod　　si　　etiam　　a　　parentibus suis

him ænig þinc gesend　　　　he na gedýrstlæce underfon þæt
ei quicquam directum fuerit :　non presumat suscipere illud. nisi

ærest buton hit beo ge·æd þam abbode þæt gif he hæd
prius　indicatum　fuerit　abbati ;　Quod si　juserit

beon underfangen　　　sig on * anfealde þam þe he þæt
. suscipi.　in abbatis　sit　potestate.　cui　illud

hæt　sýllan　7 he na si gedræfed　þam þe hit biö
jubead dare :　et　non contristetur frater　cui　forte 5

gesent　　þæt na si geseald intingu þam deofle se öe ge-
directum fuerat　ut non detur　occasio　diabolo ;　Quia

dýrstlæcö　elles　　　　regolicere　stire　he
(152 b.)　autem　aliter　|　presumserit　discipline　regulari sub-
underfon
jaceat ;

be hrægel þenum 7 scceoh þenum gebroöra
DE VESTIARIIS ET CALCIARIIS FRATRUM. (CAP. LV.)

[b.] reaf　[c.]　[d.] æfter stowa [e.] gehwýlcuýsse [d.] þær
Vestimenta fratribus secundum locorum　qualitatem　10

þær hi eardiaö　　　　beon gesealde forÖam on cealdum
ubi abitant. vel aerum temperiem　dentur.　quia in frigidis

eardum　[l.]　swýÖor þe behofaö on wærmum [n.]　læs　[a.]
regionibus amplius indigetur. in　calidis vero minus ; Haec

þeos foresceawung [a.]　mid þam abbude is　[a.]　[b.]
ergo consideratio :　penes abbatem est ;　Nos　tamen

on medenlicum stowum [c.] genihtsumian [c.]　[c.]　munecum
mediocribus　locis　sufficere　credimus monachis

geond ænlepige [f.] * culam 7　tonican　* culam on wintre
per　singulos　cucullam et　tonicam ; Cucullam in hieme 15

þicce [h.]　on sumere þinne [k.]　oööe　ealdnesse　7
; villosam.　in　estate　puram.　aut　vetustatem :　et

scapularian　for　weorcum [o.] * fiandreaf [b.]　fota
scapulare　propter　opera ;　Indumenta　pedum.

3. hæd, d or t.　4. anfealde, read anwealde.　13. foresceawung,f might be r.　15. culam, read culan (twice).　17. flandreaf, see note.

5. jubead dare, MS. jube ad dare.　9. LV. In the MS. this is found before vestimenta.　9. CALCIARIIS, MS. CALCIARIS.　11. temperiem, MS. temperium.　16. vetustatem, MS. vetustantem.　The other texts have vetustam for which vetusta(n)tem is an old mistake, having been glossed as though a substantive.

---

soccas 7 hosan [c.]   þara þinga   eallra be bleo
pedules et   *caligas; De quarum rerum omnino de colore*

ne oððe gretnýsse [d.] na   cidan   [b.]   ah swa swilce
aut   grossitudine non causentur monachi.   sed quales

swa magan beon gefundene   [f.]   on scira [h.] on þam þe hi
*   inveniri possunt   in provincia   qua habi-*

wuniað oððe swa hwæt swa waclicor [m.] beon wiðmetene mæg
tant.   aut   quod   vilius   comparari   potest;

   [c.]   [b.]   be gemete   foresceawige þæt na beon [e.]
5 *Abbas* autem *de mensura   prevideat   ut non   sint*

gescýrte þa sýlfan   reaf   brucendas hi ah gemetlice
curta   ipsa   vestimenta utentibus. ea sed mensurata;

nimende niwe þa ealdan   [b.] hi agifan on andwerdum to
Accipientes nova   vetera   semper reddant in presenti loco re-

geleohgenne   on rægel huse   for   þearfan genoh bið
ponenda   in   vestiario.   propter pauperes; Sufficit

   [b.]   munece twa   tunican 7   twa   cuflan habban
enim monacho duos tonicas. et   duas cucullas habere

   for   nihtum   7   for   þweale þæt þæt
10 *propter   noctes.   et   propter lavationem. Jam quod*

   to lafe bið   beon ofadon   [a.]   7   meon
supra fuerit superfluum est. amputare decet; Et pedules:

   7 swa hwæt swa his   eald   [b.] 7 hi agildan þonne
et   quodcumque est retustum: semper   reddant

hi underfoð þonne hi underfað niwe   . rec þas þa þa
*   dum | accipiunt novum; Femuralia hi qui in* (153 a.)

   [f.] beoð asende on hrægelhuse niman þa hi gecýrrende
via diriguntur de vestiario accipiant qui revertentes

geþwagenu þara agenbringan [b.] cuflan [a.] 7 tonican [c.]
15   *lota ibi restituant;   Cuculle et   tonice*

beon oðerhwilen sýnd gewnnede sunt habban æthwigan beteran
sint aliquanto   solito   quas habent modice meliores;

---

8. *geleohgenne*, h above line. 13. *underfoð* (a dittographical gloss to *accipiunt*), o or a! . rec, one letter not clear, probably b; this would make it *brec*. 15. *geþwagenum*, w corr. from r. *cuflan*, see note. 16. *sunt* in hand of glossator.

---

1. *colore*, MS. *calore*. *de?* cf. note to 10. 7. 2. *aut*, MS. *uit*. *causentur*, MS. *causenter*, with a u over the *er*. 7. *Accipientes*, MS. *Acoipiens*. *loco* in none of the other texts; the MS. has *locc*. 11. *decet*, MS. *dedet*. 13. *dum*, the MS. has *divine dum*. *novum*, MS. *novem*, but e corr. into u. 16. *solito*, MS. *solitis*.

*þamman utgangende   þoune hi underfon of hrægelhuse
quas   *exeuntes*   *in viam*   *accipiant*   *de vestiario.*

7 gecýrrende 7 hi agenbringan bedreaf   [b.]   bedda geniht-
et   *revertentes restituant ;*   *Stramenta* autem *lectorum : suf-*

sumiað [e.]   7 hwitel 7 wesline 7 heafudrægel þa   bed
ficiant matta et *sagum.*   *lena*   et *capitulæ.*   *Que tamen lecta*

ofer rædlice [a.]   sind to smeagenne   for   weorc
frequenter ab abbate   *scrutanda*   *sunt : propter* opus

sindor   þæt hine si gemett 7 gif ænigum   gett   býð
peculiare   *ne inveniatur ;*   *Et si   cui   inventum fuerit* 5

fram þam abbude   he ne underfehð þære healicosta stire [b.]
quod   ab   abbate non acceperit : gravissime   discipline

he underþeodde 7 þæt sig þisne leahtor sinderlices *grimpionge
subjaceat ;   et *ut hoc vitium peculiare   radicitus*

ofadon beon gesealde [c.]   [b.]   þa þe sýnd nýdbehefe
amputetur ; Dentur ab abbate omnia que sunt necessaria.

þæt is cufle [g.] tanecan [h.] meon hosan earmslife   sex
id est cuculla.   tonica.   pedules. calige. bracile. cultellus.

græf [m.] nædl [u.] mýshrægel [p.] wexbreda [q.] þæt ælc [q.]
gravium.   acus.   mappula.   tabule.   ut   omnis 10

si gefýrsod nepearfnesse beladung [q.] from þam [c.]   [c.]
auferatur necessitatis. excusatio ; A quo tamen abbate

[b.] [a.] si foresceawod se   cwýde   dæda þæra apostola
semper   consideretur   illa sententia actuum apostolorum :

for þam þe wæs *geald ænlepium beðam þe gehwýlcum [i.]
quia   dabatur   singulis prout   cuique

neod weorc   7 [a.] se [a.] foresceawige   untrum
opus   erat ; Ita et abba   consideret   infirmitates

beþýrfendra   na   ýselue   wýllan   niðfulra. andigendra
indigentium. non malam voluntatem invidentium ; 15

1. *þamman,* probably *þa niman,* as gloss to *accipiant.*   7. *grimpionge,*
read *grundlonge.*   9. *tanecan,* a corr. from *o?* probably it was intended
to be corrected into *u.*   11. *nepearfnesse,* for *nedpearfnesse.*   13. *yeald,*
read *geseald*   14. *se* over *et;* I think it is meant for *se (abbod)* over *abba.*
untrum for *untrumnessa.*

2. *revertentes,* MS. *reverentes.*   5. *inventum,* the MS. has *inventa, ŭ*
written over *a,* and after that *inve* crossed out.   6. Second *b* of *abbate* above
line.   7. The MS. has *peculiares.* The other texts have partly *peculiaris,*
partly *peculiare,* which latter would seem to be right from a Latin stand-
point; but the gloss points to a genitive.   11. *necessitatis,* MS. *necestatis.*
15. *malam,* MS. *malum.*

on   eallum   [b.]   his domum   [e.]   godes   edlean
In   omnibus   tamen   judiciis   suis;   dei   retributionem
he þence
cogitet;

DE MENSA ABBATIS.   (CAP. LVI.) | (153 b.)

. . nisan [c.]   mid ælþeodigum   7   [e.] cuman * sýð
MENSA   ABBATIS   CUM   PEREGRINIS   ET   HOSPITIBUS   *sit*
simble   swa of swa   þeahhwæðere   læs [i.]   sint [g.]   [h.] gýstes
5 *semper;   Quoties   tamen   minus   sint   hospites:*
ða þa he wile of gebroþrum [b.] geclýpian   his   sig
quos vult   de   fratrilus   vocare   in   ipsius   sit
on * anfealdre ealdres [b.]   ænne oððe twegen   æfre   mid
potestate;   Seniores tamen   unum   aut   duos   semper   cum
gebroðrum to forlætene   for   lare oððe stire
fratribus   dimittendum propter   disciplinam;

DE ARTIFICIBUS MONASTERII.   (CAP. LVII.)

* cræfican [b.] gif sind on   mýnstre   mid   ealre eadmod-
10 ARTIFICES   SI SUNT IN MONASTERIO: CUM   OMNI   *humili-*
nesse hi don   þa sýlfan cræftas   gif   geþafað   se abbud
tate   faciant   ipsas artes.   si   permiserit   abba;
þæt [a.] gif bið ænig [a.] [b.]   upahafan [a.] for ingehide
Quod   si aliquis   ex eis   extollitur   pro scientia
his cræftes   þeah þe he beogæsæwen sum þinc þurhteon
artis   sue eo   quod videatur   aliquid   conferre
on minstre þes swýlce si upahræred fram þam sýlfan cræfte
monasterio.   hic talis   erigatur   ab   ipsa   arte
7 oðer siðan þurh hine   he na fare buton wennnge geead-
15 *et   denuo   per eam   non transeat. nisi   forte   humi-*
mettum   [p.]   hatte gif hwæt [a.]   [b.] of weorcum
liato   ei iterum abba jubeat;   Si   quid   vero ex operibus

---

4. Erasure before . . . *nisan,* read *misin. sýð,* read *sýy* or *býð.*   5. *of,*
for *oft.*   7. *anfealdre,* read *anwealde.*   10. Read *cræfticau.*   13. *beo-*
gæsæwen, sæ under the rest, a contemporary addition.

---

3. LVI. in the MS. before *mensa,* in line 4.   6. *ipsius,* MS. *ipsis.*
8. *dimittendum,* MS. *dimittendo.*   The word *procuret* of the other texts
completing ours is omitted in the MS.   9. ARTIFICIBUS, MS. ARTICIBUS.
LVII before *Artifices* in l. 10.   12. *ex eis* in glossator's handwriting.

wyrhtena   is   to   sillanne   warnian   hi   sylfe   þurh
artificum   venundandum   est ;   videant   ipsi   per

ðara handa þe sýnd to sýllanne   þæt hina gedýrstlæcan
quorum   manus transigenda sunt   ne aliquam

ænig facen   [k.]   on gebringan   hi   gemunon   æfre
fraudem   presumant   inferre.   Memorentur   semper

                þæt hine   [e.]   [f.] þe hi   on lichaman
annanie. et saphire   ne forte mortem   quam   illi in corpore

þolodan [f.]   þas   [h.]   oððe ealle   ænig facen   [l.]   of
pertulerunt: hanc   isti   vel   omnes qui aliquam fraudem de 5

þingum   mýustres   þaðedoþ   [d.]   þolian   [c.]   on
rebus ;   monasterii   fecerint   in   anima   patiantur ;   In

þam sýlfum   [b.]   sceattum ne undersmuge   gitsunge   ýfel
ipsis   autem   pretiis   non   subripiat avaritie malum.

ah   sige   æthwega   waclicor   seald   þonne   fram   oðrum
sed   semper aliquantu'um   vilius   detur   quam   ab   aliis

woruldlicum þingum þæt sig eallum gewuldrod gode
secularibus | ut in omnibus glorificetur deus ;

(154 a.)

DE DISCIPLINA SUSCIPIENDORUM FRATRUM. (CAP. LVIII.)   10

niwan [f.] cumenne ænig to gecýrrednesse ne si him eðelic [b.]
NOVITER VENIENS QUIS AD CONVERSIONEM. non   ei   facilis

forgifen in færeld [c.] ac [i.] swa swa sæde   [i.]   [k.]fandiað
tribuatur   ingressus.   sed sicut ait :   apostolus.   probate

gastes gif hi of gode sind [m.]   [a.]   cumende gif he þurh-
spiritus si   ex   deo   sunt.   Ergo si veniens persevera-

wunað cnuciende 7 gif he on gebrohtum teonum 7 unfrodnýssa
verit   pulsans et inlatas   sibi injurias.   et difficultatem

inagan   [l.] æfter feowerdagum   [m.]   [m.] 7 bið
ingressus   post   quattuor   aut quinque   dies   15

gesawen [n.]   [d.] geþýldelice beran 7 þurhwunian his bene [t.]
visus   fuerit patienter portare. et persistere   petitioni

[q.] [m.] si forgifeu in agan in færeld   [r.] on huse mid-
sue : annuatur   ei   ingressus :   et sit in cella hos-

9. *gode, g* partly erased, instead of *c*, which was most likely intended to be erased.

1. *ipsi*, added by glossator. 10. SUSCIPIENDORUM FRATRUM, MS. AD S. F., which may also indicate that AD SUSCIPIENDOS FRATRES was in the original. LVIII in the MS. before *Noviter*. 12. *ait*, MS. *ut*. 13. *veniens*, MS. *inveniens*.

---

cumendre on feawum dagum sýððan [e.] [b.] sig on huse
pitum paucis diebus; Postea autem sit in cella

nicnmendra þær he smæge [g.] 7 he ete 7 he slæpe [i] [a.]
novitiorum: ubi meditetur et manducet et dormiat ;

[a.] ealdor him [b.] swilc 7 si betæhte se sig [d.] gelimlic [e.]
Et senior ei talis deputetur : quia aptus

    [f.] to gestiynenne [f.] sauwla [g.] [h.] [i.] ofer [i.] him ne [l.]
sit ad lucrandas animas : qui super eum

eallunga [k.] geornlice si begeme 7 hohful [m.]
5   *omnino curiose intendat ; et sollicitus sit. revera deum*

    [q.] [r.] to godes weorce to gehýrsumnesse [t.]
querit si solicitus est ad opus dei : ad oboedientiam :

7 to hospa beon gebodenne ealra heardnessa [c.] [c.] 7
ad obyrobria ; Predicentur ei omnia dura. et

stiðnissa [d.] þurh þæt he si gefaren to gode [a.] 7 gif he behæt
asyera per que itur ad deum ; Et si promiserit

be his staþolfæstnessa [c.] [c.] anrædnessa æfter twegra
de stabilitate sua persererentiam : post du-

monðum [d.] onbrine [a.] si geræd [b.] him [c.] þes
1c *orum mensium circulum legatur cui hec*

regol be endebýrdnessa [d.] 7 si geæd him efne her is
regula per ordinem : et dicatur ei ecce lex :

under þære þeowian þu wilt gif [c.] þu miht [i.] gehealdan [k.]
sub qua militare vis ; Si potes obserrare

infaran gif þu na miht [n.] [m.] [q.] frige [p] aweggewit
ingredere. si vero non potes. liber discede ;

gif [e.] þa git [f.] he stint þonne *he* si gelæd on þam fore-
Si adhuc steterit. tunc | Cucatur in supra- (154 b.)

sædan [c.] huse [c.] nicumenra 7 he si fandod [q.]
15 *dictam cellam novitiorum: et iterum prcbetur*

on eallum geþýlde 7 æfter sýx monða [c.] embrine 7 si ofor-
in omni patientia ; Et post sex mensium circulum rele-

ræd him regol [c.] þæt he wite to þan ingange [g.] 7 gif
gatur ei regula, ut sciat ad quod ingreditur ; Et si

---

5. *si* (Latin), *i* corr. from *e*.   10. *on brine*, read *embrine*.   14. Second *he*
not clear.   15. *fandod* stands so close upon margin that something before
it may have been cut away.

---

2. *meditetur*, MS. *medicetur*.   5. *rerera deum querit*, MS. *rererendum
quem*.   8. *per que itur*, MS. *persequentur*.   13. *discede*, MS. *disscede*.
14. *ducatur*, *d* cut away.   15. The contraction for *pre* stands over *pro*
of *probetur* in glossator's hand as if he wished to correct it thus.

he þa git stýnt   eft   si geræd him
adhuc stat: *post quattuor menses iterum. legatur ei*

se ýlca regol   7 gif * habban * ðretioðinge   he be
eadem regula; Et si habita   secum   deliberatione pro-

hæt   hene ealle þinc gehealdan   7   ealle bebeodenlice
miserit   se   omnia   custodire: et cuncta   sibi

þinc   7 gehealdan 7 he si underfangen on gegæderunge
imperata   servare;   tunc suscipiatur in congregatione

witende under lage regolas   * gescendne   7 þæt ne sig
sciens   se sub lege   regule constitutum: et   quod   5

     gelýfed   utgan of minstre   nato swýran
ei ex illa die non   liceat egredi de monasterio nec   collum

sceacan under geoce regoles þæt si under swa langsumum
excutere de sub jugo regule: quam   sub tam morosa

frigedome gelifed   wið sacan oððe underfon se underfonlica
deliberatione. licuit ei excusare: aut suscipere. Suscipiendus

[b.] on cýrican [a.] toforan eallum gebroðrum behate be his
autem in oratorio: coram   omnibus: promittat de

staðolfæstnessa [f.] 7 drohtnunge heora· þeowa 7 gehýrsum-
stabilitate   sua. et conversatione morum suorum: et oboedien- 10

nesse toforan gode 7 his halgum   þæt gif he deþ æt
tia   coram   deo et   sanctis eius: ut si ali-

sumum cýrre elles [q.]   [o.]   hine sýlfne fordemed
quando · aliter fecerit: a   deo   se damnandum

[b.] he wite hwæne he gebýsmrige be þam his behate [c.] [c.]
sciat   quem   irridet;   De qua   promissione sua

he do [a.] [b.] gewrit [d.] 7 naman halgena þare lafe þe sind
faciat   petitionem ad   nomen sanctorum   quorum re-

halidomas þara sind 7 þæs andweardes abbodes þæt gewrite
liquie   ibi sunt: et   abbatis presentis; Quam petitionem 15

mid his agenre hand he awrite oððe soðes gif he na can
manu sua scribat;   aut certe si non scit

stafas oðer fram him [h.] gebeden [g.] write 7 se nicumena [b.]
litteras. alter ab eo   rogatus   scribat; Et   ille novitius

---

2. *habban ðretioðinge,* see note.   5. *gescendne,* read *gesætne?*   6. *nato,*
to is part of gloss to *excutere* in l. 7.   7. *regoles, o* corr. from *u* contemporarily.
8. *frigedome,* as if the lemma were *liberatione?*

---

4. *imperata,* MS. *imperate.*   5. *sciens,* MS. *siens. sub* not found in the
MS., but necessitated by the gloss.   6. *illa,* MS. *illi.*   8. *excusare,* MS.
excusere.   10. MS. *conversione.*   12. *se,* MS. *sed.*   16. *scit,* omitted
by Latin scribe.

mearce   do   7 mid his handa hit ofor þam weofode
signum faciat: et   *manu sua eam   super   altare*
he lecge þæt gewrit þonne he læigd agenne se nicumena sona
ponat ;   Quam dam posuerit. | *incipiat ipse novitius mox* (155 a.)
þis fers :   [b.]   [c.]   [c.]   æfter þinre [d.]   spræce
hunc   versum ; Suscipe me, domine   secundum   *eloquium*

[d.]   7 ic libbe na gescýnd þu me   fram minre anbidunge
tuum et *vivam :* et *ne   confundas   me ab   expectatione*

[h.]   þæt   fers   eall seo gæderung þriddan siðan
5 *mea ;   Quem   versum   omnis congregatio   tertio respondeat*
to geþcodenne mid   [f.]   [b.] se nicumena broðor [c.]   si
adjungentes. gloria patri ; Tunc ipse frater novitius proster-
apreht ænlepigra [d.] fotum   þæt hi biddan for him   [a.]
natur   singulorum   pedibus   ut   orent   pro eo ; Etiam
of þære tide   on gegæderunge he si geteld gif he hwýlce
ex illa   hora in congregatione   reputetur. Res si quas
þinc hæfð þæt heiaspendæ [c.] ær þearfum [d.] oððe geworden
habet :   aut   eroget   prius   pauperibus.   aut   facta
simbollice   sýlene   he forgife minstre   [k.]   him sýlfum
10 *solempniter donatione conferat monasterio. nihil   sibi*
na healdende of eallum witodlice se ðc of þam dæge [q.] neto
reservans   ex omnibus. quippe   qui ex   illa   die nec
*ontigenum lichaman *andfealde wite sana [b.]   on cýrican
proprii   corporis potestatem sciat; Mox   ergo in oratorio
he si unscrýd agenum þingan Mid þam þe wælgescrýd [c.]   7
exuatur   rebus propriis   quibus   vestitus est : et
he si gescrid mid þingum minstres þa [b.]   reaf [b.]
induatur   rebus monasterii ;   Illa   autem   vestimenta
mid þam þe he wæs unscrid   beon gelogodre on rægelhuse
15   *quibus exutus   est   reponantur   in vestiario*
to gehealdenna æt suman cýrre tihtendum deofle gif he þafe
conservanda :   ut si aliquando suadente diabolo   consen-
þafað þæt he utga of   minstre   unscrýd
serit,   ut egrediatur de monasterio quod absit : tunc exutus

---

8. *of,* o crossed, perhaps corrected from *e.*   11. *neto,* see note.   12. *onti-*
genum, see note. *andfealde,* read *anwealde.*   15. *gelogodre,* see note.
16, 17. *gif he þafe þafað,* read *gif he þafað.*

---

8. *quas,* MS. *quod.*   13. *exuatur rebus,* MS. *exuaturibus.*   14. *Illa,*
MS. *Illi.*

þingum   [r.]   he si ut adræfed   þæt   þchhwæþere
rebus   monasterii   proiciatur ;   Illam   tamen

gewrit [c.] his þæt he nam uppan [f.] þan weofode [f.] [g.]
petitionem eius   quam   super   altari   abbas

underfond he na underfo [h.]   ac hit si gehealden
tulit   non recipiat   sed in monasterio   reservetur ;

DE FILIIS NOBILIUM AUT PAUPERUM QUI OFFERUNTUR.

(CAP. LVIIII.)   5

gif hwa [d.] [b.] of æðelborenum offrað ł dat his *carn
SI QUIS   FORTE DE NOBILIBUS   *offert   filium   suum*

gode on   minster   gif he þæt sylfe cild on iunre ylde
(155 b.) *deo in   monasterio : si   ipse   puer | minori*

is his magas   don   gewritt swa swa we bufan
aetate est. parentes eius faciant petitionem quam supra

             mid   ofrunge   þæt   gewrit   hand
diximus. et cum oblatione ipsam petitionem. et manum

cildes 7 he be fealde on weofodsceatan
pueri   involvant in   palla   altaris. et sic eum 10

7 hi geofrian of heora æhtum   oððe on andweardum
offerant ; De   rebus   autem suis : aut in presenti

gewrite hi behatað under aðsware þæt hi næfre ne þurh
petitionem promittant sub jurejurando ;   quia numquam

hi sylfe   ne þurh gewenedne had ne mid nanum
per se : numquam per suffectam personam :   nec quo-

gemett him æt ænigon cirre æni þinc syllan oððe hi
libet modo   ei   aliquando aliquit dent. nec tri-

forgifan intingan to habbenne oððe soþes   þæt don
*buant occasione*m *habendi ; Vel certe si hoc facere* 15

gif hi nellað 7 ænigþincg offrian 7 hi wyllað to ælmæssan
noluerint : et   quid   offerre voluerint in elemosina

on minstre for heora mede hi don of þingum þa þe hi
monasterio pro mercede sua : faciant ex rebus quas

willað syllan mynstre.   sylene   gehealdenum
dare volunt monasterio donationem.   reservato

2, 3. *nam*, gloss to *tulit* (l. 3) ; *underfond*, originally marginal note to *he underfo*? 6. *t dat* in hand of glossator. *earn*, a letter blotted before it; read *bearn*. 13. *gewenedne*, see note. 14. *gemett* or *gemete*?

4. MS. OFFERUNT DE F. N. A. P. QUI. 6. SI, erasure between S and I. *nobilibus*, second *i* corrected from *u* by erasure. 7. *in* omitted by Latin scribe. 12. MS. *promittat*. 13. *suffectam*, see note. 18. *donationem*, *m* corrected from two other letters.

H 2

him sýlfan   swa gif hi willað   landare   7 beon * behýdda
sibi.   si ita   voluerint,   usufructuario ;   Atque ita

ealle þinc   * dedre   þæt ænig to hopa na belife þam cilde
*omnia   obstruant*ur   *ut   nulla suspicio remaneat   puero*

þurh   þa bepæhð losian he mage þæt fcor sig þæt mid afun-
per quam deceptus perire possit   quod absit ;   quod experi-

dennesse welleorniaþ swa gelice soðlice swýlce þa þearflicran
mento   didicimus ;   Similiter   autem :   et pauperiores

don   gif   mid ealle hi naht nabbað   anfealdlice
5 *faciant ; Si qui vero   ex toto   nihil habent :   simpliciter*

gewrit   hidon   mid ofrunge 7 hi ofriað heora cildra ætforan
petitionem faciant. et oblationem   offerant filium suum coram

gewitnessum
testibus ;

DE SACERDOTIBUS QUI VOLUERINT IN MONASTERIIS HABITARE.
(CAP. LX.)

gif hwilc be endebýrdnesse * mæssepreostrum on   minstre
10 *Si   QUIS DE   ORDINE   SACERDOTUM   in monasterium   se*

beon underfangen   [e.]   [a.] ne sig   [b.]   hrædlice
suscipi   rogaverit :   non   quidem | ei citius

geþafod   [b.] gif eallunga he þurhwunað   [c.] on þissere
assentiant ; Tamen si omnino   perstiterit. in hac suppli-

halsunge he wite ealle lare regules þeahfæstnýsse to healdenne
catione.   sciat   se omnem regule   disciplinam   servaturum ;

nene ænig þinc   si forgifen þæt hesig swa swa hit awriten
Nec   aliquid ei relaxabitur ut   sit   sicut   scriptum

is eala þu freond to hwam comeþu sý geunnen him
15 *est ;   Amice.   ad quod renisti ; Concedatur   ei tamen*

æfter þam abbote standan   7   bletsian oððe mæssen healden
post   abbatem   stare.   et benedicere aut missas   tenere.

gif [b.]   hæt [g.] hi him * hellas [a.]   nateshwon he nege-
si tamen   jusserit   ei abba ; Sin alias   nullatenus   pre-

___

1, 2. *behýdda ealle þinc dedre, behýdda* and *dedre* probably belong together, and read, *behýddedre,* thus eliminating the consequences of a partial ditto-graphy ; see p. 98. 15.   4. *welleorniaþ,* i. e. *we leorniaþ.*   10. *mæsse-preostrum,* read *mæssepreostra* ; see note.   13. *þeahfæstnýsse,* read *þeaw-fæstnysse,* *h* corrected from other letter, possibly *w.*   17. *hellas,* read *he elles.*

___

1. *voluerint, n* corr. from *ti.*   6. *offerant,* MS. *offreat.*   8. MS. VOLERINT.   11. *ei citius,* MS. *excitius.*

dȳrstlǣce ænig þing [d.] hine　regolicere　stire　underþeodne
sumat　aliqua '　sciens　se discipline regulari　subditum :

7 swiðor eadmodnesse　bȳsna　eallum he sȳlle 7 gif wenunge
et magis　humilitatis　exempla omnibus　det ; Et si　forte

hades hadunge　oððe　æniges þinges　　　intingan　bið　on
ordinationis　aut　alicujus　rei　causa　fuerit in

minstre　þa stowe þæne stȳde 7 he begime on þære þe he
monasterio.　illum　locum　attendat :　quando

inferde　[c.]　[c.] on minstre [d.]　ne þæne se þe　for
ingressus　est　in monasterium non illum qui ei pro 5

arwȳrðnesse preosthades þæs geunnen is　preosta　gif
reverentia　sacerdotii　concessus　est ; Clericorum autem si

hwylce　þære ȳlcan　gewihunge on minstre beon gefærlæhte
qui　eodem　desiderio　monasterio　sociari

willað　on medomlicere stowe　[a.]　[c.] 7 hi　[d.]
voluerint :　loco　mediocri　collocentur.　et　ipsi

[f.]　gif hi behatað　behealdsumnesse regoles oððe agenre
tamen si　promittunt　de observatione　regule vel propria

staþolfæstnessa :
stabilitate ;　　　　　　　　　　　　　　　　　10

De monachiis peregrinis. (Cap. LXI.)

gif ænig　　　of ælþeodigum mannum of fȳrlænum scirum
Si quis monachus　peregrinus　de longinquis

becimð　gif forcuman　he wile wunian　on
provinciis supervenerit : si pro hospite voluerit habitare in

minstre　7　gepæf　7 he bið on gewunan　[u.]
monasterio et　contentus　fuerit consuetudine loci　quam

[u.] [q.] [o.]　mid his oferflowodlicnysse [q.] [q.]
invenerit et non forte　superfluitate　sua 15

7 he ne gedrefð　minster　ahh　lice　gepeef is
(156 b.)　*perturbat　monasterium. sed | simpliciter contentus est*

þæt þæt þæt he gemet　he si underfangen on swa langre
quod　invenerit.　suscipiatur　quanto

---

9. *behadað* or *behatað*.　14. Over the words . . . *tudine loci quam invenerit et non forte*, the gloss has probably been erased.　16. *ahh* . ., a letter erased?　17. Three times *þet*, thus the MS.

---

5. *ei* above line.　6. *Clericorum*, MS. *clericum*.　8. MS. *collocetur*.　9. *de*, MS. *ded.*　11. peregrinis, MS. peregrinio.　16. *perturbat*, MS. *perturbet*, with *a* written over *e* of ending.

tide   swa he gewilnað gif he gewistlice gesceadwislice 7
tempore   cupit ;   Si qua   sane   rationabiliter et
mid eadmodnesse soðre lufe hwylce þinc repað oððe geswutalað
cum humilitate   karitatis   reprehendit   aut   ostendit.

smæge [b.] snotorlice þe læs forþan sylfan þingan hine
tractet abbas prudenter ne forte   pro   hoc   ipso   eum

    [c.]   sænde gif he wile syððan [o.] his staðolfæstnesse
dominus direxerit. Si   vero   postea voluerit   stabilitatem

    [d.] getrýmman na si forwýrned swýlc   willa   7 swiðest
5 *suam firmare.   non renuatur talis voluntas.* et *maxime*

     forþan   cumliðnesse þe mihte his lif [h.] beon acnawan
quia tempore hospitalitatis potuit   eius vita   dignosci.

þæt gif bið gemet oferflowende oððe leahterfull [g.]   [g.]
    Quod si superfluus   aut   vitiosus inventus fuerit

on tide   [g.]   [b.] þæt an [b.] hena scel beon gefærlæht gefer-
tempore hospitalitatis: non solum non debet   sociari cor-
roddene mynstres ac eac swylce   si gesæd arwýrðlice þæt he
pori monasterii. verum   etiam dicatur ei honeste   ut

aweggewite [p.] mid[r.] his ýrmða[r.]   cðre [q.] [p.]
10 *discedat : ne   eius   miseria etiam alii vitientur.*

þæt gif he na bið   swýlc gecarnige beon ut adræfæd
  Quod si non   fuerit talis qui mereatur   proici

     þæt an gif he bitt he si underfangen gegæderunge
non   solum   si petierit   suscipiatur   congregationi

to geferlætenne ac eac swýlce he si gelæred þæt he stande [p.]
  sociandus verum etiam   suadeatur ut stet   ut

mid his bisne oððre beon gelærede 7 sig on ælcere stowe
eius exemplo alii   erudiantur ; Et quia in omni loco

anum drihtne þæt gepeowod anum cinge 7 si gecampod
15 *uni domino   servitur ; uni regi   militatur ; Quem*

gif [k.] þýlne beon ·besceawiað [h.] sigelifed him   on
si etiam talem esse perspexerit abba. liceat   eum in

uferan æthwega [d.] gesettan stide [n.] [o.] [o.]
superiorem aliquantulum constitueret. locum. non solum autem

---

10. ýrmða, *a* of much larger size than the other characters.

---

4. *direxerit*, MS. *dixerint*. 6. MS. *hospitalis*. 9. *monasterii*, MS. *monasterio*, but last *o* underdotted, and *i* written over it. 11. *proici*, MS. *projiciunt*. 15. *servitur*, MS. *serviatur*. 17. *autem*, MS. *aut.*

[p.]　　ah　　[q.]　　of　　þam　foresædum　gradum　　[s.]
monachum.　sed　etiam　de　　superscriptis　　gradibus sacerdotum.

oððe　preosta　gestaþolfæstan　mæg　[x.]　on　maran　whænne
(157 a.) *vel　clericorum　　stabilire　　potest abbas　in | maiori　quam*

　incode　stede gif　he hig　besceawad　þæt lif　[w.]　wærnige
ingreditur　loco　si　ejus talem perspexerit　vitam.　esse.　Caveat

　[b.]　　[c.]　　þæt　æhwænne　of　oðrum　cuðum　mýnstre
autem　abba　ne　aliquando　de　alio　noto　monasterio

　[e.]　　　　to wunigenne　he ne underfo　buton　geþafunge
monachum　ad　habitandum　　suscipiat :　　sine　consensu 5

abbotes　his　[i.]　stafum　oððe gegretlicum　forþam　þe hit is
abbatis　ejus　aut　litteris　commendaciis ;　　Quia　scrip-

awriten　　þæt þæt　þe sýlfan　þu nilt beon ne du oðrum
tum　est ;　Quod　tibi　non vis fieri.　alii　ne

feceris ;

DE SACERDOTIBUS MONASTERII. (CAP. LXII.)

gif ænig　[b.]　him sýlfan　mæssepreost oððe [l.]　diacon
SI QUIS ABBAS　SIBI　　PRESBITERUM　VEL　DIACONEM. 10

beon gehadod geornð　of his geceose se wýrðe sýg preosthade
Ordinari　petierit ; de suis eligat qui dignus sit sacerdotio

brucan se gehadoda [b.]　warnige upahafennesse 7 modig-
fungi ; Ordinatus autem　careat　elationem.　atque super-

nesse　ne he ne ge ænig þing dýrstlæce　butan þæt þe him
biam ;　Nec quicquam presumat :　nisi　quod ei

fram þam abbode bið beboden witende　micele swýðor　stýre
ab　abbate precipitur :　Sciens se multo magis discipline

regollicere undeiþeodne [a.]　intingan preost　ne he na for-
regulari　subditum ;　Nec occasione sacerdotii　oblivisca- 15

gimeleasne regoles gehýrsumnesse 7 þeawfæstnesse ac swiðor
tur　regule　oboedientiam　et　disciplinam : sed　magis

7　swiðor on godc he geþeo　stede þæne [b.]　　[c.]
hac　magis in　deum proficiat ; Locum vero illum semper

he begýme on þam þe he in * neode　[d.]　on mýnstre toforan
attendat　quo ingressus　est in　monasterium ; preter

---

3. *besceawad, a* indistinct.　15, 16. *forgimeleasne,* read *forgimeleasie.*
18. *in neode,* read *inn eode.*

---

2. *clericorum,* MS. *declericorum.*　10. *presbiterum,* MS. *presbiteri.*
14. *ab abbate precipitur,* MS. *abba teprecepitur,* and *i* written over second *e*
of *precepitur.*　17. *rero,* MS. *vera.*　18. *monasterium, u* corrected from *a.*

þenunge weofodes oððe gif *wile* gecorenes gæderunge 7
officium altaris ; Aut si forte electio congragationis et
willa þæs abbodes lifes forgearnunge him wendan oððe
voluntas abbatis pro vite merito eum promovere
stiran [a.] se [l.] regol fram decanum oððe fram
voluerit qui tamen regulam a decanis vel pre-
pravostum him sylfan gesetne gehealden [i.] wite þæt gif
positis sibi constitutam servare sciat ; Quod si
he elles gedyrstlæcð na sacerdos ac hwiðercora ac beo geme-
5 *aliter presumpserit : non sacerdos sed rebellio judice-*
demod [a.] gelome geminegod gif he ne bið geþreadd [b.]
tur ; Et sepe ammonitus si non correxerit. etiam
[b.] si gegearcod [d.] on gewitnesse þæt [a.] gif he hit
episcopus | adhibeatur in testimonium ; Quod si nec (157 b.)
swa [a.] ne ge bett [a.] [d.] he si utadræfed
sic emendaverit : clarescentibus culpis proiciatur
[c.] gif hwile [h.] bið his toþundennessa [g] þæt
de monasterio : si tamen talis fuerit ejus contumacia ut
he beon underþeod oððe gehyrsumian þam regole nele.
10 *subdi aut obedire regule nolit ;*

DE ORDINE QUO CONGREGATUR. (CAP. LXIII.)

heora endebyrdnesse [d.] swa hi gehealden swa swa
ORDINES SUOS IN MONASTERIO ITA CONSERVENT ut con-
gecyrrednesse tima [g.] earnunge swa swa asyndrað
versiones tempus et vite meritum discernit.
7 swa swa se abbod hit gesette sene [a.] abbod [a.] ge-
utque abbas constituerit : Qui abbas non
drefe [a.] befæste him sylfum heorde ne swilcum freolicum
15 *conturbet gregem sibi commissam : nec quasi libera*
brucenne * anfealde unrihtlice he ne gedihte [e.] ac he þænee
utens potestate injuste disponat aliquit sed cogitet

---

1. *wile, w* above line. *gecorenes,* i. e. *gecorenness.*   5. *sacerdos.* The
scribe wrote *sacerdos* by mistake; corrected *o* into *h,* put *o* over *s,* and *de*
under it; the whole is meant for *sacerdhades.*   5. *beo, b* corr. from *g.*
5, 6. *gemedemod,* probably *gedemed* is the original reading.   16. *anfealde,*
read *anwealde.*

---

2. *vite,* MS. *ivvite.*   3. MS. *propositis.*   7. *si nec,* MS. *sinet.*
11. QUO not in the MS., nor in any other Latin texts. These read: DE
ORDINE CONGREGATIONIS.   13. *et vite meritum,* MS. *ut vi temeritum.*
15. *commissam,* MS. *commissim.*   16. *utens,* MS. *ut nos.*

simle þæt he be eallum his * domumum 7 weorcum be his
semper quia de omnibus judiciis et operibus suis
is to gildanne [b.] [d.] [m.] æfter endebyrdnesse
redditurus est deo rationem. Ergo secundum ordines

[i.] þa þa he gesette oððe þa þa habbað þa sylfan gebroðran
quos constituerit. vel quos habuerint ipsi fratres

hi ne genealæcan [b.] to huselgange to on sealmum
si accedant ad pacem. ad communionem. ad psalmum

ginnende on choro standende 7 [e.] [o.] eallunga
imponendum: in choro standum; Et in omnibus omnino 5

[e.] yld na si gesindrod on endebyrdnesse ne he ne foredeme
locis etas non discernatur in ordine nec prejudicet.

forþam [g.] [h.] [h.] cnihtas preostas þe demdon [b.]
quia samuel et daniel pueri presbiteros judicaverunt; Ergo

þisum asindrodum þa þa ge swa swa we bufon sædon mid
exceptis his quos ut diximus altiori

maran ræde [h.] reeð oððe [l.] of gewissum
consilio abbas pretulerit. vel degradaverit certis

intingan ealle þa oðre swa swa hi beoþ gecyrde swa
ex causis. reliqui omnes ut convertuntur ita 10

beon swilce ic swa cwæðe seþe æt þære oðran tide cymð to
sint. ut verbi gratia. qui secunda hora diei venerit in

minstre ginran hine hecunne his beon seþe [x.] [y.]
monasterium juniorem se noverit illius esse qui prima

on þære forman tide swa hwylcere ylde oððe wurðscipe
(158 a.) *hora venerit diei cujus | libet aetatis. aut dignitatis*

hesi cildra [b.] geond ealle þing fram eallum gebroðrum styr
sit. Pueris vero per omnia ab omnibus disciplina

si gehealden þa ginran iornostlice heora yldran arwurþian
teneatur; Juniores igitur: priores suos honorent; priores 15

lufian on þære sylfan clypunge namena
minores suos diligant. In ipsa autem apellatione nominum:

ænigum na si gelefed mid agenum naman genan ac þa yldran
nulli non liceat alium puro nomine apellare sed priores

---

1. *domumum*, read *domum.* 4, 5. *on* in l. 4 belongs to *ginnende* in l. 5.
5, *choro*, Latin influence. 17. *na* in the margin. *genan*, beginning of
genamian.

---

6. A letter erased before *ordine*. In *ordine*, *i* has been corr. from
a or *u.* 10. *reliqui*, MS. *relinqui*, but *n* nearly erased. 12. *juniorem*,
MS. *juniorum.* 13. *venerit*, MS. *cenirit. aetatis*, MS. *cecitatis. diguitatus*
in MS. 16. *minores* not in MS.

heora ginran   nemnan þa ginran   þa ỹldran
  juniores   suos fratres nominent   juniores autem priores suos
arwurðe hi gecian þæt bið to understandenne mid fæderlicere
  nonnos   vocent ;   quod intellegitur   paterna
arwurðnesse [d.]   for þam ðe þa spellunga is gelỹfed
  reverentia ; Abbas autem quia   vices christi   creditur
don   si genemned na mid his underfangennes
  agere dominus et abbas   vocetur ;   non sua   assumtione.
ac on wurðmente 7 mid christes lufan   he sỹlf   þence
5 *set   honore   et   amore   christi. ipse autem cogitet et*
hinc 7 he gearcie   weorðe þæt he si   swilcum wurðmente
  sic se exhibeat. ut dignus ut dignus sit.   tali   honore.
swa swa   ongeancumað   se ginra fram þam caldre
  Ubicumque autem sibi obviant fratres junior   a priore bene-
bletsunge bidde   se læssa aris 7 he sỹlla
  dictionem petat. Transeunte majore. minor surgat : et det ei
rỹmet to sittenne ne ne gedỹrstlæce se ginra   sittan   buton
  locum   sedendi ; Nec presumat   junior consedere nisi ei
hate   his ealdor þæt beo   on wurðmente
10 *precipiat senior suus   ut fiat quod scriptum est   honore*
         * foahrædigende   geongra cildra oððe   ginran
  invicem prevenientes. Pueri parvi vel adolescentes
        oððe æt meosan mid þeawfæstnessa heora endebỹrd-
  in oratorio. vel ad mensas. cum   disciplina   ordines
nesse   fỹlian   wiðutan hi beon   oþ þæt hi heordrædene
  suas consequantur foris   autem vel ubicumque   custodiam
hi habban 7   to lare   oððæt hi to   andgitfullere ỹlde
  habeant : et disciplinam usque ad intellegibilem etatem
becumen
15 *perveniant :*

DE ORDINANDO ABBATI. (CAP. LXIIII.)

      þæs abbodes on hadunge þæt [b.] si forasceawod gescead
  In   abbatis   ordinatione illa semper consideretur | ratio. (158 b.)
      her þæt si gesæd þone þe him sỹlfum eal seo gesibsum
  ut hic constituatur.   quem sibi omnis

---

11. *foahrædigende,* read *forahrædigende.*

---

5. *christi,* MS. *episcopi* (the scribe read *Ēpi* for *Xp̄i*). *amore,* MS. *amor.*
6. *ut dignus,* repeated thus in MS.   9. *presumat,* MS. *presumant.*

gegæderung   [æ.]   æfter   godes   ege   sit oððe
concors   congregatio   secundum   timorem   dei :   sive

eac swýlce þeah þe he gehwæde   dæl   gegæderunga   mid ge-
etiam   pars quamvis   parva   congregationis   saniori

wissum geþeahte gecýsð   be iarnunge 7 wisdomes
consilio   elegerit ; Vite autem   merito :   et sapientiae

lare   he si gecoren se þe is tohadgenne   þeah æfter
doctrina   elegatur   qui ordinandus est : etiam si ultimus

þe he beo on endebýrdnesse   gegæderunge   þæt
fuerit in ordine   congregationis ; Quod si etiam 5

for his leahtrum þæt feor   * sit
omnis congregatio   vitiis suis   quod   qu em absit

geþafienne   had   mid gelicum geþeahte gif gecýsð 7
consentientem   personam   pari consilio   elegerit :   et

þa sýlfan leahtras æthwega on   cýðe biscopis becumon to
vitia   ipsa   aliquatenus in notitiam episcopi pervenerint ad

þæs   scir þegena   gebýrað   seo stow   oððe   to
cujus   diocessim   pertinet   locus   ipse   vel   ad

abboddum oððe þa cristenan uýhgeburum geswuteliað hi for-
abbates   aut   christianos   vicinos   claruerint.   pro- 10

beodan þwýrlicra swýþrian geþafiunge ah * hwiwræddene
hibeant pravorum prevalere   consensum sed   domui   dei

wurðe gesetton   dihtneran   witende for þi hi to under-
dignum constituant dispensatorem.   scientes pro hoc se recep-

fonne   méde [b.] gode gýf þæt clænlice 7 mid ande don hi
turos mercedem   bonam. si illud   caste et zelo dei faciant :

eall swa þær togenes   synna   gýf hi forgæwað gehadod
sicut   e contrario   peccatum si   neglegant ; Ordinatus

soðlice   he þence æfre hwilce býrdena he underfeng 7
autem alba cogitet semper quale honus suscepit :   et 15

hwam he is to agendenne gescad his gerefsciran   7 wite he
cui   redditurus est   rationem   villicationis suę Sciatque

him sýlfan o gedafenian freman swiðor þonne derian him gebýrað
sibi oportere prodesse :   magis quam preesse ;   Oportet

---

1. *oððe, o* corr. from *e.*   6. *sit,* read *sig.*   9. *þegena,* i. e. *þegnunga !*
10. *geswuteliað, t* corrected from *l ?*   11. *hwiwrædenne,* read *hiwrædenne.*
12. *underfonne, o* corr. from *u* or *n.*   14. *togenes,* first *e* corr. into *æ.*
forgæwað, see note.   15. *byrdena, d* corr. from some other letter ?
17. *gedafenian, a* corr. from *e.* I cannot account for the *o.*

---

2. *pars, r* above line. *saniori,* MS. *samori,* but *m* is dotted under the
second stroke, so as to indicate the reading *saniori.*   8. *notitiam,* MS. *notetiam.*
pervenerint, MS. *perveniam.*   10. *vicinos,* MS. *ricinis.*   11. *dei* above line.

soðlice hinc beon gelæred on godcundlicra æ þæt he wite 7 he
ergo   eum   esse   doctum   lege divina :   ut   sciat   et sit

si hwanon he forð teo niwe   7   ealde   clæne [n.] sefre
unde   proferat   nova   et   vetera ;   Castum. sobrium.

mildheortnesse 7   æfre   he upahebbe   on
misericordem | et semper   superexaltet   misericordiam (159 ʀ)

dome   þæt he þæt ylce   begyte   hatige he lehtras
judicium   ut idem   ipse consequatur.   Oderit   vitia

lufige he gebroðra on þare sylfre soðlice þreatinge snotorlice
5 *diligat   fratres ;   In ipsa autem   correptione prudenter*

he det 7 nan þing ofer swiðe þæt he na to swiðe ne gewilnige
agat. et   ne quid nimis.   ne dum nimis cupit

upawyrtlian rust oððe om si tobrocen fæt   7 his   tydder-
eradere   eruginem.   frangatur vas : suamque   fragi-

nysse æfre ge. em. hydi sy 7 geþence   reod   forþrest
litatem semper   suspectus sit. memineritque calamum quassatum

ne sy to bryd   on   þam   we ne secgað þæt w beon for-
non conterendum.   In quibus non dicimus,   ut   permittat

lætanne beon gefed leahtras ac snotorlice 7 mid þare soðra
10 *nutriri   vitia sed prudenter et cum karitate*

lufa þa he of acerfa swa swa hem þynce ænige gelettan
ea amputet.   prout   viderit   cuique expedire.

ealswa we ær sædon 7 hogie he swyðor beon gelufon þænne
sicut jam diximus ; Et studeat plus   amari.   quam

beon ondrædod ne sy he adrefað 7 * anc sam ne sy he
timeri ;   Non sit turbulentus et anexius ;   non sit

swiðlic 7 andan wille ne sy he nyð full 7 swiðe wenende
nimius et obstinatus   non sit zelotipus et nimis suspiciosus :

for þy   næfre   he ne gercsteð on þam sylfan bebodum
15 *quia numquam   requiescit ; In   ipsis imperiis   suis*

forgleaw 7   forseone   oððe   æfter gode oððe   æfter
providus et consideratus : sive secundum deum. sive secundum

---

6. *det*, for *deþ*; influence of Latin ?   7. *upawyrtlian*, see note. *fæt* or *fæd*
in MS. ?   9. *w beon forlætanne beon gefed.* I think *w* is either a 'paving'
letter or the beginning of *we*, a dittography of the *we* going before, in which
case *beon* is attributable to the same cause, viz. to a dittography of *beon*
in l. 10. *forlætenne* is a mistake for *forlæte* = permittat.   11. *hem*, e or o ?
It is crossed out in the MS.   13. *anc sam*, corr. from or into *anx sum*,
probably — from a palæographical point of view — the former ; from an
etymological point of view, the latter. *anexius* is glossed as if it were
angustus.   14. *andan*, i. e. anan.

---

14. *obstinatus*, MS. *obstinandus. nimis*, MS. *in misu.*

wurulde he sȳ þa weorc þe he ge þeod he gesýndrige 7
seculum sit ; Opera que injungit discernat et

gemetȳge þencende gescad þæs halgan iacobes secgende
temperet. cogitans discretionem sancti jacob dicentis.

   mine heorde swiðor oððe on gange gif ic do swingan
Si greges meos plus in ambulando fecero laborare :

hi swȳltað ealle on anum dæge þas oðre gecýðnýssa gewitnessa
morientur cuncti una die ; Hec ergo aliaque testimonia

smæiunge moder mihta nimende ealle þinc gemetic æt
(159 b.) *discretionis matris virtutum sumens : sic omnia temperet | ut* ₅

he si strang þæt þæt hi gewilniað 7 þa *uncruman hi na
et fortis sit quod cupiant : et infirmi non

forfleon 7 healicost þæt he andweardne regol on eallum
refugeant ; Et precipue ut presentem regulam in omni-

þingum gehealde þonne he þenað þæt he gehýre
bus conservet. ut dum bene ministraverit. audiat

   þæt þe gehýrde se goda þeowa seðc aspende
a domino quod servus bonus qui erogavit triticum

his efcnþeowan on his tide soðlice ic secge eow sæde
conservis suis in tempore suo ; Amen dico vobis ait. 10

ofor ealle his godu he geset
super omnia bona sua constituet eum.

DE PREPOSITO MONASTERII. (CAP. LXV.)

oftrædlice witodlice hit belimpð þæt þurh hadunge prafostes
SEPIUS QUIDEM CONTINGIT *ut per ordinationem prepositi*

hefilice ætswicunga on mýnster þonne bið sume
scandala gravia in monasteriis oriantur. dum sint aliqui

mid þam awýridan gaste modignesse *tobedde 7 wenende
maligno spiritu superbie inflati. et estimantes 15

hine oðre beon nimende him gewin
se secundos esse. abbatis assumentes sibi tyrannidem.

æswicunga hi fedað 7 twȳrednysse on gegaderunga hi doð
scandala nutriunt. et dissensiones in congregatione faciunt ;

7 swiðost on þam stowum þær fram þam ýlcan oððe
Et maxime in illis locis. ubi ab eodem sacerdote. vel

5. The *m* is indistinct in *gemetie.* 6. *uncruman*, read *untruman.*
14. *hefilice, l* corr. from *s. tobedde,* read *tobrædde.*

2. *dicentis,* MS. *dicentes.* 3. *fecero,* MS. *fecere. laborare,* MS. *baborare.*
4. *cuncti,* MS. *cuncta. Hec,* MS. *Her.* 6. MS. *forte. fortis,* for which
other MSS. have *fortes,* is postulated by gloss. 8. MS. *conscrrent.*
12. MONASTERII, MS. MONASTERIO. 14. *sint,* MS. *fuit.*

fram þam abbotum þa þa abbod hadiað   7
ab eis abbatibus qui abbatem ordinant. ab ipsis etiam et

se prafost þe ær bið gehadod þæt bið hi fullice hit is
prepositus ordinatur ; Quod quam sit absurdum

eþelice undergiten forþam þe byð fram þam sylfan anginne
facile adfertitur. quia ab ipso initio ordina-

hadunge ontimber gesceald to motgenne þonne hit bið getiht
tionis : materia ei datur superbiendi. dum ei suggeritur

fram his geþohtum [m.] [m.]
5 *a cogitationibus suis exutum eum esse a potestate*

his abbotes forþam þe he wæs * gehæle from þam
abbatis sui : quia ab ipsis est ordinatus. a quibus

se abbod heonen beoð astyrede andan geflit * stalu
et abbas ; Hinc | suscitantur invidie. rixe. detractionis (160 a.)

efestes twyrædnesse unhadunge 7 hwænne þwyrnessa
emulationes dissensiones. exordinationes. et dum contraria

heom betwynan 7 se prafost geþafiað 7 heora neod is
sibi invicem abbas prepositusque sentiunt. et ipsorum necesse

sawla under heom
10 *est sub hac disentione animas periclitari. et hi qui sub*

þænne hi lyfetað dælmælum færað uton forspilled-
ipsis sunt. dum adulantur partibus eunt in perdi-

nesse þæs frecednessa yfel heom * lucað on anginne
tionem ; Cujus periculi malum. illis respicit in capite

[a.] ða swilcum on hadunge doð ealdras forþi
qui talibus in ordinatione se fecerunt auctores ; Ideo nos

foresceawiað fremman for sibbe 7 þære soðre lufe hyrdræ-
previdimus expedire propter pacis karitatisque custo-

dene þæs abbodes standan on cyre hadunge minstres his
15 *diam in abbatis pendere arbitrio ordinationem monasterii sui ;*

7 gif mæg beon heora decanus si geendebyr swa swa * weg
Et si potest fieri ; per decanos ordinetur sicut ante

bufon ælc nytwyrðnesse mynstres be þam þe
disposuimus omnis utilitas monasterii. prout abba

---

6. *gehæle, ælc* crossed out, and *hadod* (sic) has been substituted for it in
the margin. 12. *lucað*, read *lociað*. 16. *decanus*, copied from Latin?
wey, read *we ge*; the verb is left out.

---

2. *absurdum*, MS. *obsurdum*. 7. A hole in parchment before *rixe*; it
does not affect the text at all, having evidently been there before the MS.
was written on. 11. MS. *perditione*. 12. *illis*, MS. *illi*. 13. *fecerunt*,
MS. *fecunt*, and *e* corrected from *r*. 17. *disposuimus*, MS. *disposimus*.

diht   þæt   þænne   magon hit byð befæst   an   ne
disposuerit.   ut   dum   pluribus committitur.   unus   non

modie   þæt gif oððe stow gyrnð oððe gegaderung
superbiat; Quod si   aut   locus   expetit.   aut   congregatio.

bit gescadwislice mid cadmodnesse [g.] se   demð
petierit rationabiliter cum   humilitate.   et   abba judicaverit

gefremman swa hwænne swa geccost   mid geþeahte
expedire   quemcumque   elegerit   abba cum   consilio

ondrædendra gode hadige hesylf   prafost   se
fratrum   timentium   deum ordinet ipse sibi prepositum; Qui 5

se prafost   mid arwurðnessa þa þe fram his
tamen prepositus illa agat cum   reverentia   que   ab

abbode   læhte beoð naht ongen   wyllan   7 had-
(100 b.) *abbate suo ei injuncta fuerint nihil contra volun | tatem et ordina-*

ung þæs donde forðam þe   oðrum
tionem abbati faciens   quia   quanto prelatus est ceteris. tanto eum

gedafenað carfullicor healden beboda regoles se pra
oportet   sollicitus observare precepta regule; Qui prepositus

gif he bið gemet   leahtres oððe upahafennes beswicen
si   repertus   fuerit   vitiosus   aut   elatione   deceptus 10

modignes   forhicge þæs haligan byð   fandod
superbie   aut   contemptor sancte regule fuerit approbatus

si geminegod mid wordum oð feowersiðan gif he hit na
ammoneatur   verbis   usque   quater; Si non emenda-

gebet si gegearcod þræiung regolicere styre
verit adhibeatur   ei   correptio   discipline   regularis;

he si adræfed of endebyrd-
Quod si neque sic correxerit; tunc   deiciatur de   or-

nesse pravostscire   seðe   is   stete his
dine prepositure. et alius qui dignus est in loco eius subro- 15

7 gehyrsum
getur; Quod si postea in congregatione quietus et oboediens

---

9. *pra*, for *prafost* or *pravost*.   10. *leahtres*, should have been *leahterful*, but either the scribe's eye was caught by the *s* of Latin ending, or by the ending of *upahafennes*.   15. *stete*, i. e. *stede*.

---

3. *petierit*, MS. *petitierit*.   4. *quemcumque*, MS. *quecumque*.   6. *ab* omitted by Latin scribe.   7. *ordinationem*. Between *r* and *d* the same hole in parchment obtains, as spoken of before (see note to p. 110. 7).   8. *prelatus*, MS. *relatus*.   13. *ei*, MS. *que*.   15. *alius*, MS. *aliter*.

he na byð   of mynstre he si utadræfed þence
non fuerit: etiam de monasterio expellatur ; Cogitet tamen
                  to iýldenne
abbas se de omnibus judicis suis deo redditurum rationem : ne
          andan   æfestes lig forbærnde sawla
forte zeli aut invidie flamma urat animam ;

DE OSTIARIIS MONASTERII. (CAP. LXVI.)

   æt geate   mynstres   si geset eald wita   se wite cunne
5 *Ad portam monasterii   ponatur senex sapiens qui sciat acci-*
underfon andswore 7 agifan þæs geþungennes hine ne
  pere responsum et reddere. cuius maturitas eum non
geþafige worian se geatweard hus scýll habban wið þæt
  sinat vagari ; Qui porterius cellam debet habere juxta por-
geat þæt cumende   andweardne gemeton frem hwam
tam ut venientes semper presentem inveniant. a quo
andswore underfon 7 sona þænne cnucað oððe þearfa
responsum acipiant ; Et mox ut aliquis pulsaverit | aut pauper (161 a.)
  clýpað goda þanc he andsware oððe bletsige 7 mid
10 *clamaverit. deo gratias respondeat aut benedicat. et cum*
ealre manþwærnesse godes eges heagilde andsware   ofstlice
omni mansuetudine timoris dei reddat responsum festinanter :
mid wýlme þæresoðre lufe se geatweard   helpe
cum fervore karitatis ; Qui portarius si indiget solacio :
ginran broðran underfo   mýnster soðlice gif hit mæig
juniorem fratrem accipiat. Monasterium autem si   possit
beon   sceall beon gesett þæt ealle neod behefness þæt is
fieri ita debet constitui. ut omnia necessaria. id est
wæter   mýll   orceard   bæcern   oððe mistlice cræftes
15 *aqua molendinum ortus pistrinum. vel artes diverse*
wiðinnan   minstre   beon geganne þæt nesig   neod
  intra in monasterium exerceantur. ut non sit necessitas
munecum werigende wiðutan for þam
monachis vagandi foris quia omnino non expedit
heora sawlum   þysne   oft we wýllað
animabus eorum ; Hanc autem regulam sepius volumus

---

11. *manþwærnesse, w* corrected from another letter ?

---

2. *se de,* MS. *sed.*   4. MONASTERII, MS. MONASTERIIS.   7. *juxta,* MS.
justam.   11. *timoris,* MS. *moris.*   13. MS. *accipiant.*   14. *fieri,*
MS. *fierii. id est,* MS. *idem.*   15. (*h*)*ortus,* MS. *ortu.*   17. *foris,* a non-
contemporary *a* has been put over the *i* in the MS.

---

        beon geræd   ænig   gebroðra   be nytennyssa
in congregatione   legi :   ne quis   fratrum   se de ignorantia
þæt na belædie
excuset;

DE FRATRIBUS IN VIAM DIRECTIS. (CAP. LXVII.)

þa sendlican gebroðra   on   wege   ealra gebroðra   [h.]
DIRIGENDI FR*ATRE*S   IN VIAM.   OMNIUM   FRATRUM *vel*

[b.] [e.] gebed   befæstan   ⁊ æfre   æt þam æftemc-
abbatis   se orationi commendent; Et semper ad   ora- 5

stan gebede   godes   weorces   gemynd   ealra   and
tionem ultimam operis   dei.   commemoratio   omniu m ab-

weardra   ⁊ beo   þagencyrrendan   gebroþra   of   wege
sentium   fiat;   Revertentes   autem   de   via fratres;

on þam dæge   on þam þe gehweorfað geond ealle minsterlice
ipso   die   quo redeunt.   per omnes canonicas

tida   þonne   bið gefylled   godes weorc   astrehð   moldan
horas   dum   expletur   opus dei   prostrati   solo

oððe eorðan fram eallum gebroðrum biddan   gebed   forgime-
oratorii :   ab   omnibus petant   orationem propter 10

leaste   þæt ænig þinc ne undersmuge on wege gesyhðe oððe
(161 b.) *excessum :   ne quid forte | subripuerit   in   via visus. .aut*

lyst   þinces   oððe idelre   spræce   ne ne gedyrstlæce
auditus   male   rei   aut   otiosi sermonis;   Nec presumat

ænig   oðrum gereccan swa hwylce þinc swa he gesyhð wið-
quisquam   aliis   referre   quecumque

utan   on mynstre   oððe   he gehyrað forþam þe hit is
foris   monasterio viderit.   aut   audierit   quia

mænifealt   towurpon   [a.]   rego-
plurima   destructio   est; Quod si quis presumpserit vin- 15

licre waclicre   oððe stire   he underþeodde swa gelice ⁊ se ðe
dicte   regulari   subjaceat :   Similiter   et   qui

---

7. *þagencyrrendan*, read *þa ayencyrrendan.*   8. *gehweorfað, g* corr. from
some other letter.   15. *towurpon*, for *towurponnesse?*   *regolicre, r* corr.
from *a.*   16. *waclicre?* see note.

---

3. DIRECTIS, MS. DIRECTUS.   4. *omnium fratrum*, MS. *omniam fratres,*
but *ū* above *res,* as if to indicate the correction.   9. *prostrati*, MS.
prostratu.

I

gedẏrstlǽcð clẏsunga   minstres   utgan oððe awẏder faren oððe
presumpserit claustra   monasterii egredi : vel quoque ire   vel
ænig þing   þeh þe   litel   buton   hæsc   þæs abbotes
quippiam   quamvis   parvum   sine   jussione   abbatis
don
facere ;

Sɪ ꜰʀᴀᴛʀɪ ɪɴᴘᴏssɪʙɪʟɪᴀ ᴊᴜʙᴇɴᴛᴜʀ.   (Cᴀᴘ. LXVIII.)

gif hwilcum breðer   ænig   hefincs oððe *unacumendalice
5 Sɪ   ᴄᴜɪ   ꜰʀᴀᴛʀɪ ᴀʟɪǫᴜᴀ *forte gravia   aut   inpossibilia*
beoð geþeodde   he underfo witodlice bebeodendes bebod .
injunguntur   suscipiat   quidem   jubentis   imperium
mid ealre   manþwærnesse   7 gehirsumnesse þæt   eallunga
cum   omni mansuetudine. et   obedientia ; Quod si omnino
heora mægena   gemet gif he gesẏhð   began
virium suarum mensuram   viderit   pondus oneris excedere
his   unacumenlicnesse   se þe gewis
     inpossibilitatis   sue causas   ei qui   sibi   preest
      7 gedafenlice   na   modigenne oððe wið-
10 *patienter et   oportune suggerat ; non superbiendo : aut   resis-*
standende   æfter his tihtinge
  tendo : vel contradicendo ; Quod si post suggestionem suam
on   his   cwẏde   bebod   þæt gif þurhwunað
in   sua   sententia prioris   imperium   perduraverit :
wite se gingra swa him selfan gefremman 7 of soðre lufe
sciat junior   ita sibi   expedire :   et ex karitate
getruwigende be godes fẏlste   gehẏrsume |
confidens   de adjutorio dei   obediat : |

15   Uᴛ ɪɴ ᴍᴏɴᴀsᴛᴇʀɪᴏ ɴᴏɴ ᴘʀᴇsᴜᴍᴀᴛ ᴀʟᴛᴇʀ ᴀʟᴛᴇʀᴜᴍ
        ᴅᴇꜰᴇɴᴅᴇʀᴇ.   (Cᴀᴘ. LXVIII.)

            mid ænigum intingan ne gedẏrstlæce oðer
Precavendum est ne   quavis occasione   presumat   alius
oðerne bewerian   oððe swẏlce gescẏldan
alium defendere monachum in monasterio. aut   quasi   tueri

---

5. *unacumendalice,* read *unacumendlice*?   7. *manþwærnesse,* œ or a?
9. *þe, þ* corrected from *g.*

---

2. *parvum,* MS. *parvium,* but *i* underdotted.   6. *imperium* (= *imprum*),
MS. *impium.*   15, 16. Heading not in the MS. ; supplied from the list of
chapters.

þeah þe hig mid ænigre mæg sibbe blodes sibbe beon ge
etiamsi qualibet consanguinitatis propinquitate jun-

þeodde ne ne mid ænigum gemete fram munecum
gantur ; Nec quolibet modo id a monachis

si gedýrstlæcð forþam þe mæg þanon seo hefegoste intinga
presumatur : quia exinde gravissima occasio

æswicunga unaspringon þæt gif for ænig gemelcasað
scandalorum oriri potest ; Quod si quis hec transgressus

　　　　*arlicor hi si gebread
fuerit : acrius coerceatur.　　　　　　　　　　　5

UT NON PRESUMAT ALIQUIS ALIUM CEDERE. (CAP. LXX.)

forboden æle dýrstignýsse intinga we ge-
VETETUR IN MONASTERIO OMNIS PRESUMPTION*is occasio ; Or-*

endebýrdað 7 we gesettað alýfed ænigne heora
dinamus atque constituimus ut nulli liceat quemquam fratrum

gebroðra amansumian oððe slean buton þam þe mihte
suorum excommunicare. aut cedere. nisi cui potestas ab

　　　bið geseald ða syngendan ætforan eallum gebro-
abbate data fuerit ; Peccatores autem *coram omni-*　　10

ðrum beon geþreade oðre ogan þæt habban cildum
bus arguantur : ut ceteri metum habeant ; Infantibus

　　　oð þone fifteoðan gear ýlde lare oððe
vero usque ad quintum decimum annum aetatis disci-

stýre geornfulnessa si gegearcod hýrdrædene
pline diligentia ab omnibus adhibeatur. et *custodia sit :*

ac eac swýlce mid eallum gemete 7 gesceade soðes strangran
sed et hoc cum omni mensura et *ratione ; Nam in fortiori*

ýlde se de gedýrstlæcð æthwega butan bebode þæs abbodes oððe
aetate qui presumpserit aliquatenus sine precepto abbatis : vel 15

on þam sýlfan cildan butan smegunge onstingð regolicre
in ipsis infantibus sine discretione exarserit : | *disci-*

stýre he underhnige þe
pline regulari subjaceat : quia scriptum est ; Quod tibi

sýlfan þu nelt beon ne oðrum ne do þu
non vis fieri : alii ne feceris ;

(162 b.)

---

3. *mæg*, gloss to *potest*, in l. 4.　　4. *for ænig gemelcasað*, read *ænig for-
gemeleasað.*　　5. *arlicor*, read *tearlicor.*

---

2. *id*, supplied by glossator. *a*, MS. *ad.*　　3. *quia*, MS. *qui.*　　4. *hec*,
MS. *hic.*　　6. Heading not in the MS.; supplied from the list of chapters.
13. *custodia sit*, MS. *custodiat se.*

UT OBEDIENTES SIBI SINT INVICEM FR*ATRES*.   (CAP. LXXI.)

gehýrsumnesse god   na þæt an   þam abbade is togearcienne
OBEDIENTIAE BONUM NON SOLUM.   ABBATI   EXHI*bendum   est*

        heom * betwýnanan   hi gehýrsumian
ab omnibus. sed etiam sibi   invicem   ita   oboediant

    witende for þisne gehýrsumnesse weg him sýlfne to
fratres : scientes per hanc   obedientiae   viam : se

farenne to gode on ðam fore sædon   prafosta
5 *ituros ad deum ; Premisso ergo   abbatis atq*ue *prepositorum*

þa þa fram him beon gesette bebode þam we ne geþafiað
qui ab   eo constituuntur imperio. cui non permittimus

asindrodum beboda beon foreset þær to eacan ealle þa gingran
privata imperia   preponi : de cetero   omnes juniores

heora ýldrum   on   ealre soðre   lufe hohfulnesse
prioribus   suis   omni karitate.   et   sollicitudine

hi gehirsumian þæt gif ænig   sacful fuerit byð gemet
obediant ;   Quod si   quis contentiosus, repperitur :

he si geþread gif hwýlc broðor   for ænigum gehwædum intinga
10 *corripiatur ; Si quis* autem *frater* pro *quavis minima causa*

      oððe for gehwýlcum ealdre his beoð geþread
ab abbate vel a quocumque priore suo   corripitur

mid ænigum mete oððe gif he leohtlice undergit mod ealdres
quolibet modo : vel si   leviter senserit animum prioris

      ongen him wrað oððe astiredne þeah þe
cujuscumque   contra se iratum   vel   commotum quamvis

æthwega sona buton ýldinge swa lange astreht on corðan
modice : mox sine mora tamdiu prostratus in terra

toforan his fotum   ac he licge gebetende oððe þæt bið
15 *ante pedes   ejus   jaceat satisfaciens: usque dum*

bletsunge gehæled seo stýrung   gif he forhogað don
benedictione sanetur illa commotio ; Quod si contempserit facere :

oððe he lichamlicere wrace þæt gif forsihð oððe gif anmod
aut   corporali vindicte   subjaceat : aut si contumax

he bið of minstre he si utadræfæd
fuerit de monasterio   expellatur. | (163 a.)

---

3. *betwýnanan*, read *betwýnan*.   7. *asindrodum beboda*, see note.   9. *fuerit*, added by glossator.   11. *for*, read *from*.   17. *þæt gif forsihð*, I suggest that this was originally written in the margin as supplementary gloss to *gif he forhogað*. It was then copied into the text in the wrong place.

17. *vindicte*, MS. *rindincte*.

De zelo bono quem debent monachi habere. (Cap. LXXII.)

swa is [h.] se ýfela biternesse anda   7
Sicut est zelus amaritudinis malus qui separat a deo et

læd to helle   is se goda anda se ðe sýndrað fram
ducit ad infernum ita est zelus bonus qui separat a

leahtre 7 læt to gode   þýsne   andan
vitio et ducit ad deum et ad vitam aeternam ; Hunc ergo zelum

mid þære wealdestan   began   mid
ferventissimo amore exerceant monachi id est ut ;

wýrðmente   forhradian heora untrumnessa oððe
honore se invicem preveniant; Infirmitates suas sive

lichama oððe þeawa gepýldelicost forþýldian gehirsumnesse
corporum sive morum patientissime tollerent obedientiam

him sýlf geflitmælum   hi beodan   na ænig þæt þe he
sibi certatim   impendant ;   Nullus quod sibi

nýtwýrdlice deme folgie   swiðor oðrum þa soðe
utile judicat sequatur ; sed quod magis alio ; Carita-

lufe broðor rædene mid clænre hi beodan lufe hi on
tem fraternitatis casto impendant amore ; Deum 10

drædan heora abbud   mid sifre 7 eadmodre soðre *lare
timeant. abbatem suum sincera et humili caritate

hi lufian cristes eallunga naht hi forasettan sege ætgædere
diligant; Christo omnino nihil preponant. qui nos pariter

[g.]   [g.]   bringe
ad vitam aeternam perducat ;

De hoc quod non omnis justitie observatio in hac sit regula constituta. (Cap. LXXIII.)   15

þýsne regol   we awriton   healdende on
Regulam autem hanc discripsimus, ut hanc observantes in

minstre æthwega oððe arwurðnesse þeawa oððe anginn
monasteriis. aliquatenus vel honestatem morum aut initium

drohtnunge us *þe geswutelian habban oðra haligra to ful-
conversationis nos demonstremus habere ; Ceterum ad per-

fremednessa drohtnunge   sýnd lare
fectionem conversationis qui festinat. sunt doctrine sanctorum

---

11. *lare*, a misreading for *lufe*.   18. *þe*, read *we*.

---

6. *Infirmitates*, MS. *Infirmites*.   14. QUOD, MS. QUO. OMNIS, MS. OMNES.

---

fædera   þara   gehealdsum   gehealdsum   ne   gelæd   mannan   to
patrum.   *quarum* | *observatio*   *perducit*   *hominem   ad* (163 b.)

healdsumnessa   fulfremednessa   la   hwylc   tramod   oððe   hwylc
celsitudinem   perfectionis ;   Que   enim   pagina   aut   quis

spræc   godcundlice   ealdordomes   ealdre   7   niwe   gecyðnesse   nis
sermo   divine   auctoritatis   veteris   ac   novi   testamenti   non

se   rihtoste   bysen   lifes   mennisces   oððe   la   hwilc   boc   haligra
est rectissima norma vite humane : Aut   quis   liber sanctorum

rihte   fædera   þæt   na   sweg   mid   rihtum   rine
₅ *catholicorum   patrum   hoc   non   resonat   ut   recto   cursu*

we   becumende   to   urum   scyppende   eac   swilce   7
perveniamus   ad   creatorem   nostrum ;   Nec   non   et

þurhtogenessa   7   gesetnessa   heora   lifes   ac   eac
conlationes   patrum   et   instituta   vite   eorum.   sed   et

swylce   regol   basilius   hwæt   elles   sind
regula   sancti   patris   nostri   basilii :   quid   aliud   sunt.

butan   wel   libbendra   7   gebirsumera   munecca   7   gesetnessa
nisi   bene   viventium   et   obedientium   monachorum   instituta

mihta   us   asolcenum   7   yfel   lybbendum   7   gime-
¹⁰*virtutum.   nobis   autem   desidiosis   et   male viventibus atque neg-*

leasum   scame   gescyndnysse   swa   hwilc
legentibus   rubor   confusionis est ;   Quisquis   ergo   ad   patriam

þu   efast   þysne   þane   læstan   *acunnednesse   regol   awric-
celestem   festinas.   hanc   minimam   inchoationis   regulam   dis-

tenne   fylstendum   criste   þu   gefremme   7   þu   ætnyxtan   to
criptam   adjuvante   christo   perficias :   et   tunc   demum   ad

maran   þe   wiðufan   we   gemundon   lare   lare   7   mihta
majora   que   supra   commemoravimus   doctrine   virtutumque

geþincðe   godes   scildendum   becimð   wyrcendum   þas þinc
¹⁵*culmina   deo   protegente   pervenies ;   Facientibus   hec   regna*

geopenað   þa   ecan.
patebunt   aeterna ;

FINIT REGULA SANCTI BENEDICTI.

1, 2. *gehealdsumnessa* in l. 2 is the proper gloss to *observatio* in l. 1, and
the *gehealdsum, gehealdsum* in this line, I am unable to explain except as a
double dittography.   2. *-sumnessa*, first stroke of *m* erased.   12. *acunnednesse*, read *acennednesse*.   14. *lare* was first put over the ending of *commemoravimus*, then erased and written again over *doctrine.*

1. *quarum*, MS. *quorum.*   2. *Que enim*, MS. originally *Qu. enim*, from
which *Que enim* has been corrected.   7. *patrum*, third stroke of *m* erased.
10. *desidiosis*, MS. *desidiosus.*   11. *rubor*, MS. *robur.*   12. *festinas*,
MS. *festinans.   regulam*, MS. *regula.*

NOTES.

1. 5. *fremfi*. After this word there is a gap in the MS., so that some letter or letters may have been there, which are now gone. Read *fremfullice*.

1. 8. *roluptatibus*. This reading, for which nearly all other codices have *roluntatibus*, is supported not only by two of the Latin MSS. (G. U.), but also by the gloss.

2. 8. Above *dicente*, a little to the right, ū is found in the MS. I presume it is the ending of *secgend*, which gloss was filled out by a copyist in its proper place, and thus written twice.

3. 3. -*eond*, as gloss to (*proh*)*ibe*. The other texts have *forhafa* (Schröer, Die Prosabearbeitungen, 2. 21), except S. (W. V. 5. 15), which gives *heald*. Neither of these suggests a reading for our text. Possibly the *e* is a misreading for a *t* (which suggestion is favoured by the palæographical evidence), and the gloss was *forstond*. I am happy to acknowledge my indebtedness to Professor Cosÿn, of Leiden, for this and other suggestions.

3. 11. *gebroht*, as gloss to *perducatum*, is in itself undoubtedly right. Only *per ducatum* was wrongly taken as one word; see context. Similar cases where a misreading of the MS. produced a wrong gloss—wrong so far as the context is concerned—are numerous. See e.g. *sægde*, as gloss to *ait*, which is wrong for *aut* (78. 1).

3. 16. *Habitavit*=*habitabit*. See Sweet, O. E. T., p. 185.

5. 10. *de habitatore* (MS. habitatorum), glossed by *be wunungum*. The other texts have '*be þæm bugendum* his *eardungstowe*' (Schröer, Die Prosabearbeitungen, 4. 22). But the Winteney Version, which is independent of our text, has '*be þam wuniunge his eardingstowe*' (7. 27). That the original also had *wunungum* is made (at least) likely by the MS. reading *habitatorum* for *habitatore*, which may be owing to the -*um* of the gloss. But whence the form *wunungum*? To read *wunigendum* (see ib., l. 11) is an easy way out of the difficulty, but scarcely the right one. We must have very good reasons indeed for assuming that a commoner form made room for a rarer one. Considering that the earliest examples given by *Koch* (I², p. 342, § 61), of participial forms in -*ing* are from the A-text of Layamon's Brut., i. e. about the year 1200 (see ib., p. 10), I should not dare to think that we had here an early instance of it, if this form stood alone in our text. But we also find *latens* glossed by *lettincg* (80. 10). There would not seem to be the shadow of a doubt concerning the ending -*incg* being

that of a participle; but I would again not lay too much stress on
this instance by itself, since I am not sure as to the meaning of the
gloss itself. But if we find *monstrante* glossed by *swijtelunge* (35. 3),
we may perhaps look upon the others too, as evidencing a participle
in -*ing* [1].

I cannot leave the matter alone without going at some length
into detail as to the origin of the form in -*ing*. I may at once state
that I look upon it as a direct and phonetic representative of the A.-S.
form in -*ende*. Whatever be the origin, whether the above view will
prove to be the correct one, or whether we must continue to view it
with Prof. Max Müller (Lectures on the Science of Language, II) as a
'corruption' of a verbal substantive in the dative, we are alike struck
with the fact that for a long time, down to Gower and Chaucer, nay,
to early in the fifteenth century [2], the forms -and, -end, -ing continue
to be found parallel in the same authors. Now, though a hundred
and eighty years more of parallelism may increase our wonder, they
need not materially alter our view of the case.

Let us now turn to our text, and see what the frequent occurrence of
-*enne* by the side of -*ende* for the pres. part., as well as for the gerund
or participium necessitatis (Introd., V, § 89), gives us a right to conclude.
If we may lay down anything, it will be this, that the ending
-*ende* has dwindled down into a combination of a certain vowel (of
no definite phonetic value) + the nasal which occurs before dentals, and,
be it remembered, a *voiced* nasal before the voiced *d*. I denote this
voiced nasal by ñ. This ñ was sometimes continued, i.e. lengthened;
but sometimes the stop was undone with a jerk, occasioning the
explosion which is symbolised by *d*. Now the only difference between
this form eñe and -*inye* is that the dental nasal is replaced by the
guttural nasal, which I denote by *ñ*, surely in itself no very great
change, especially as analogues are by no means wanting. We must
look to vulgar speech for some of these analogues. An *orphan* becomes
an *orfling* (sometimes a *horfling*), etc. See *H. Baumann*, Londinis-
men, Slang und Cant. (Berlin, 1887), Introduction, § 5, sub 3 (p. xci),
from which passage it must not, however, be supposed that this
pronunciation is peculiar to London. I may also instance the
'peculiar' pronunciation of the French nasals in the mouths of badly
taught Germans, and—what is more interesting at this conjunction—
English children. I distinctly remember the contortions that some
untrained pupils of mine in an English school had to make their
mouths undergo, when they had to pronounce 'je demande, tu

---

[1] Cf. Bosw. in v. *wellicung*; also Cant. Ps. 149. 4. (See the forthcoming
edition, by Mr. Fred. Harsley.) Reluctantly, I must draw attention to the
ending, -*e*, which is not that of an A.-S. participle in the dative. Can the
glossator have taken *monstrante* as a gerund, = *monstrando*?

[2] I was strengthened in my conviction by a correspondence on this subject
with Mr. C. Stoffel, of Nymegen, the results of whose extensive reading are
always so kindly placed at the disposal of his correspondents.

demandes,' etc. The words invariably became je demangde, tu demangdes, nous demángdons, etc., no doubt in all respects a fit analogue.

6. 3. *we hihtaꝺ*. Evidently a marginal gloss got in the wrong place, instead of over *speramus*. See note to l. 5 on page 6.

9. 18. *dan. orseclena*, as gloss to *anachoritarum*. Read *onsetlena*. But what does *dan.* mean ? I suspect that *d* is a paving or sequence letter, and that *an* indicates that instead of *onsetlena* we may also read *ansetlena*. Thus interpreted, *-an* would be another case of merography, a part put for a whole (Introd., V, § 4).

9. 19. *conversationis*, MS. *conversionis*. The same corruption obtains in six other MSS., but both context and gloss show *conversationis* to have been the original reading.

10. 1. *frore* for *frofre*. The dropping of the *f* (after it had become voiced), i.e. the merging of it into the *o*, may very well be a phonetic process. See also *Ellis*, E. E. P., II, pp. 513, 514.

10. 7. *vel oꝺꝺe*. I think that originally the gloss to *experientia* was ꞇ *afundennessa*. (For this use of ꞇ = id est, see Skeat's ed. of Matthew passim, and l. 1 on p. 25 where *oꝺꝺe* ꞉ ꞇ occurs after the word ; see note to 29. 15 ; 55. 2.) A second glossator, who did not see that ꞇ meant the same as .i. (=id est), or as 7 (cf. 20, 2 ; 20. 3 ; 84. 9, etc.), added the lemma *vel*. For other cases where part of the gloss was wrongly translated into Latin, I refer to (92. 1). *Colore* was here glossed by *be bleo* ; a second glossator adds *de*, as supposed lemma to *be*. Cf. also (93. 3) *et sagum*. where *et* may have a similar origin.

12. 1. *geondsprecend*. If it means anything, *geondsprecan* = to address or to make anyone hear, which in this place has no meaning. Read *geondsprēcend* = *geondsprencend*. See Introd., V, § 70.

15. 5. *bennꝥe* stands over *ne he*, and *ne he* over *Neque*. *bennꝺe*, as gloss to *neque* is unintelligible ; read *bemiꝥe*, and take it as gloss to *dissimulet*. Cf. Corpus gl. 681, and Wright-Wülker, 388. 31, 32 (Dissimulare, bemiþan oꝥe yldan).

16. 9. *for forht taliendre*, as gloss to *parri pendens*, is corrupt ; it is very likely that *forht* was misread for *nawht*, which is a not infrequently occurring form of *nawiht*.

17. 15. *est*, a little erased. The fact is that *faciat* is found in other MSS. in this place, but in our MS. lower down (l. 16) erased. Someone who did not understand the words *et quod utilius judicaverit* in the context tried to restore sense by adding *est*.

18. 4. *hwonlicor*, as gloss to *salubrius* ? Read *hahrendlicor*.

20. 10. *factam*, MS. *factum*. Of the other texts (Schmidt, p. 13), none has *factum* (but the collation of our text is very imperfect. our reading *i.a.* not being given ; see Schröer, Die Prosabearbeitungen, p. xxvii): they read *factam, factas*, or *facta*. Originally, I suppose, our text had *factam*, agreeing with *injuriam*. Hence the gloss *gedonne*, agreeing with *tregan*. In this state our text must have been copied out, and the copyist, by an absolute blunder, or mislead by the masc.

termination of the gloss, wrote *factum*. After that, some one added
the gloss *dǽde* to the new lemma *factum*.

20. 13. *Ƶe modig*, as gloss to *desuperbum*, *đ=debere*, must have been
copied into the Latin as though it were part of *superbum*.

21. 13. *frǽdlice*. *Rǽdlice* (=hrǽdlice) (cf. Wright-Wülker, 243. 1 :
frequenter, celer) must have been there first, and *f* added by the
influence of the Latin. Or we must take *o* to be no paving letter, and
read ofrǽdlice = oftrǽdlice.

26. 6. *sylfsyne*, as gloss to *rara*. *seldsyne* was probably there originally. The corruption is easy to understand if we suppose *selƿsyne*
(cf. Introd., V, § 55) to have been there.

27. 2. *c. us. y̆.*, as gloss to *nobis*. Do *c, y* perhaps form part of the
gloss to *nobis*; and must we consequently look upon it as a misreading
for *us. y̆. c.*, i.e. *usic*? It would be quite in accordance with the usual
practice if more or less uncommon forms were misunderstood, and
consequently mutilated. It is true that forms in -*ic* are found only in
the accusative, whilst a dative form is postulated by the lemma ; but
first, this rule holds good only for the classical periods of Anglo-
Saxon (cf. Sievers [2], § 81, Anm. 2), and secondly, the acc. may be
explained as dependent upon *clypad*.

28. 12. *a, an*, over *inseruit*. *a* may of course be a gloss-letter, but
an ? I have thought of the following explanation : that *a, an*, as indicating the weak nom. and gen. ending (or acc. plural) were put over
ascendendos. Afterwards the full gloss was added. A case in point
may be adduced here from a Leiden MS., where we find *lucubro* glossed
by *brasbrat*. The explanation—see *Goetz-Loewe*, Glossae Nominum,
Leipzig, 1884, p. 161—is given by *Vossius* as lucubro, (lucu)bras,
(lucu)brat. The gloss to *inseruit* is *gesætt* in l. 10.

29. 11. *asmaidan*. Is this a corruption of *asmaiand = asmeagend*?

29. 15. *sodes oððe secge*, as gloss to *dicat*. *sodes* may be a mere
repetition of the *sodes* in l. 14, and then *oððe (secge)* simply means the
same as the .i. or the 7 found over Latin words to introduce the gloss.
But there is also the possibility that in *sodes* we have a remnant of
the verb *seðan*, to affirm.

30. 9. *insint*? Must we read 7 *sint gewordene* as gloss to *facti sunt*,
and *in* as gloss to (or repetition of ?) Latin *in* ?

30. 17. *þæt he oseo*. Read, as pointed out in the foot-note, *þæt he seo*.
If the *o* is not a solitary paving letter—which, see above, p. xxxiii, is
not altogether a contradiction in terms—the only explanation to fall
back upon is, that an original had *heo seo* ; *heo* under the influence of
the following *seo*.

31. 14. *under* should stand over *þæt*; it is part of the gloss to
subdat in l. 15.

34. 7. *wursan*, gloss to *vermis*. How *wurm* can be corrupted into
wursan I fail to understand. The unfortunate *s* makes it alike
impossible to assume either a mistake of the eye or of the ear.

54. 4. *swyrige*? The only way out of the difficulty I know is

to assume that *swýrige* is somehow or other misread for *scyrige*, and
that this should be gloss to *partiat* as well as *todæld*.

55. 2. *þelæs þe hi wýrdan odde gewundode.* The first glossator put ł
gewundode over *vulnerentur* (cf. note to 10. 7). Another added the
auxiliary, and wrote *odde* for ł.

56. 8. *gemedemod*, read *gemet.* Probably *med* (for *met*) was found
there first by a copyist, who, not understanding this, or not deeming
it sufficient, put *gemed* before it. This *gemed med* was copied out as
gemedemod=temperatur.

58. 4. *gesewene.* I think we have a remnant here of the rare verb
geseon, for which see Grein, in voce. Also in v. *séon*, and Bosworth,
ed. 1838, in v. *seon*.

59. 14. *for* belongs to *swýrian* (=swyᚱrian, cf. Introd., V, § 57), and
an is possibly a wrongly transcribed dittography for *na* of naht.

61. 2. *gehealdenne*, gloss to *sanentur.* Either a copyist found
gehealde ~ gehælde (Introd., V, § 17) or *sanentur* was glossed by *salventur*, and this by *gehealdenne.* Subsequently this middle gloss was
omitted. This kind of double glossing occurs very frequently, e. g.
in Bouterwek's Aldhelmglosses (H. Z. 9).

64. 1. *anwealde* is gloss to *potestate*, and not to *voluntate*; and in no
way can I suppose *anwealde* to be corrupted from any word meaning
potestas. And the Latin texts T. U. G., i. e. exactly those that agree
most in particulars with our own Latin text, also have *voluntate*,
whence it is likely that our text must have originally presented this
reading. Otherwise we might suppose our text to have been corrected
by another (which had *voluntate*), after the original *potestate* had been
glossed by *anwealde.* Cf. note to 88. 6.

69. 9. *frum anginne*, as gloss to *incipiente.* I cannot quite make
this out; we must expect a dative or a nominative (Introd.,
V, § 3) of the present participle. Professor Cosÿn suggests *fruman
anginne*, which is certainly the best I can think of, although it is not
entirely satisfactory.

69. 12. *drenc* as gloss to *musitatio?* Several explanations suggest
themselves. *d* may be a paving letter, in which case *rene* may stand
for *ryne*=mysterium, or better still *rene*=*ryne.* Cf. Grein in v. *rýn.*
Cf. Introd., V, § 27. If we take *d* to be part of the word we may
think of *drem*=*dream.* Cf. Introd., V, § 30.

70. 4. *seo wuca þen.* If we had not Sievers, § 337, Anm. 2, and supra,
§ 84, to refer to, where other instances from the above text are given,
we might possibly be induced to look upon *seo* here as a solitary proof
of a feminine origin of our text, which would then be in the same
plight as Schröer's texts (cf. Die Prosabearbeitungen, p. xxix). But
by these references this phantom vanishes into thin air.

73. 11. *belippendan = continuanda.* If we may suppose *continuanda*
to have been misread for *concernanda.* *belippendan* would stand for
belimpendan (cf. Introd., V, § 39). But this explanation does not
seem entirely satisfactory.

82. 3. This word cannot be otherwise explained as *gif forcrafað* (cf. Introd., V, § 70); *gif*, as gloss to *si*, in l. 2.

86. 3. I had thought *bigænge* to be a dittographical gloss to *in itinere*, which had got into the wrong place. However, Professor Cosÿn suggests that *m. g. bigænge*=under religious worship, should here be understood. I suspect that we shall have to combine the two explanations, because there is no lemma, which, taken by itself, could occasion the gloss *under religious worship* (unless it be cum *tremore* divino?). A copyist put *bi gænge* in the margin, and another, misled by the frequency of the occurrence of the expression, mid godcundum bigænge, put this over *divino*. It must, however, be admitted that the train of thought, the association of ideas, may very well have given rise to the error of mistaking these two words (*b. g.*) for one.

86. 17. *egelod*, as gloss to *condatur*. This is the reading of the MS., but we may detach *e* as a 'paving letter' from the body of the word, and thus *gelod* remains to be explained. The lemma suggests a connection with *gelogian* (cf. e. g. 98. 15), of which the past part. would be *gelogod*. This might easily become *gelowod* (cf. Introd., V, § 68), and this could be contracted into *gelod*. But since I have no other instances of such 'contractions' I prefer to look upon it as a mere scribal error.

88. 6. *mæð*=humilitas, which is in the other texts. Compare for the probable origin the notes to 64, 1; 99, 13.

91. 17. *fiand reaf*? Perhaps corrupted from *færeld reaf*? or from *fierdreaf*? But, writes Professor Cosÿn, what would monks do with those? To add another possibility, I suggest that it is from *fot reaf*. Cf. the reading of the other texts *fotgewradum*.

97. 2. *habban ðretioðinge*, as gloss to *habita . . . . deliberatione*. We may perhaps assume *habban* to be an infinitival gloss (cf. Introd., V, § 3) to a verbal inflection, which would seem to be of rare occurrence, and therefore liable to corruption, and then *ðretioðinge* would be a corruption of *ymbðriodunge*. This can be more easily accounted for if we think of the phenomenon which I discussed in the Introduction (V, § 4).

98. 15, and 100. 1, 2. I have stated, Introd., V, § 93, that I fail to understand these forms. The first *o* in *gelogodre* is indistinct; for the verb, cf. note to 86. 17. The only explanation I can think of is, that in each case the *r* was misread from an original *n*. This would yield perfectly intelligible forms; and palæographically speaking, the corruptions are very likely to occur. The puzzling *mæssepreostra* for *mæssepreostrum* (see note to 100. 10) may be in the same plight.

99. 4. MS. 'Offerunt de filiis nobilium aut pauperum qui.' The original must have read,

Offerunt'

De filiis nobilium aut pauperum qui.

The copyist read *offerunt*' first, although it was meant for the last word, and not seeing the MS. sign for *ur*, he copied the word as *offerunt*.

99. 13. *suffectam* would seem to be the right reading, although as many as nine other texts have *suspectam* (C. D. G. H. K. L. S. T. U). At one time or another this must also have been in our text (cf. note to 64. 1), or *suffectam* must have been misread as *suspectam*. With this word the gloss corresponds. How little *suffectam* was understood is proved by the fact that our text would seem to be the only one that had preserved it, since A. O. P. Q. R. have *subjectam*.

100. 10. *mæssepreostrum*. In § 36 of the Introd. (V) I have stated that the *r* was inserted. Professor Gallée, of Utrecht, suggests that the word **preostr* may have existed, in which case I should have to cancel the above statement. I can only add that, although I have not found any traces of it, it is extremely likely, considering the Greek origin, and the analogue of the Dutch and German form *priester*. But see note to (98. 15).

108. 7. *awjrtlian*, a legitimate form for *awjrtwalian*? The gloss reads as if the lemma were *eradicare*.

113. 16. *waclicre oððe stjre*. Cp. 115, 12, 17; and 116, 17, and read *regolicre wrace, lare oððe stjre*.

116. 7. *asindrodum beboda*. As it is not likely that we can look upon *beboda* as a crude form in the plural (cf. Introd., V, § 3), I suspect that *beboda* was misread for *bebodū* = bebodum.

www.ingramcontent.com/pod-product-compliance
Lightning Source LLC
Chambersburg PA
CBHW020535270326
41927CB00006B/589